"*Policy as Practice* brings fresh perspectives to the complexity of making and implementing policy. Stressing the importance of problem identification and framing, it moves beyond didactic instrumental management as the fundamental tool of the policy enterprise."

Adam Graycar, *Professor of Public Policy, University of Adelaide, Australia*

Policy as Practice

Colebatch, Castles, and a collection of policy practitioners and scholars investigate the process of policymaking through a range of current policy issues in Australia.

With case studies including childcare, educational policies, mental health, and environmental policies, the expertise and experience of policy practitioners and academic observers offer an empirical understanding of what makes for policy work in practice. From problematising to participating, structuring to judging, the authors reflect on the significance of the practices of governing in relation to current policy issues in Australia. They also present a robust conceptual framework for making sense of how we are governed to draw meaningful inferences about policy as a practice.

A practical guide for students and practitioners of policymaking, which goes beyond the policy cycle model to look at how real policies are really made and how they really work.

H.K. Colebatch has taught and researched in the field of public policy and administration in Australia, Papua New Guinea, East Africa, Southeast Asia, and Europe for over four decades.

Calista Castles is an Adjunct Fellow and a social researcher in mental health theory and practice at Griffith University, and has 20 years' experience working in government and non-government organisations.

Policy as Practice
Making Sense of Governing

Edited by H.K. Colebatch and Calista Castles

LONDON AND NEW YORK

First published 2024
by Routledge
4 Park Square, Milton Park, Abingdon, Oxon OX14 4RN

and by Routledge
605 Third Avenue, New York, NY 10158

Routledge is an imprint of the Taylor & Francis Group, an informal business

© 2024 selection and editorial matter, H.K. Colebatch and Calista Castles; individual chapters, the contributors

The right of H.K. Colebatch and Calista Castles to be identified as the authors of the editorial material, and of the authors for their individual chapters, has been asserted in accordance with sections 77 and 78 of the Copyright, Designs and Patents Act 1988.

All rights reserved. No part of this book may be reprinted or reproduced or utilised in any form or by any electronic, mechanical, or other means, now known or hereafter invented, including photocopying and recording, or in any information storage or retrieval system, without permission in writing from the publishers.

Trademark notice: Product or corporate names may be trademarks or registered trademarks, and are used only for identification and explanation without intent to infringe.

British Library Cataloguing-in-Publication Data
A catalogue record for this book is available from the British Library

ISBN: 978-1-032-43718-7 (hbk)
ISBN: 978-1-032-43717-0 (pbk)
ISBN: 978-1-003-36856-4 (ebk)

DOI: 10.4324/9781003368564

Typeset in Times New Roman
by KnowledgeWorks Global Ltd.

Contents

List of illustrations ix
List of contributors x
Preface xii

1 **Introduction** 1
   H.K. COLEBATCH AND CALISTA CASTLES

2 **Policy as a process** 8
   H.K. COLEBATCH

3 **Problematization in school education policy: Underperformance and parent hyperactivity** 16
   SARAH WARNER

4 **Local governments as policy shapers** 27
   SARAH de VRIES

5 **It's just the way we do things around here: How policy worlds influence the implementation of policies** 39
   PRUDENCE R. BROWN

6 **The evidence base for policy: Changes in the use of data, information and knowledge within government** 50
   FIONA McKENZIE

7 **When government is not the only option for setting public performance standards and ensuring compliance** 60
   RICHARD CURTAIN

8 **Evaluation as a governing practice: Judging the outcomes of policy and practice** 70
   CALISTA CASTLES

9 Contested viewpoints on the management of social problems: The case the Australian Child Support Scheme 81
KAY COOK

10 Performing the policy cycle 92
COSMO HOWARD

11 Public value and complex problems in pluralistic settings and the *Meriba Omasker Kaziw Kazipa* (for Our Children's Children) Act 2020 103
PRUDENCE R. BROWN AND SARAH WARNER

12 Stocktake and future agenda 115
H.K. COLEBATCH AND CALISTA CASTLES

Index *122*

Illustrations

Figures

9.1	Divergent views on the technical management of social problems	84
11.1	The strategic triangle	105

Tables

3.1	The *What's the Problem Represented to be?* analytic framework	18
4.1	Democratising local governments	34
4.2	Local government voice	34
10.1	Jungian archetypes and traits	96
11.1	Philosophical underpinnings of value	104
11.2	Differences between public value, responsive and public values approaches	104
11.3	Public value and the *Meriba Omasker Kaziw Kazipa* legislation	109

Contributors

Prudence R. Brown (PhD) is a non-Indigenous scholar with an interest in government responses to complex problems. Prior to their current academic career, they moved from a previous academic career to spend more than 15 years working in the Northern Territory, Commonwealth and (briefly) Queensland governments in a broad range of senior policy roles, mostly in remote Indigenous policy. As such, their beliefs are now firmly grounded in practice and come from my long experience in, and reflection on, Indigenous affairs in Australia. Prue acknowledges that the practices of colonialism are embedded in Indigenous policy and practice and acknowledges their place within these mainstream processes.

Calista Castles (MPol & Policy) is an Adjunct Fellow and scholar at Griffith University, Queensland, Australia, where she researches and teaches in the areas of mental health theory and practice, and wellbeing. Prior to working in academia, Calista has worked in both (state) government and non-government organisations in multiple areas from land management and administration to social justice and homelessness services. Her research presently focuses on various elements of work, labour and employment including subjectivity and structural (in)justices in related politics and policy, organisational well-being and mental health, the Lived Experience (Peer) Workforce, and political theory.

H. K. Colebatch (PhD), editor of the original *Beyond the Policy Cycle*, has taught and researched public policy and administration in Australia, Papua New Guinea, East Africa, Southeast Asia, and Europe, for over four decades. His focus on governing as the outcome of a range of distinct but interacting practices has helped to draw together what practitioners knew from experience and what scholars knew from research, which has helped to integrate both sources of knowledge in preparing people for their place in the process of governing.

Kay Cook (PhD) is a Professor and the Associate Dean of Research in the School of Social Sciences, Media, Film and Education at Swinburne University of Technology, and a member of the federal Economic Inclusion Advisory Committee. Her research explores how new and developing social policies such as welfare-to-work, child support and child care policies transform relationships between individuals, families, and the state. Her work seeks to make the personal impact of these policies explicit in order to provide tangible evidence to policy-makers to affect more humanistic reform.

Richard Curtain (PhD) prior to retiring, was a Research Fellow with the Development Policy Centre, Crawford School of Public Policy, the Australian National University, 2018–2022. Richard was the lead labour mobility analyst for the 2014 independent review of the Australian government-funded Australia-Pacific Technical College, and between 2011 and 2018 has worked as a labour market analyst for assignments in the Pacific and Timor-Leste for the Asian Development Bank, the Australian High Commission to Solomon Islands, the International Labour Organisation, and the Governments of Samoa and Vanuatu to identify opportunities for domestic and overseas employment.

Sarah de Vries (MU & EnvP) is an Adjunct Research Fellow at the Centre for Policy Futures at the University of Queensland and an experienced policy practitioner in the Department of Environment and Science. She has worked in various roles relating to World Heritage, climate change, and environmental planning, with previous experience in the Victorian Government in urban planning and community development. Her existing research interests are in local governance, community engagement, environmental policy change, and circular economies.

Cosmo Howard (PhD) is an Associate Professor in the School of Government and International Relations and Centre for Governance and Public Policy at Griffith University, Australia. His research focuses on the politics of expertise, policy responses to inequality, and comparative public administration.

Fiona McKenzie (PhD) is an Honorary Research Fellow at RMIT University in Melbourne and a Fellow of the Regional Studies Association and the Royal Geographical Society. She has spent over 30 years working in applied socio-economic and spatial research within government and has authored over 50 research reports including government publications and journal articles. Prior to retiring from the public service in mid-2022, she spent 18 months working with the Victorian Commissioner for Environmental Sustainability, bringing social science perspectives to State of Environment reporting. Fiona's holds a PhD from the University of South Australia, a Master's degree in Regional and Urban Planning Studies from the London School of Economics, and a Master's degree in Geography from the University of Melbourne.

Sarah Warner (PhD) is a policy scholar in the School of Political Science and International Studies at the University of Queensland. Her work focuses on the intersections between policy and politics. Dr Warner is interested in how policy is experienced by citizens and policy subjects and the possibilities and implications for democratic practices arising from this intersection. Prior to coming to academia, Dr Warner worked in a range of policy environments including in Indigenous policy in the Queensland Government, in the NSW Government, and in the community sector. Dr Warner is a non-Indigenous policy scholar and acknowledges the ongoing processes of colonialism that are embedded in government policy and practice.

Preface

This book is the successor to *Beyond the Policy Cycle: The Policy Process in Australia*, published in 2006 to complement (and correct) the then-dominant account of policy in use in Australia, Bridgman and Davis's *The Australian Policy Handbook* which set out a model of policy as a process of systematic, authoritative instrumental choice (AIC). Since *Beyond the Policy Cycle*'s original conception, there has been a lot of 'new' thinking and scholarly work exploring how governing occurs and the implications for how we understand policy practices and processes. There have also been several editions of *The Australian Policy Handbook*. When Routledge proposed to produce a new edition of *Beyond the Policy Cycle* to once again complement a new edition of *The Australian Policy Handbook*, it seemed appropriate to not just update the original text, but to explore some of the 'new' thinking and (re)theorising within the context of contemporary policy issues. Along with a new co-editor, this edition contains all new content from a suite of authors with a variety of individual and collective academic expertise, innovative insights, and professional experience in the field of policy – scholarship and practice – spanning public policy, governance, political science, humanities, environmental, social science, and professional expertise in policy development. The book has been organised to enable readers to engage with and explore the assemblage of policy practices – from problematising to participating, structuring to judging, and managing and analysis – and reflect on the significance of the practices of governing in relation to current policy issues; drawing on a variety of expertise, perspectives, and contexts to understand what makes for policy work. Rather than supersede *Beyond the Policy Cycle*, this edition is designed to sit alongside it as a valuable addition to any policy practitioner or scholar's collection. It is our hope that readers not only enjoy the contributions but also find them useful for understanding what makes for policy work and how it contributes to how society is governed.

1 Introduction

H.K. Colebatch and Calista Castles

When we talk about 'policy', the focus is usually on the object of policy: what the problems and solutions are and how governments attempt to address particular issues deemed to be problematic. Or perhaps our attention is directed to particular policy topics: environmental policy, health policy, policies relating to caring for children, transport, or taxation. The process of policy gets relatively less attention. That is, how activities and practices associated with policy are understood and carried out. This has begun to change over the last decade or so since the predecessor to this text, *Beyond the Policy Cycle: the policy process in Australia*, was published on 2006. *Beyond the Policy Cycle* was produced to complement (and correct) the then-dominant account of policy in use in Australia, Althaus, Bridgman, and Davis's *The Australian Policy Handbook*, which set out a model of policy as a process of systematic, authoritative instrumental choice (AIC): the political leaders determined what the government's objectives are and make clear decisions about how they want to achieve them (Althaus, Bridgman, and Davis 2020). The policy process is seen as an exercise in problem-solving in which an issue is identified as 'a policy problem', information is gathered, people are consulted, possible approaches are analysed and compared, and advice is provided to those in positions of authority. While at times, it is generally recognised that this perspective is not an empirical description, many involved in teaching policy felt, and still do, that a corrective that was both analytically sound and of practical use was needed. Thus, *Beyond the Policy Cycle* was born.

But *The Australian Policy Handbook* has continued to be the dominant account of policy in Australia and has since gone through multiple editions and acquired an extra co-author. Like many other mainstream texts, it still presents policy as the exercise of instrumental authoritative choice, even if at times it recognises this as an ideal to be aspired to, rather than a description of contemporary practice. However, there is a widespread questioning of this account of governing. Scholars ask themselves (even if only privately) 'why do we keep talking in these terms when we know we need more than this for an adequate account of policy practices and governing?'. And practitioners of governing see the authoritative choice account as 'the theory', which needs to be supplemented by 'practical' knowledge gained from experience. This edited collection is the successor to *Beyond the Policy Cycle* and seeks to provide (again) accounts of policy process that complement (and correct) the dominant account. It does this by bringing together some of the 'new' ways of thinking about the process of policy and governing and draws on the tacit practitioner knowledges ('observer accounts') of policy practice and theoretical understandings to build an approach to the work of policy, which is both intellectually sound and practically useful. In this introductory chapter we provide context for the accounts of 'policy' discussed in the following chapters and some of the questions and thinking that have informed the alternative approach offered.

DOI: 10.4324/9781003368564-1

The work of policy as a sense-making process

'Policy' is a central concept for making sense of and explaining the ways we are governed. Like many such concepts, there is no agreement on exactly what it means, but it is clearly significant in validating some forms of governing (rather than others). Within government, policy has developed an identity as a distinct function, quite separate from other technical knowledges, and a specialist occupation. Over time, it has come to reflect a belief that we are governed in an ordered and predictable way, which rests on choices made by appropriate people: 'the government'. This is not the only way that governing can be understood (as we shall see), but it is 'a good account', which is consistent with our normative understanding of our collective life. It is also recognised that there are many players or actors in the policy process, which contribute to the complexity and challenges of policy work. Moreover, not all those actors read from the same script when it comes to what policy is and what makes for policy work.

To make sense of 'policy', we need to address two questions – analytically distinct, but inseparable in practice: what is it that people do that 'makes policy' – the various activities that form part of 'policy making' – and what is the significance of some things (but not others) being recognised as 'policy'? The task is to investigate how we make sense of governing, and how 'policy' comes to form part of this sense-making, both in the doing of governing and in describing the process. And having done this, rather than assume that the aim is to find a 'correct' definition, we recognise that 'policy' is a 'concept in use' and ask *how* it is used – by participants (of different sorts) and by observers (commentators and the media, as well as scholars).

It is possible to make sense of policy as practice and as an organising concept. As a practice, policy produces such a diversity of activity and participants; as an organising concept in government, 'policy' designates organisational units, position titles, and knowledges. For example, 'health policy' involves health ministers and their bureaucratic subordinates, but also experts in related fields such as employment, education, cultural change, and so on. These 'fields of expertise' are typically treated as distinct and disconnected. Thus, policy comes to be recognised as discrete bodies of knowledge and expertise, and as a base for the activities of specialists in those fields. This then directs us to the ways in which models of governing set up the questions that must be asked in order to make sense of it: what do the models direct our attention to and what do they deflect attention from?

There are multiple organising models associated with 'policy', but two tend to stand out: the dominant AIC and the collective managing of the problematic (CMP). The dominant AIC model directs our attention to authority:

> "it seems obvious that governing is done by 'the government,' and policy is 'whatever government decides chooses to do or not to do'"
>
> (Dye 1976, 1; Colebatch and Hoppe 2018, 1)

Policy as a process is understood as an exercise in informed problem-solving and draws attention to the way that concerns are recognised as needing to be governed: the formal practices of problem identification, authoritative choice, and decision-making as presented in notions of systematic policy cycles, and how each of the stages relate to patterns of institutionalised practice, both governmental and non-governmental. It points, too, to the ways in which different forms of practice – governmental and other – shape the outcome, and in consequence, the importance of relating different modes of shaping practice to one another: often breezily labelled 'coordination'. And while this tends to be seen as calling for negotiation between organisations, often the task seems to be to communicate with a wider audience, who have to be persuaded of the need to change: 'the public'. Moreover, the AIC model points to policy objectives, the intended outcomes of governing, and the ways in which the 'success' of the policy is evaluated, and what impact this has on future policy. Additionally, the AIC model tends to see 'the policy-makers' as a single voice, whereas both practitioners and researchers report that, usually, there are multiple participants, concerned about the situation for different reasons, from different perspectives, and with different standings in the governmental process.

Recognising that there are many participants sees policy as a continuing activity of collective sense-making. The focus is on the practices through which the problematic is identified and governed and the ways in which official forms ('the government' and 'policy') become part of this process. Within a CMP model, as put forward in this edited collection, 'the government' is seen less as an actor, more as an arena, an assemblage of policy participants through which collective activity is generated, shaped, and flows. It also acknowledges the constructed and changing nature of society and societal forms: that what is considered problematic and in need of governing (and how it is governed) is contextually contingent. Participants in policy work (particularly the more experienced ones) are likely to be conscious that governing is a continuing process, and while they may seek specific outcomes of particular contests, they will also have an interest in the sense-making process: maintaining the CMP and, in particular, having 'a place at the table' themselves. Both the AIC model and the CMP alternative can be significant in shaping practice, and practitioners tend to be aware of the tension between collaboration and autonomy, and the potential outcomes of practice.

What to expect in this collection

In this edited collection, our focus is on policy as continuing practice where policy is understood as a 'concept in use' in governing. We see a number of identifiable forms of practice that can help make sense of policy in this way: problematisation, structuring activity, managing the process, judging outcomes, and mapping and analysis of practice. These forms of practice are weaved throughout this book. While each chapter can be read and used as a standalone contribution to help make sense of particular aspects of governing, as a collection, the chapters highlight that the study of 'government' cannot be reduced to discrete, finite cycles of activity. Rather, governing is a continuous practice in which assemblages of diverse elements come together in heterogenous and unique ways to make the world thinkable and the conduct of conduct governable. In this present volume, there are several examples of the five interrelated forms of practice though which situations are proposed as being of collective concern (advocacy), explored (what is known and who has standing), supported/disputed, and come to be expressed in specific programmes of action.

The collection starts by acknowledging that what is to be governed is the current outcome of a process of problematisation – sometimes conscious, sometimes so buried in the taken-for-granted that it seems 'only sensible'. Hal K. Colebatch (Chapter 2) examines how the care of young children became a problem, for whom, what was seen as acceptable and problematic, and what kinds of action are possible. Sarah Warner (Chapter 3) examines the way underperformance of school systems becomes problematic, but also how the process of problematisation produces problems of particular kinds amenable to specific solutions. Sarah de Vries (Chapter 4) and Prudence R. Brown (Chapter 5) guide readers through *organising processes*, how the structuring of activity associated with policy effects participation and vice versa. That is, who is (or should be) involved in the management of particular concerns, who is seen to have the 'right' knowledge, and on what is this knowledge based? Who has authority, and on what basis? Who has the capacity to effect changes in practice? And are there potential participants who do not participate, or who are excluded? De Vries explores how local governments are often best placed to influence public policymaking in relation to climate change but are often left out of policymaking at the national level because of the way policymaking processes are structured. Brown's chapter examines the multi-layered policy world of Indigenous policy and how existing ways of working can inhibit meaningful participation, but importantly that policy worlds are contingent and can accommodate diverse understandings, even when they seem stable and fixed. How concerns, interests, institutions, authority, and resources are drawn together in practice has implications for the CMP.

Generating acceptance of a pathway for the settlement of contested issues is test of the participants' skill at *managing the process* in order to arrive at a mutually acceptable outcome. However, as with the framing of the problematic and structuring the activity, the way in which the problematic is managed depends on the framing being used by participants, and who participates and contributes to how the problematic is problematised. When exploring the management process, the focus is on the various ways concerns, interests, institutions, authority, and resources are drawn together in practice; the relationships between how policy issues are structured and who gets to participate in problematising, responding, and analysing the problematic; and the various effects that may be produced in the process. Managing the process is about an iterative interconnectedness of processes and practices, rather than the linear sequencing, of the policy process. Fiona McKenzie (Chapter 6) highlights how technological changes can transform the way information and knowledge is managed, but also has implications for how information is used, interpreted, and applied. Richard Curtain (Chapter 7) comparatively examines two model of governance relating to Australia's seasonal worker programme in the Asia-pacific region: a centralised model and a regional and collaborative model. The comparison highlights the difference between the AIC model that is state-centric with government at the heart of policy and a CMP model in which participants collectively produce a mutually acceptable outcome, which can then be 'enacted' by authoritative action.

Whether or not the process has been successful is a matter of judgement – which covers all the ways in which participants (and the watching public) form opinions about the worth of the activities being done to advance this policy concern (or of the concern itself); this includes both formal practices of evaluation, and the more diffuse attempts to identify the multiple and overlapping focuses of justification in practice. *Judging the success of policy* involves a number of related questions which have become a distinct field of social and political science: *evaluation*, which is now seen as an integral part of the policy process. Of course, there are many observers – Royal Commissions, government inquiries, think-tanks, the media, academics, and the general public all engage in various forms of evaluating and judging the worth of policy in their own way. Claims from social scientists of systematic evaluation of policy often rest on the expectations contained in the initial document: to what extent have these expectations been achieved and what explains any non-achievement? Thus, the judgements of policy practitioners tend to fall within a 'performance review' model – what is working best, what needs to be improved, and what can be learnt from this experience. Both these forms of evaluation share the AIC assumptions, but some forms – seeing policy in CMP terms – recognise that there are many interested parties and that they may have different ways of judging success, and this needs to be considered when analysing the process of evaluation. 'Evaluation' as a technique of governing has implications that reach far beyond identifying administrative failures and setting reform agendas.

Calista Castles (Chapter 8) explores the normative power of evaluation as a technique of governing, and the potential for evaluation as a practice to reorient and reform the mental health sector. After all, what is measured gets done, and if those measures do not measure what matters, then policy becomes stuck. This is further highlighted by Kay Cook (Chapter 9) through the case of child support in Australia. Cook explores the interconnected ways through which interest, evidence, and authority come to define policy problems and their technical solutions in ways that reinforce the gendered status quo. The various policy actors – politicians, programme administrators, parents, and front-line workers – bring different insights, experiences, and interests which inform their assessment of the programme, but some dominate while others are subjugated. This has implications for how the system is reviewed, what (if any) changes are made, who benefits, and who becomes disadvantaged. Importantly, how the interests of various policy actors become aligned and function to depoliticise child support influence the ongoing managing of a 'wicked' social problem.

Sooner or later, all writing about policy has to face the question of the relationship between analysis and practice: the analysis is dawn from the contemplation of practice, the search for generalisation, and the quest for a beneficial outcome of practice – but it is not practice, and there is always a question of the relationship between the modelling and the doing – between 'theory' and 'practice'; or as practitioners like to put it, between what you might do 'in theory' and what you would do 'in practice'. 'The theory' is seen as having a normative element: it is what you *ought to* do, but may be unable to do for several 'practical' reasons. Bailey (1969) saw this as a distinction between 'normative' rules and 'pragmatic' rules: what you might do to accomplish the outcome you wanted. Bridgman and Davis saw the 'policy cycle' in their *Australian Policy Handbook* as an ideal which practitioners could strive to achieve, even if they often fell short. Moore (1995) saw it as a challenge for managers: how to get the capacity needed and the support required (from superiors and other participants) to create additional 'public value', recognising a triangle in which organisational capacity, legitimacy, and public value interact with one another through the work of policy participants. In Chapter 11, Prudence R. Brown and Sarah Warner show how this approach expands the perception of 'the public' and helps policy participants to address forms of order which do not depend on the statute book. Brown and Warner do this through the case of the Meriba Omasker Kaziw Kazipa (for our Children's Children) Act 2020 and highlight the importance of recognising traditional cultural practices.

The point here is that while the model of AIC assumes a single decision-maker, there are many participants, and cohesion is often manufactured. This requires a search for a way of talking about practice that will not appear to threaten the ambitions of other participants. Goffman (1959) argued that the creation of order had both a 'front stage', where the actors were in public view, and a 'back stage', where a small number of key participants could assert their claims, and through their interaction, prepare for a resolution front-stage, a sufficiently acceptable outcome which would be 'enacted' by being announced as a 'decision' by an appropriate authority. And Cosmo Howard (Chapter 10) has developed this point to address the question of why the policy practitioners continue to pay deference to the AIC model, even though they know it is not enough as a guide to practice. It does, he argues, by becoming a tool for organising and structuring communication of both the policy process and the role particular participants take within it; offering not just a way of locating what they do in a model of the policy process, but one which casts them in a heroic mould, as the people who made it happen.

While Howard proposes that the scripts policy participants (politicians) use are consciously chosen, it is also acknowledged that they become part of the norms associated with policy work: they are, in effect, constitutive *of* policy processes and constituted *within* them as the participants choose and perform their roles. The roles, narratives, and performances direct out attention to 'the government' and the characters within it. Other participants roles are marginalised and risk being left out of analysis. An example not explored in this collection, but worth noting, is the role of external consultants who are contracted by government to provide advice and analysis. However, the consultancy firm is rarely considered or implicated in the analysis of policy or held to account for any missteps and mistakes that result from their advice. The organisational complexity of policy work presents a great challenge to the analysis of the work of policy in how we are governed. A multiplicity of participants, organisations, interests, and knowledges are involved and emerge as a consequence of the practices and technologies of governing. Understanding the work of policy as a continual process of generating collective activity for governing society is a more useful approach for making sense of governing practices.

This introduction has been outlining and explaining the approach to understanding policy which is developed in this book, but there are two big questions which might be asked: first, how does this approach relate to the rest of the literature on policy, and secondly, as the concept of policy has been developed in Western liberal democracies, does it have any relevance in other forms of political order? There is a large and constantly expanding literature on policy, which is periodically surveyed (see, for instance, Cairney 2013; Schlager and Weible 2013; Petridou 2014; Trousset et al. 2015), and we see no need to attempt a comprehensive survey. Rather, we seek to equip the reader with the questions to ask of writing on policy. Seeing policy as a continuing process of making sense of governing gives us some core diagnostic questions. First, what is the *stimulus* to practice? What provokes (or sustains) action? Secondly, who *participates* in the issue, whether as officials or as outsiders (including the subjects of the action). Then, what is the *practice* in which the participants engage? And finally (logically, anyway), what is the *outcome* of this practice – and, therefore, of the policy?

As we have outlined, there seem to be two contrasting archetypal patterns for answering these questions in the literature: one sees policy as an instrument in a process of official problem-solving and the other sees policy as the product of a continuing process of the CMP. Scholarly writing tends to formally recognise both accounts, but some give more attention to instrumental action – the selection and pursuit of goals – and some puts more stress on the number and diversity of 'stakeholders', the complexity of the interaction, and the difficulty of achieving a mutually satisfactory outcome. We have tried to recognise both the significance of authoritative goal statements and the need to maintain a 'negotiated order' in the policy process. By starting with 'problematisation' as an activity, rather than on pre-existent 'problems', we focus on what frames, presuppositions, and situations as 'problems' demanding attention, and what sort of action becomes an appropriate response. But it has to be acknowledged that policy studies have struggled to escape its liberal democratic, social-improvement origins. It can be seen as having arisen as the US was trying to establish a post-war order which would erase the trauma of the Great Depression, and liberal intellectuals wanted to see governing as more than partisan allocation and bureaucratic routine, and presenting it in instrumental terms – 'what is the government trying to achieve?' – was appealing. But if our concern is to use policy as an analytical concept in explaining the patterns of governing, then these questions about why or how particular situations become the focus of policy, who participates, what actions follow and what are the consequences and how are they assessed, and to what extent is the way in which public authority is applied known and predictable are just as relevant. In this way, we are using 'policy' as an analytic construct, not as a unique feature of parliamentary democracies.

Our exploration has raised questions about 'policy', not simply as an analytical construct, but as part of the lived experience of all the participants in the process of governing; and (we hope) contributes meaningfully to how we come to understand and make sense of governing.

References

Althaus, C., P. Bridgman, and G. Davis. 2020. *The Australian Policy Handbook: A Practical Guide to the Policy-Making Process*. Abingdon: Routledge.

Bailey, Fredrick G. 1969. *Stratagems and Spoils: A Social Anthropology of Politics*. New York, NY: Schocken Books.

Cairney, P. 2013. Standing on the shoulders of giants, *Policy Studies Journal* 41 (1): 1–21. https://doi.org/10.1111/psj.12000

Colebatch, H. K., and R. Hoppe. 2018. "Introduction: Policy, Process and Governing." In *Handbook on Policy, Process and Governing*, edited by H. K. Colebatch, and R. Hoppe. Cheltenham, UK: Edward Elgar.

Dye, T. R. 1976. *Understanding Public Policy*. Englewood Cliffs, NJ: Prentice-Hall.

Goffman, E. 1959. *The Presentation of Self in Everyday Life*. New York, NY: Anchor.

Moore, M. 1995. *Creating Public Value: Strategic Management in Government*. Cambridge, MA: Harvard University Press.

Petridou, E. 2014. Theories of the Policy Process: Contemporary Scholarship and Future Directions. *Policy Studies Journal* 42 (S1): S12–32.

Schlager, E., and P. Weible. 2013. "New Theories of the Policy Process." *Policy Studies Journal* 41 (3): 389–96.

Trousset, S. et al. 2015. "The 2015 Public Policy Yearbook: Tracking Research in Public Policy." *Policy Studies Journal* 43 (S1): S1–11.

2 Policy as a process

H.K. Colebatch

Introduction

This book sees policy as an idea which shapes action: people use it in making sense of the way in which discourses and practices and institutions seem to produce order, which is called 'governing'. In this chapter, we will take one issue in social practice – the care of children – to ask how the concept of policy helps us to make sense of the way it is governed. Our empirical material is Australian, but there is nothing to indicate that our experience has been markedly different from comparable advanced industrial countries, or that the questions we are asking are not relevant in most polities.

In taking this 'social construction' approach, we ask first how attention is focused, which people and organisations are involved, what they see as acceptable and what as problematic, and what sorts of action are possible. These questions are all linked to one another, and the links run both ways: how we understand the problem shapes who we think should be involved in addressing it, and who is raising the issue shapes what sort of a problem it is seen as being. So, we start with the question of how the issue is problematised and move to how it is structured, how issues are managed, and how the outcome is judged. But while it is convenient to identify these as distinct forms of activity should not be taken to imply that the practitioners saw them in these terms, that these are 'stages' in the policy process, or that they occur in any order.

Problematisation: How something becomes a concern to be governed?

Some creatures seem to have offspring who can, more or less, fend for themselves almost as soon as they arrive, but human offspring are dependent, and need much protection, nurturing and skill before they reach adult life. But there is a diversity of opinion and practice about what the young need in these years, how they might acquire it, and to what extent this involves collective responsibility and state authority. How much is this about protection, how much about the development of the self, and how much about learning? Is the learning need about skills, or about abstract knowledge, or about identity, norms, and socialisation: 'who am I, and how should I conduct myself?' And from whom will they learn what they need to know? The kin group? The old and the wise? Siblings and other contemporaries? Specialist professionals?

In Australia, there has been little assertion of a collective responsibility for the protection and development of the young, compared to the early Israeli confidence that this was a responsibility of the whole community, the *kibbutz*; instead, there have been many voices with answers to these questions. Kinship groups have been important in the continuing supervision of the young, especially among the indigenous Australians. For the settlers, this role fell more particularly to mothers, and ethnic links were less important (except in the development of schools). But there

DOI: 10.4324/9781003368564-2

have also been multiple and overlapping forms of professional knowledge and practice, centred on belief, on health, on welfare, and on schooling.

So how is the care of the young governed and to what extent does 'policy' play a part in this? The 'official' response, from state institutions, has tended to reflect all of the claims, though not equally. The foundational assumption was the primacy of kinship: parents were seen as legally responsible for the care of their children. In an early (and foundational) judgement in the new federal governing of industrial relations, it was ruled that the 'basic wage' should be sufficient to sustain not only the worker (who was assumed to be male) but also a wife and two dependent children. (In practice, of course, kinship links were invoked beyond the nuclear family in organising caring, e.g. to grandparents, or even within it, to older siblings.)

There were also voices focused not on the child, but on the adult carer. In the kinship discourse, thus was nearly always the mother, and feminists sought to contest the assumption that a woman who had given birth to a child should spent some years caring for it; for them, organising child care was a way of restructuring gender roles and relationships. There was a parallel concern from those surveying the operation of the labour market, who saw young, skilled members of the work force dropping out of it to become the unpaid carers of a single child and regarded institutionalised child care as a way of enabling these absentees to return to 'the workforce' – i.e., paid employment.

There were many institutional structures offering care. Religious congregations, networks of parents and local entrepreneurial carers set up 'kindergartens'. Organisations emerged to offer 'community child care', sometimes involving parents or other community members in the caring, raising questions both about how caring was understood, and 'the community' was represented in their activities. The enthusiasm for market-like responses to social needs was also felt in relation to child care. Links between similar child care centres became networks, and sometimes companies, which owned chains of centres. In 2021, one such company, which owned 22 centres in and around Melbourne, and claimed to have a management team of 'seasoned industry professionals' seeking to expand its business through the 'targeted acquisition of established Childcare centres with potential for growth against agreed criteria including … profitability', bid $39.2 million for 14 centres owned by a smaller company, in the expectation that these centres would generate a cash flow of $8 million a year. And there was already a periodical addressed to the child care 'sector' (presumably 'of the economy').

But the main institutional contender for the care of children was the education industry. Through the 19th century, schools emerged, sometimes started by teachers, mostly by ethnic and religious groups, to reinforce the identity of 'their' children. By the end of the century, it had become an issue in governing, and the colonial governments made attendance at school compulsory for children from about the age of six, and set up school systems themselves. This established a clear assertion of governing the care of younger children to be the responsibility of their parents, but older children were to be in schools, which would be inspected to ensure their compliance with established standards. Some in the teaching profession sought to expand their domain by designating the care of four- and five-year-olds as 'Early Childhood Education and Care' (ECEC), and many care centres re-labelled themselves centres for 'early learning'.

But while we might think that problematisation would clarify what needed to be governed, there was very little discussion of what sort of care young people need, and how it could be met. There seemed to be a shared but tacit belief that young people 'don't know anything', but no discussion of what young people need to know, and how could they could learn this. It seemed to be assumed that children would acquire an acceptable level of shared norms and practices from interaction with family, peers, and the community, and anything else could be learned by instruction from adults at school. There was a counter-discourse that children need to develop their own ways of apprehending the world and dealing with its challenges, and that this autonomous capacity is not necessarily advanced by instruction from adults.

It is worth noting that Finland, which seems to be at or near the top in most international comparisons of learning, does not start school until age 7, and the year of pre-school which precedes it consists of 'play-based learning' rather than instruction. But in Australia, there was little discussion of need on how it could be met; there was an established institutional answer, and extending it to cover earlier years of life would enable women to rejoin the paid workforce and meet some institutional claims of the teaching profession. There are occasional reports of innovative exercises in schooling where the students learn innovation through practice, defining the learning task and how to go about it, but these are the exception to a norm of adult instruction (and assessment) on a prescribed curriculum.

This does raise an important issue about how we understand policy. Bacchi (2009) makes a clear case for seeing policy as a systematic response to a known problem, but in the case of the care of children, it was not clear that the existing order was a problem, or if it was, why it was, and what would be better. In this case there is evidence of what Béland and Howlett (2015) call an 'instrument constituency', advocates of particular sorts of action, whatever the problem. Teacher unions and faculties of education favour schooling, as do public figures confronted with behavioural problems among young people, who call for these to be addressed by the school system.

Organising governing: Structuring

There have been a number of voices on the needs of the young, with different concerns and different claims to authority. Some are already part of the pattern of governing; some may be trying to join it. We need to ask how the governing is *structured* and recognise the process by which some matters (but not others) are seen to be in need of governing, and why, and who understands what is needed, and can be trusted to carry it out. Problematisation has to be related to the pattern of governing. Is there a need for collective action, and does it involve the application of authority? The process of governing involves different institutional forms, including (obviously) the family, but also ethnic identities, religious affiliation, and cultural formations, including 'cause' groupings.

The first question is whether this is about practice that needs to be governed by state authority, and if it is, which forms would be involved. The 'official' institutional forms tend to reflect function (e.g. 'health'), activity, ('education'), or sometimes intended beneficiaries ('Veterans'). 'Locality' seems to be less significant in Australia than elsewhere, perhaps because the states were originally self-governing settlements with their own spatial identity. There are systems of local government, but local councils all are dependent on state governments, which can (and do) abolish elected councils and replace them with more acceptable bodies, in particular, with merged, larger bodies more like (and compatible with) the functional bureaucracies of state government and less concerned with local preferences.

So, in this perspective, the question for governing is 'whose problem is this?' – that is, 'which institution could be expected to deal with this?' Children five and five years old are seen as being governed by 'the family', and there is no government agency to deal with them, though welfare agencies (mostly governmental) were able to intervene if the parental care was seen as inadequate. But it was not clear that the socialisation of children – how they developed relationships with adults outside the family, and with other children – was seen as a matter to be governed.

Of course, there were institutions offering forms of organised care for young people, at least for parts of the day – some community-based, not-for-profit, others as commercial enterprises.

Both federal and state governments responded to this development, and there was a complex web of regulation and support for the institutions and the parents who used them.

Most Australian children attended one or more of these at some stage before reaching school, partly for education, partly for the social contact, and partly to allow a parent to re-enter the paid workforce. They encountered aspects of the school model of practice – organisation by adults, clustering by age, gathering in specific rooms, etc. – in these institutions, which sometimes called themselves 'pre-schools'. These were regulated by state governments, but eventually the federal government established an Australian Children's Education and Care Quality Authority (ACECQA), to regulate them through a network of state government agencies – perhaps recognising that while the federal government may have a national vision and the money to encourage it, it has very little experience of actually governing social practice and needs the involvement of the states.

So, the structuring of this policy issue – care for young people – was shaped by the existing institutional framework, and the cognitive and normative base on which it rested. The institutional form it took initially had some resemblance to the family and increasingly came to resemble the school. There is not much evidence of public discussion of what outcomes might be expected from any particular mode of care. That children learn in other ways – from peers, for instance, and social interaction – was admitted, but this did not lead to the avoidance of adult-controlled instruction that we saw in Finland. The evaluation done under the authority of the ACECQA appears to focus on institutional forms and practice rather than outcomes, but children who have been in pre-school are said to adjust better to school than those who have not (AIHW 2020).

While it is common for policy to be seen as 'how the government responds to a problem', we should not assume the existence of such an actor, or that it is the only player in the game. We need to ask who is addressing this question, what (if anything) they see as problematic, and why, and what they would see as an appropriate response – and where, and by whom, action might be taken. There was no 'obvious' institutional base for governing the care of young people. Legal responsibility remained with the family, but was becoming less relevant, and adult family members might not be anxious to be carers. Schooling advocates might be happy to recognise 'pre-schools' as preparation for 'real' school, but for education bureaucracies adding two more years to their task was not welcome. Participants who might have sought a greater policy role were content to rest in the ambiguity of the situation.

But while new policies have to negotiate an accommodation with existing patterns of governing, it is open to participants to propose new forms of governing, and de Vries, in her chapter, gives a number of examples, in the tradition of 'place-based' governing. This is much-discussed in the reform literature, but the dominant assumption in Australian government is functional specialisation, with a parallel assumption that bigger is better, and if bigger means more bureaucratic and less attentive to public voices – well, that is better, too. I recall a critic arguing that the state of New South Wales, which then had about 150 local councils, 'had too many', and should reduce the number as Premier Kennett had done in Victoria. Why this would improve the quality of government in NSW was not stated, nor has there been any demonstration that the reduction since then to 128 has improved the quality of governing. Nor has there been any interest in comparing NSW with, for example, Switzerland, which has about the same population as NSW (though it is one-twentieth the size), and has not only 2,136 local councils, but is a country, and (like Australia) a federation, with 26 cantons rather than six states. This suggests, not that governing in NSW is more 'efficient' than governing in Switzerland, but that the Swiss value locality, difference, and the responsiveness of government to the governed as well as cost

Organising governing: Managing

So, when a situation is seen as needing to be governed, there may be a diversity of voices about the nature of the situation, why it is problematic, and what might be done about it. How do the participants generate from this diversity and conflict an order, and a sense that the matter is being appropriately dealt with – that it is 'being *managed*'? Structuring generates a sense of hierarchy – which organisations are seen as the normal custodians of order, but even so, they may generate multiple and competing claims, which need to be managed.

In this managing, two sorts of claim are likely to be made, one focused on *authority* and one focused on *knowledge,* and participants are likely to draw on both. The simplest form of 'authority' argument is a constitutional one: there is a government with authority to make decisions in the common interest, so if it has made a decision, the matter has been governed. But authority is also claimed on the basis on kinship – most of all, by parents – whose authority is recognised in law, and who are not subject to effective supervision and control by 'the authorities'. Authority is also claimed on cultural grounds, e.g. over gender and practice, by religious and ethnic leaders.

This means that the question should perhaps be 'who would people in authority look to for an understanding of the situation, and for an appropriate response – and what knowledge would be drawn on?'. Would it be functional (e.g., education, health, child development); or cultural (e.g., derived from ethnicity, class, or religion) or locational (e.g., what is appropriate in that area)? Even the secular bureaucratic claim that 'the right thing to do is what works' draws on assumptions about the problem and evidence of impact of responses, with a diverse array of answers, and advocates for each.

So the Australian answer for the care of children has been age-determined: for children of six and over, the appropriate activity is seen as institutionalised instruction by adults in a school, whose form and practices are subject to regulation. For younger children, participation is less learning-focused, and there is no agency claiming to govern the activity of children under six, and no consensus on what they most need – self-care, socialisation, skills, or knowledge – or how they might get it. The federal government has now set up an Australian Early Childhood Education and Care Quality Authority, with national standards, state-level inspectors, and self-assessment, but perhaps the most significant governing forces are parent expectations, corporate form (child care centres often being part of a network), and market competition.

What does this say about policy for the care of children? Is there a problem, and if so, is it being managed? Some would say that it is for parents (or, sometimes, the children themselves) to decide what these young people should do. If they choose to send them to a care centre, there are public agencies which regulate the number (and to some extent, the suitability) of the adult carers. Some were arguing that the young need more instruction, but this was as much reflecting the parental desire to have both parents in the paid workforce. And this got strong political support: there was a joint announcement in 2022 by the two largest (by population) states that one year of pre-school would be made compulsory for all children and undertook to spend $5.8 billion over the next ten years to achieve this.

Judging the worth of policy

A key question for 'policy' as part of governing is assessment: 'how do we tell if it's doing the job?'. This, too, depends on how we think about the task. In the authoritative instrumental choice (AIC) account, policy is seen as a way of achieving a known outcome, the goal of the policy. In the collective managing of the problematic (CMP) account, it's more about process: responding to the problem in a way that most people are content with. In the case of caring for children, there was not much concern to clarify the nature or extent of the problem or the extent to which the need would be met by the action proposed. There was a data-informed discussion about which sort of schooling is most effective, but no comparable comparison of schooling with other ways for children to develop their abilities (and their persona). Data could have been used, but was not.

In *Beyond the Policy Cycle*, Fiona McKenzie discussed the way that institutions within government used different sorts of data used to justify policy decisions and attempts to develop more 'place-based' data. In this volume, she reviews the way data collection and display has advanced in the last couple of decades – but it is still largely used to justify action being proposed and supported for other reasons (largely to do with the workforce).

So, there were a number of overlapping reasons prompting official action to provide an institutional frame for the care of young children, and schooling was seen as a familiar, and the most accessible, answer, and the government as the most obvious source of both provision and finance. What, then, does this mean for the task of judging the 'success' of the policy? Here, again, it depends on how 'policy', as such, is understood. In the AIC account, when policy is presented as the choice made by the authorised leader to achieve some desired outcome, it might seem that assessment should be relatively simple (though it might break it into two questions: (a) were the activities chosen carried out? and (b) did they achieve the desired outcome?).

Since these questions are obviously important, how the policy would be assessed becomes a significant element in policy argument and an essential part of a policy proposal. This led to the emergence of a new mode of applied knowledge and bureaucratic specialisation: 'evaluation'. This was seen as a process which should be specified before the policy was introduced (*ex-ante*) as part of the policy design and carried out once it was in force (*ex-post*) to help determine whether the policy should be continued, amended, or replaced. In this perspective, a well-prepared policy would include a clear (traditionally quantitative) expression of its objectives – e.g. 'to reduce drop-outs from the program by 25% by the end of next year' – and consultants became skilled at offering expert, 'objective' evaluations of policies and programmes.

In the CMP account, though, policy emerges from the interplay of a number of participants, who might not have the same view of why the situation is problematic and what might be done about it, but can agree that something should be, and find the action proposed acceptable, at least at this point in time. So, they form a 'coalition of support' for the policy and can accept that there might be 'official' forms of evaluation, but have their own ways of determining how successful it is in their terms. These might be in terms of outcome ('fewer people are dropping out of the program') or in terms of process ('we are now doing more to prepare people for the demands of the programme so that they are less likely to drop out' or even 'we told the boss that this was a problem and for once, he listened to us and did something').

The chapter by Castles is a searching examination of evaluation as a mode of practice in the pursuit of governing. It recognises that there are many voices in the conversation and that even if the mode of evaluation has been specified (which is far from normal practice), there are criteria and timetables to be determined, ambiguities being exploited – and the person or organisation responsible to be appointed. In other words, the evaluation is part of policy practice, not a separate activity at the end.

Analytic models and practice

Finally, we have to face the question of the relationship between analysis and practice: does it describe practice, offer guidance for practitioners, or identify the questions needed for a complete understanding of the activity? Analysis is drawn from the contemplation of practice, the search for generalisation, and the quest for a beneficial outcome of practice – but it is not practice, and there is always a question of the relationship between the modelling and the doing – between 'theory' and 'practice' – or as practitioners like to put it, between what you might do 'in theory' and what you would do 'in practice'. 'The theory' is seen as having a normative element: it is what you *should* do, but may be unable to do for a number of 'practical' reasons. Bailey (1969) saw this as a distinction between 'normative' rules and 'pragmatic' rules: what you might do to accomplish the outcome you wanted. Bridgman and Davis (2000) saw the 'policy cycle' in their *Australian Policy Handbook* as an ideal which practitioners could strive to achieve, even if they often fell short, but one experienced policy worker said:

> ... this model would not be of great use. ... if that's where you left it, you might as well be sacked tomorrow. These words are so neutral. It's not about consultation. It's really about stakeholder engagement.
>
> (Howard 2005, 10)

So, it seemed to be about practitioner skill. Authoritative leaders could make their preferences clear, but practitioner skill was needed to bring them into effect. Moore (1995) saw it as a challenge for managers: how to get the capacity needed and the support required (from superiors and other participants) to create additional 'public value', recognising a triangle in which organisational capacity, legitimacy, and public value interact with one another through the work of policy participants. In their chapter, Brown and Warner show how this approach expands the perception of 'the public' and helps policy participants to address forms of order which do not depend on the statute book.

The point here is that while the model of authoritative instrumental choice assumes a single decision-maker, there are many participants, and cohesion has to be manufactured. We note Goffman's (1959) distinction between 'front stage' and 'back stage', where the representatives of the most significant participants could meet to negotiate in private (back stage) what could be announced publicly (on the front stage). This involves developing a shared account of the situation to be dealt with, which reflected both the specific concerns of the various participants, and their common interest in seeing the 'problem' resolved through the exercise of authority. In the AIC model, there is a significant role for all of the participants: applicants, established stakeholders, and official regulators. This makes it an appropriate way to talk about the process, and to act – e.g., by assembling a data-based application and by responding to competing claims with informal critique. This is not the only way that applicants will press their claims, but they know that this is the appropriate way and should not be neglected.

Conclusion

In this book, we try to recognise the different perceptions that the participants bring to policy activity, in a way that strengthens both the participant and the observer. We stand back from the practice, as observers, and we recognise that this gives us a different perspective on practice, but there is a good reason to believe that if practitioners do stand back and think about their practice, they can be more effective. And if students of governing do this, they will be better analysts and better practitioners.

References

AIHW. 2020. *Australia's Children*. Canberra: Australian Institute of Health and Welfare.
Bacchi, Carol. 2009. *Analysing Policy: What's the Problem Represented to Be?* Frenchs Forest, NSW: Pearson Education.

Bailey, Frederick G. 1969. *Stratagems and Spoils: A Social Anthropology of Politics*. Oxford: Blackwells.
Béland, Daniel, and Michael Howlett. 2015. "How Solutions Chase Problems: Instrument Constituencies in the Policy Process." *Governance* 29 (3): 393–409.
Bridgman, Peter, and Glyn Davis. 2000. *The Australian Policy Handbook*. Sydney: Allen & Unwin.
Goffman, Erving. 1959. *The Presentation of Self in Everyday Life*. New York, NY: Doubleday.
Howard, Cosmo. 2005. "The Policy Cycle: A Model of Post-Machiavellian Policy Making?" *Australian Journal of Public Administration* 64 (3): 3–13. https://doi.org/10.1111/j.1467-8500.2005.00447.x
Moore, Mark H. 1995. *Creating Public Value*. Cambridge MA: Harvard University Press.

3 Problematization in school education policy
Underperformance and parent hyperactivity

Sarah Warner

Introduction

This chapter explores the problematization approach to analysing policy developed by Carol Bacchi. This approach starts its analysis not by looking at policy as a process of finding solutions to policy problems, but rather by seeing policy problems as being discursively shaped. This approach to problematization draws from Foucauldian scholarship, which considers the discursive practices which allow things, people, and subjects to become the focus of attention and, in doing so, constitute them (Terwiel 2020). A key insight of this problematization approach is the claim that we are governed through problematizations (Bacchi 2009). While Foucault's work on problematization is useful in providing an entry point into the concepts and the analysis required to identify and understand problematization, Carol Bacchi provides a way to operationalize problematization in policy analysis through the systematic application of a series of interrelated questions she calls the What's the Problem Represented to be (WPR) approach (2009).

School education is a large and significant policy area for contemporary governments. What happens in schools, the way school education is conducted and the social infrastructure it produces are key areas of policy activity of the state in Australia and many other countries. New policy directions are reshaping school education, and this chapter uses the problematization approach to explore the implications of these changes for parents as key policy subjects. This chapter considers the problem representation of 'underperformance' in school education policy and focuses on a tranche of policies relating to the underperformance of the school system. Whilst the impacts of these policies are multi-fold, this chapter focuses specifically on how policies act on parents and caregivers. It argues that the problematization of underperformance discursively shapes parents and caregivers to act to try to ensure successful school education outcomes for their children. Success in education becomes an activity that has to be strategized for by parents and caregivers, rather than simply delivered through the schooling system.

The remainder of the chapter is structured to first consider the definition, historical use, and ways in which problematization is used. Second, Bacchi's WPR approach is introduced before applying it to a case study of school education policy reform in Australia. The central problematization of 'underperformance' is discussed with reference to Bacchi's approach. The case study looks at how underperformance is utilized as a mechanism of rule and draws out the political implications of the problematization of underperformance. Finally, the chapter draws together some of the implications of this analysis for understanding how concepts of public and private, and collective and individual responsibility are reshaped by this problem representation.

DOI: 10.4324/9781003368564-3

A problematization approach

A problematization approach describes the way 'problems' are constituted in response to the very issues they are attempting to address. In this way, we can think of policies as producing the problems that they are designed to fix (Bacchi, 2009, 3). These 'problems' have particular meanings that impact what does and does not get done by government and how people live their lives. Focusing on problematizations provides an approach to understanding how we are ruled. By contrast, it is not an approach to finding the best policy solutions (Bacchi 2009).

Problems have become central to many forms of policy analysis. As Bacchi notes, problems can be understood in different ways and associated with a variety of analytical strategies, from interpretivists who focus on social actors as 'problematising agents' and in the approach used here drawing from a post-structuralist approach to "problematizations as the products of governmental programs" (Bacchi 2015, 3). Bacchi's approach operates in contrast to other problem focused approaches which locate problems as existing materially in the world. In those accounts, governments, are 'reacting' to problems when they generate policy (Bacchi 2009, 1). The problematization approach, used in this article, upends this central contention by showing instead how problems are 'made' through attention to what government finds important. In this way, the problematization approach offers an epistemologically and ontologically different approach to the way 'problems' are understood. Whilst positivist ontology, associated with problems existing in the material world, sees the world as 'external', objective and epistemologically knowable through observation, the problematization approach sees the world as discursively created and therefore as knowable only from within its construction. This difference allows problems to be thought of only as a representation of the way that knowledge is deployed within the field in which they are occurring.

A post-structural problematization approach to policy analysis is contextualized by Foucault within the broader approach to problematization. Foucault identifies problematization as the historical process of producing objects for thought (Deacon 2000). One way to understand Foucault's approach to problematization is through one of his major areas of inquiry: madness. Foucault asked how and when madness came to be identified as problematic and subject to 'governing strategies', which then constitute what 'madness' is understood to be. Linked to this is what kind of deportments, characteristics, and activities were labelled as 'mad'. He showed that labelling a behaviour or activity as mad actually serves to constitute madness itself (Foucault 2003). Moreover, madness is contingent on the discursive strategies it is embedded within: there is no intrinsic 'madness' but rather it is made up of a plurality of socially constructed and socio-historical context-dependent meanings. Governmentality scholars operationalized Foucault's understanding of problematization to show how governing in advanced liberal democracies has become linked to practices of self-government and individual responsibility (Miller and Rose 2008). Bacchi narrowed the analytical focus of governmentality from governing 'rationalities' broadly to policies specifically. However, she continued to emphasize the importance of problematization. Using the key insight that problems do not exist naturally or intrinsically but are constituted by the solutions developed, Bacchi developed a systematic way of analysing policy called the What is the Problem Represented to be Approach? (WPR) (2009), a question-based approach that unpacks the problematizations lodged in policy proposals. The questions Bacchi poses (see Table 3.1) provide an analytical strategy for unpacking problematization in policy and form the approach to problematization used in this chapter. The overall contribution that a study of problematization makes is to "make the politics, understood as the complex strategic relations that shape lives, visible" (Bacchi 2012, 1).

Table 3.1 The *What's the Problem Represented to be?* analytic framework

Question 1: What's the problem (e.g., of "gender inequality", "drug use/abuse", "economic development", "global warming", "childhood obesity", "irregular migration", etc.) represented to be in a specific policy or policies?
Question 2: What deep-seated presuppositions or assumptions (conceptual logics) underlie this representation of the "problem" (*problem representation*)?
Question 3: How has this representation of the "problem" come about?
Question 4: What is left unproblematic in this problem representation? Where are the silences? Can the "problem" be conceptualized differently?
Question 5: What effects (discursive, subjectification, lived) are produced by this representation of the "problem"'?
Question 6: How and where has this representation of the "problem" been produced, disseminated, and defended? How has it been and/or how can it be disrupted and replaced?
Question 7. Apply this list of questions to your own problem representations.

Source: Bacchi and Goodwin (2016, 20).

However, while problematization remains an important tool for policy analysts, critiques of the approach question its ontological premise, arguing that discourse alone is not constitutive of society and consequently a focus on discourse alone limits the WPR approach's capacity to analyse society (Feely 2020). Newer approaches to policy analysis which draw from problematization continue to emerge. Some of these approaches such as 'new materialism' adopt problematization as a strategy without the adherence to discourse alone (Davies 2016). Moving away from discourse alone opens up the use of problematization to a broader audience. Nonetheless, the WPR approach continues to provide a useful and relatively simple approach to unpacking underlying political perspectives in policy. The following section explores a case study of problematization in school education policy in Australia.

Problematization in school education policy

School education is a significant site of governmental activity and a site of recent reforms. It is so important to contemporary societies that it can be described as a paradigmatic institution in society (Peim 2013, 175–176). However, this was not always the case, institutionalized school education provided by the state is just over 150 years old in Australia (Campbell and Proctor 2014). School education emerged in the late nineteenth century as an arm of state building (Green 2013) and a form of social administration (Hunter 1994). Although there is a great deal of specificity to school education policy, the central thrusts have been to educate children for the purposes of social discipline and economic need within the construction of the modern state. These themes have been replicated in school education policy as it has changed over the years. Whilst the provision of school education is considered to produce benefits for the individual, it is also acknowledged that there are significant inequalities built into the system. For example, Connell (2012, 2) notes that the inequalities in the system have changed historically, moving from inequality based on institutional segregation to inequality based on market mechanisms. The way in which these inequalities emerge and the role of policy within them is an ongoing site of academic attention. This case study contributes to this analysis by exploring the role of the problem representation of underperformance in restructuring school education. Although it is acknowledged that the effects of the problematization of underperformance in school education policy are broad, this case study focuses specifically on the effects on parents as policy users.

Problematization in school education policy 19

The central impact of problematizing underperformance is that it destabilizes the certainty with which parents can assume that the state will provide a 'good' education for their children. In turn, parents are entreated to act in particular ways to secure a 'good' education, which blurs the role of private citizen and public policy actor. However, it should also be noted that parents are not a homogenous group and the way these effects play out in their lives is also governed by other factors such as their own education, socio-economic factors, race, class, and geographic location.

Recent reforms in school education at the federal, state, and local levels have shifted the arrangements in school education governance which have intensified the activities of parents in supporting their children through schooling. This case study concerns a range of policies that were introduced beginning in 2008 that have restructured school education in Australia. It explores how the essential underlying problematization of 'underperformance' has been operationalized in policy to show that school education has activated parents and caregivers as policy users. This chapter concentrates on two key policies which emerged out of federal education policy documents. The relevant policies which both constitute and address the representation of the problem and which have activated parents are the introduction of large-scale learning metrics in the National Assessment Program Literacy and Numeracy (NAPLAN) and the publication of these metrics for the benefit of parents and the community through MySchool. Though these policies are now firmly embedded in the system it is useful to reflect on them because they continue to exert influence on education policy users and generate change in the landscape of school education.

The remainder of this case study follows Bacchi's questions (see Table 3.1). In describing the strategies that can be used to undertake a WPR approach, Bacchi notes that the questions can either be used sequentially or integrated into a broader analysis (2009, 155). This chapter focuses on the questions related to representation of policy, underlying knowledges, and the conceptualizations which are left out (silences) to show how parents are shaped by this problematization.

Underperformance as the problem representation

Bacchi's first question asks about the problem representation in policy. The key problem representation can be found by working backwards from the proposed 'solutions' in policy texts. Underperformance is identified as a key issue in multiple policy texts. In 2008 the Federal Government's *Quality education: the case for an education revolution in our schools* policy document signalled the Government's interest in a reform agenda in school education. Underperformance is presented in the following way in that document:

> The performance of the Australian schooling system has been allowed to drop relative to that of other countries in the OECD. In the period between 2003 and 2006, Australia declined in both its absolute and relative performance in reading literacy.
> (Australian Government 2008, 16)

This particular policy document laid the foundation for policy changes to be implemented. However, underperformance continued to be noted in the 2011 *Gonski Report*:

> Australia must also improve its international standing by arresting the decline that has been witnessed over the past decade
> (Gonski et al. 2011, 22)

The problem representation of underperformance is again reiterated in the *Quality Schools Quality Outcomes* education policy document in 2016:

> … our performance both relative to other countries and in real terms has declined over time and there is a significant gap between our highest and lowest performing students
> (Australian Government 2016, 1)

By 2018 underperformance was even more prominent in the second Gonski Review:

> Declining academic performance is jeopardizing the attainment of Australia's aspiration for excellence and equity in school education … This has occurred in every socio-economic quartile and in all school sectors (government, Catholic, and Independent). The extent of the decline is widespread and equivalent to a generation of Australian school children falling short of their full learning potential
> (Australian Government 2018, vii–viii)

In all the policy documents mentioned here, underperformance was identified using the mechanism of quantification of school education via the OECD's Programme of International Assessment (PISA). The OECD's PISA has been influential in shaping domestic education policy and in establishing the importance of large-scale learning metrics in education as noted extensively by education scholars (Grek 2009, 2014; Gorur and Wu 2015; Lewis, Sellar, and Lingard 2016).

The problem representation of underperformance was then addressed in policy through the introduction of standardized learning metrics to measure student achievement. NAPLAN is Australia's key learning metrics, and it relies on the same underlying knowledges that are used in the OECD's PISA. The purpose of the assessment programme, as presented by the governing authority, is that it "… helps drive improvements in student outcomes and provides increased accountability for the community" (ACARA 2022b). The underlying representation encapsulated in the assessment programme is that the learning metrics through standardized testing can be used to both reveal underperformance and fix underperformance. Like the concept of madness discussed above, performance or underperformance is not an intrinsic category. Rather it only exists because it has been constructed to be so. In this way NAPLAN makes possible 'underperformance'.

The importance and influence of learning metrics have been further embedded by government policy to make the results public. Results are made public through MySchool a government website.[1] MySchool claims to do two things: first that it "supports national transparency and accountability of Australia's schools by publishing nationally consistent school-level data about every school in Australia" and second that it "helps inform discussions between parents and teachers and supports parents in making informed decisions about their child's education" (ACARA 2022a). By publicizing test scores in this way, it also specifically invites parents and caregivers into the conversation about performance in schooling. By placing the knowledge of 'underperformance' into the field of view of parents, they come to feel anxiety about the school system. Parents then use this information to become market actors by comparing, strategizing around, and choosing schools for their children. This activity of parenting is reflected in the discourses of responsibilization which identify a governing shift where risk is transferred from the state to the individual (Lemke 2011; Olmedo and Wilkins 2017).

Unpacking the conceptual logics in the problem representation

One of the strengths of the problematization approach is that it reveals the underlying knowledge assumptions in a policy, so as to reveal the political perspectives which characterize the choice of policy. These assumptions reflect the epistemological and ontological approaches adopted in policy (Bacchi 2009, 5). To reveal these assumptions in relation to school education policy requires an interrogation of how underperformance both came to be the problem representation and what makes underperformance a category which can be understood as a reflection of the quality of school education. In the case of underperformance there are two key knowledges which operate to make this representation possible. First, that school performance is quantifiable and second that comparisons make quantification meaningful. These two knowledges "construct powerful discourses about comparative and datafied approaches to educational performance as being both effective and appropriate governance mechanisms to improve educational systems" (Grek, Maroy, and Verger 2021, 5).

It is an important characteristic of the learning metrics that they be able to be used to generate comparisons. Comparative strategies have emerged as a routine practice in education policy reflected in the idea of the so-called 'comparative turn' in education (Martens 2007). Comparisons are made between cohorts, schools, and even states and countries. They are used to tell stories about performance and underperformance. Comparisons also operate to mimic market logics.

In the Australian education landscape, the public display of school level NAPLAN data is used to make comparisons between schools legible to the broader public. This in turn allows some schools to be defined as 'performing' and therefore desirable and others as 'underperforming' and therefore less desirable. Importantly, the policy outputs of NAPLAN and MySchool actually create the underperformance that they are designed to address. The public display of the data has activated parents and caregivers to engage with the performance of schools. It has created a pathway for parents to take greater responsibility for their child's schooling. This moves the risk of education from the state to the parent. Parents have internalized the importance of performance and the fear of underperformance and act to try to ensure good outcomes for their children. A key activity where this is visible is in school choice. School choice is now a widespread phenomenon both as a choice between public and private schools (Campbell, Proctor, and Sherington 2009) and more recently as choice between different public schools. Importantly, the act of choosing is not always available or able to be secured and this opens up new inequalities in school education. Whilst parents report that they choose schools for various reasons, the underlying availability and legibility of performance statistics feeds into these choices (Rowe and Windle 2012; Warner 2020). However, from a problematization perspective it is the use of the underlying logics of performance metrics which have shaped the landscape of school choice and therefore the choices made by parents. The implication of understanding problematization of underperformance, revealed and constituted by testing regimes made public, is that schooling becomes a more insecure experience. This is felt keenly by parents.

Where did the problem come from and what are its effects?

Bacchi's third question asks how the problem representation has come about. In school education the answer lies in globalization which has allowed education policy to become far more interlinked with policy in other jurisdictions (Lingard 2013; Lingard et al. 2016). This trend is so profound that scholars have noted that policy mobility has moved from policy transfer to a 'policy convergence', where like policies appear in multiple jurisdictions (Ball 2012, 2). Policy convergence in school education operates to favour a limited range of policy strategies which Sahlberg identifies as including large-scale assessments through which data is collected and used to make comparison, a concentration on core curricula which helps make comparison possible and which removes other elements of education from view (Sahlberg 2016).

Two propositions are at the core of policy convergence in education: the first is that there is an underlying set of knowledges (comparison of statistical data from standardized testing regimes) which are remaking the purpose and expression of education. The second is that international organizations, particularly the OECD, play an overarching role in disseminating education policy to member states with soft but ultimately effective ways of encouraging like policies to be adopted across jurisdictions. The role of the OECD has been highly influential in Australian education policy. In the first *Australian Education Act* in 2013 Australia committed to chasing international excellence:

> ... for Australia to be placed, by 2025, in the top 5 highest performing countries based on the performance of school students in reading, mathematics and science; (ii) for the Australian schooling system to be considered a high quality and highly equitable schooling system by international standards by 2025
>
> (2013, 3)

Lingard and Lewis show that Australia both uses and is influenced by the OECD and PISA in education policy (Lingard and Lewis 2017). Therefore, the problem representation of underperformance has importance in both linking education to the global context, encapsulated in the idea that education is key to economic competitiveness in a globalizing world, which further normalizes the idea education success as linked to standardized learning metrics and comparisons. Parents experience these themes as evidence of the uncertainty of the schooling system in its role as generating good performance.

Bacchi's fourth question allows us to see the silences: what is not considered and how could it be conceptualized differently. By representing the problem as underperformance, the answer to the problem is easily understood as driving up performance. However, this binary construction between performance and underperformance as a marker of educational success leaves out alternative ways of understanding the value of school education and the purpose of school. Biesta elaborates this point to suggest that normative validity of measurements becomes replaced by technical validity which shifts not only what we can count but what we value by asking are we "measuring what we value, or ... just measuring what we can easily measure and thus end up valuing what we (can) measure" (Biesta 2009, 35). Consequently, other aspects of education or even other approaches to school education are obscured from view and debate. The implication is that learning metrics structure the field of education in ways that limit opportunities for non-datafied education outcomes to be considered useful in determining performance and indeed assessing school experience. This, combined with the near-hegemonic role of datafication and comparison as a form of good governance in education, makes it impossible for governments to either opt out of comparative strategies or refocus education towards non-quantifiable characteristics such as creativity, imagination, or civic courage (Apple et al. 2022). Moreover, the hegemonic effect of the datafication of education impacts parents as policy users, who are only provided with limited ways of understanding merit in schooling. This obscures other socialcultural and political factors which might contribute to educational outcomes. These are the silences. Ultimately, even when parents value other aspects of education they are limited in their capacity to operationalize these values. The policy regime has contributed to their responsibilization, where parents' attempts to manage risk in education create inequalities based on their varying capacities to be successful and their varying capacities to engage in the task.

A second significant silence is that in constructing the problem representation as underperformance, other structural and systemic factors which contribute to education outcomes, such as (but not limited to) race, class, disability, sexuality, geography, and gender are minimized. An alternative analysis of school education notes that whilst it is often seen as a transformative social institution, it more commonly replicates the same inequalities which operate elsewhere in society (Bourdieu and Passeron 1990). Moreover, the inequalities are (re)produced in other ways and are structurally embedded in society, including in education. Simply targeting performance does not sufficiently acknowledge the "deep structural asymmetries of power" at play in education (Bacchi 2009, 207). This also means that as parents are activated to support their children in education, they feel responsible for perceived failures which may more rightly be attached to structural aspects of society and education.

Education policy has impacts on many different subjects, each of whom engage with education policy in diverse ways. The focus in this chapter is on considering the effects on parents and caregivers as key policy subjects in education policy. The discourse of underperformance shapes their choices and responses to school education as they seek to support their children in school education. One of the discursive effects that arises in representing the problem as underperformance is that success in schooling is no longer solely the responsibility of the school; responsibility for success or uncertainty about success has been extended to parents and caregivers.

Parents and caregivers respond to this uncertainty by trying to ensure better outcomes for their children through a range of strategies. Parents become hyperactive subjects who engage in supporting their children's success in schooling in diverse and often labour-intensive ways. Parents and caregivers do the work of supporting school students and schools in diverse ways, such as choosing schools or strategizing to get into schools, raising funds, advocating for children with additional needs, and sourcing additional tutoring. The labour which parents engage to support their children in school education, both for individual and collective purposes, recasts the role of parents not only as private citizens working strategically to manage and support their children's schooling success but also as policy actors participating in the process of executing policy goals, albeit with varying success. While the activities of parents to support their children in school education may be viewed as producing benefits for the individual and therefore be considered a private concern, they also support the broader policy agenda of driving up performance.

The analysis conducted here has shown that underperformance is a central problem representation in school education policy. While school education has always had an element of performance measurement associated with it, the concentration on underperformance tied to students, schools, and cohorts has embedded conceptual logics which normalize the idea of 'performance' and 'underperformance'. The performance of schools and students is now highly visible and is privately reported to parents and caregivers, administratively to schools and used internally in education departments and publicly through MySchool and the media. "Foucault-influenced poststructuralists emphasize how subjects are constituted (or formed) within the very discourses (knowledges) that shape understandings of 'problems'" (Bacchi 2015). This allows parents to become more immersed in the need to secure good schooling for their children. Parents and caregivers take up this role in an attempt to secure educational performance for their children. In a system where performance is everything and successful performance is not assured, parents increasingly see their own participation in their children's schooling as important to helping secure success. The body of literature which notes the hyperactivity of parenting in school education characterizes it in terms of middle-class parents having the capacities to maximize their children's success in schooling due to their socio-economic and social capital (see for example, Campbell, Proctor, and Sherington 2009; Reay, Crozier, and James 2011; Rowe

2017). However, the literature less often understands this relationship in terms of the way it ties parents and the state (in the public provision of schooling) together. An implication of this relationship is that parents become de facto policy actors, as they strategize and deliver educational outcomes for their children they also constitute the policy environment.

Conclusion

This chapter has used Carol Bacchi's WPR problematization approach to reveal the underlying problematization in school education policy. Bacchi's problematization approach turns on the idea that policy affects people's lives. Policy shapes the environments in which people live and the choices they make and how they see themselves and others. This connection between policy and people's lives is revealed through attention to Bacchi's questions. The approach shows that policy is not about cause and effect but operates through knowledges which normalize certain approaches to policy. In the case of school education and the problematization of underperformance, it is quantification and comparison which have been mobilized in the policy process. Quantification and comparison are key conceptual logics which underpin the policies discussed in this chapter; they create meanings, serve to normalize certain behaviours, and then shape the way people experience these policies. Ventilating these knowledges and their effects is a key benefit of this post-structural approach to problematization. Moreover, constructing the problem of underperformance in this way allows us to trace the impact of this problem representation on policy subjects. It shows how the underlying knowledges embedded in the performance of educational comparisons are not just inevitable outcomes but are, in fact, political choices made by government, thereby also highlighting the contingent nature of policy – where it could have been otherwise. In this way it is possible to see that parents are shaped by the policy environment in which they are enmeshed, and their actions are connected to that environment, rather than being separate to it.

Note

1 MySchool is run by the Australian Curriculum, Assessment and Reporting Authority (ACARA) established in 2008, it is a statutory authority whose work is directed by the education ministers of all Australian governments (ACARA 2008).

Further reading

Bacchi, Carol. 2009. *Analysing Policy: What's the Problem Represented to be?* 1st ed. Frenchs Forest, NSW: Pearson Education.
—. 2015. "The Turn to Problematization: Political Implications of Contrasting Interpretive and Post-Structural Adaptions." *Open Journal of Political Science* 5: 1–12. https://doi.org/10.4236/ojps.2012.21001.
Komai, Eléonore. 2021. "Constituting 'Problems' through Policies: A WPR Approach of Policies Governing Teenage Pregnancy in France." *Social Policy and Society*: 1–17. https://doi.org/10.1017/S1474746421000373.

References

2013. *Australian Education Act 2013* (Cth) (No.67, 2013). *C2013A00067*.
ACARA. 2008. "ACARA: Australian Curriculum, Assessment and Reporting Authority." Accessed March 11, 2018. https://www.acara.edu.au/home

—. 2022a. "MySchool." Australian Curriculum, Assessment and Reporting Authority. Accessed June 8, 2022. https://www.myschool.edu.au/about-my-school

—. 2022b. "NAP: National Assessment Program." Accessed September 7. https://nap.edu.au/about

Apple, Michael, Gert Biesta, David Bright, Henry Giroux, Amanda Heffernan, Peter McLaren, Steward Riddle, and Anna Yeatman. 2022. "Reflections on Contemporary Challenges and Possibilities for Democracy and Education." *Journal of Educational Administration and History* 54 (3): 245–62. https://doi.org/10.1080/00220620.2022.2052029

Australian Government. 2008. *Quality Education: The Case for an Education Revolution in Our Schools*. Canberra: Australian Government.

—. 2016. *Quality Schools, Quality Outcomes*. Canberra: Australian Government.

—. 2018. *Through Growth to Achievement: Report of the Review to Achieve Educational Excellence in Australian Schools*. Canberra: Department of Education and Training, Australian Government.

Bacchi, Carol. 2009. *Analysing Policy: What's the Problem Represented to Be?* 1st ed. Frenchs Forest, NSW: Pearson Education.

—. 2012. "Why Study Problematizations? Making Politics Visible." *Open Journal of Political Science* 2 (1): 1–8.

—. 2015. "The Turn to Problematization: Political Implications of Contrasting Interpretive and Post-Structural Adaptions." *Open Journal of Political Science* 5: 1–12. https://doi.org/10.4236/ojps.2012.21001

Bacchi, Carol, and Susan Goodwin. 2016. *Poststructural Policy Analysis: A Guide to Practice*, A Guide to Practice. New York: Palgrave Macmillan.

Ball, Stephen J. 2012. *Global Education Inc. New Policy Networks and the Neo-Liberal Imaginary*, edited by Corporation Ebooks. Abingdon, Oxon: Routledge.

Biesta, Gert. 2009. "Good Education in an Age of Measurement: On the Need to Reconnect with the Question of Purpose in Education." *Educational Assessment, Evaluation and Accountability* 21: 33–46. https://doi.org/10.1007/s11092-008-9064-9.

Bourdieu, Pierre, and Jean-Claude Passeron. 1990. *Reproduction in Education, Society and Culture*. London: Sage Publications.

Campbell, Craig, and Helen Proctor. 2014. *A History of Australian Schooling*. Sydney: Allen & Unwin.

Campbell, Craig, Helen Proctor, and Geoffrey Sherington. 2009. *School Choice: How Parents Negotiate the New School Market in Australia*. Sydney: Allen & Unwin.

Connell, Raewyn. 2012. "Just Education." *Journal of Education Policy* 27 (5): 681–83.

Davies, Bronwyn. 2016. "Ethics and the New Materialism: A Brief Genealogy of the 'post' Philosophies in the Social Sciences." *Discourse: Studies in the Cultural Politics of Education* 39 (1): 1–15.

Deacon, Roger. 2000. "Theory as Practice: Foucault's Concept of Problematization." *Telos* 2000 (118): 127–42.

Feely, Michael. 2020. "Assemblage Analysis: An Experimental New-Materialist Method for Analysing Narrative Data." *Qualitative Research* 20 (2): 174–93.

Foucault, Michel. 2003. "Madness and Society." In *The Essential Foucault*, edited by Paul Rabinow and Nikolas Rose, 370–76. New York, London: The New Press.

Gonski, David, Ken Boston, Kathryn Greiner, Carmen Lawrence, Bill Scales, and Peter Tannock. 2011. *Review of Funding for Schooling (Gonski Report)*. Canberra: Department of Education, Employment and Workplace Relations.

Gorur, Radhika, and Margaret Wu. 2015. "Leaning Too Far? PISA, Policy and Australia's 'top five' ambitions." *Discourse: Studies in the Cultural Politics of Education* 36 (5): 647–64.

Green, Andy. 2013. *Education and State Formation: Europe, East Asia and The USA*. 2nd ed. Basingstoke: Palgrave Macmillan.

Grek, Sotiria. 2009. "Governing by Numbers: The PISA 'effect' in Europe." *Journal of Education Policy* 24 (1): 23–37.

—. 2014. "OECD as a Site of Coproduction: European Education Governance and the New Politics of 'policy mobilization'." *Critical Policy Studies* 8 (3): 266–81.

Grek, Sotiria, Christian Maroy, and Antoni Verger. 2021. "Introduction: Accountability and Datafication in Education: Historical, Transnational and Conceptual Perspectives." In *World Yearbook of Education 2021: accountability and datafication in the governance of education*, 1–22. London: Routledge.

Hunter, Ian. 1994. *Rethinking the School: Subjectivity, Bureaucracy, Criticism*. Sydney: Allen & Unwin.

Lemke, Thomas. 2011. *Biopolitics: An Advanced Introduction*. Vol. 1. New York, NY: New York University Press.

Lewis, Steven, Sam Sellar, and Bob Lingard. 2016. "PISA for Schools: Topological Rationality and New Spaces of the OECD's Global Educational Governance." *Comparative Education Review* 60 (1): 27–57.

Lingard, Bob. 2013. "Historicizing and Contextualizing Global Policy Discourses: Test- and Standards-Based Accountabilities in Education." *International Education Journal: Comparative Perspectives* 12 (2): 122.

Lingard, Bob, and Steven Lewis. 2017. "Placing PISA and PISA for Schools in Two Federalisms, Australia and the USA." *Critical Studies in Education* 58 (3): 266–79. https://doi.org/10.1080/17508487.2017.1316295

Lingard, Bob, Wayne Martino, Goli Rezai-Rashti, and Sam Sellar. 2016. *Globalizing Educational Accountabilities*. New York, NY: Routledge.

Martens, Kerstin. 2007. "How to Become an Influential Actor – The 'comparative turn' in OECD Education Policy." In *Transformations of the State and Global Governance*, edited by Martens Kerstin, Alexander-Kenneth Rusconi and K. Lutz. London: Routledge.

Miller, Peter, and Nikolas Rose. 2008. *Governing the Present: Administering Economic, Social and Personal Life*. Malden, MA: Polity Press.

Olmedo, Antonio, and Andrew Wilkins. 2017. "Governing Through Parents: a Genealogical Enquiry of Education Policy and the Construction of Neoliberal Subjectivities in England." *Discourse: Studies in the Cultural Politics of Education* 38 (4): 573–89. https://doi.org/10.1080/01596306.2015.1130026

Peim, Nick. 2013. "Education, Schooling, Derrida's Marx and Democracy: Some Fundamental Questions." *Studies in Philosophy and Education* 32 (2): 171–87.

Reay, Diane, Gill Crozier, and David James. 2011. *White Middle-Class Identities and Urban Schooling*. London: Palgrave Macmillan.

Rowe, Emma. 2017. "Middle-Class School Choice in the Urban: Educational Campaigning for a Public School." In *Second International Handbook of Urban Education*, edited by William T. Pink and George W. Noblit, 945–58. Cham: Springer.

Rowe, Emma E., and Joel Windle. 2012. "The Australian Middle Class and Education: A Small-Scale Study of the School Choice Experience as Framed by 'My School' within Inner City Families." *Critical Studies in Education* 53 (2): 137–51.

Sahlberg, Pasi. 2016. "The Global Education Reform Movement and Its Impact on Schooling." In *The Handbook of Global Education Policy*, edited by Karen Mundy, Andy Green, Bob Lingard and Antoni Verger, 128–44. Chichester: Wiley Blackwell.

Terwiel, Anna. 2020. "Problematization as an Activist Practice: Reconsidering Foucault." *Theory & Event* 23 (1): 66–84.

Warner, Sarah. 2020. "State-Citizen Relations Explored through Australian School Education Policy." PhD thesis, School of Political Science and International Studies, University of Queensland.

4 Local governments as policy shapers

Sarah de Vries

Introduction

In an era where the need for community engagement in policymaking is almost universally recognised, local governments are uniquely positioned to contribute towards that goal (Herriman 2011). While critics attempt to portray the role of local governments as limited to service provision, or 'roads, rates and rubbish', it is well established that local governments' remit is much broader and includes important aspects of social and environmental policy (Dollery, Wallis, and Allan 2006; Arnold and Long 2019). The principle of subsidiarity – that central governments should perform tasks which cannot be performed at a more local level – reinforces the importance of local governments for enabling effective cooperative governance (Dovers and Hussey 2013). In attempting to conceptualise the policymaking process, the 'policy cycle' as it is traditionally represented, mirrors the design process – with stages to facilitate problem framing, design, implementation, and continual improvement – but it is largely silent on who is included and excluded from the process. Legitimate and effective policy formation must be a highly collaborative process, including those who might be impacted by a particular policy and cognisant of the values of the broader community. Local governments have unique responsibilities and decision-making powers through their planning systems and proximity to the communities they serve. They are, though, nested within a multilevel governance system whose success relies on high levels of coordination and deliberation (Daniell and Adrian 2018). The empowerment – or otherwise – of local governments to influence other levels of government in that system is, therefore, crucial.

Climate change and related environmental policies are a particularly illustrative example of local government involvement in policymaking beyond their legal remit. Local governments in Australia engage in environment-related activities well beyond their statutory requirements and in ways that are creative and innovative (Thomas 2010). Environmental matters are inextricably linked to the core business of local governments such as town planning, water and waste management as well as emerging areas of importance such as biodiversity, natural resource management, and energy use (Dollery, Wallis, and Allan 2006). Australia's national and subnational governments (state and territory) have been notoriously slow in their policy response to climate change. Despite this, many communities and local governments have continued to express their commitment to climate change action, progress the changes that they can locally and network to advocate for further action. This chapter analyses a number of Australian examples of local governments influencing environmental policy formation by higher levels of government. It identifies the practices of these local governments that made them highly engaged with their citizens and the important contributions that they made to policy formation. The ways in which policymaking processes enable and hinder this contribution are discussed before presenting a range of tools to support local governments in enhancing their engagement with their citizens and their influence over policy processes. These tools are not presented as an established theory, but rather as a provocation for additional research which is further elaborated in the concluding section of the chapter.

Local governments

Local governments can be variously described as local councils or municipalities and are the level of government closest to citizens. Their attributes vary widely, as does the role they play within communities. For example, in some countries such as the United Kingdom, local governments have a broad range of policy responsibilities including housing and community health. Australian local governments have more limited formal powers and traditionally a narrower legal remit. Local governments in Australia are subject to a high degree of oversight from higher levels of government (Coghill, Ng, and Thornton-Smith 2014). They are not recognised in the Australian Constitution, instead created by acts of Parliament by state governments, which determine their role, powers, and funding and electoral rules. There is a trend towards an expanding role for local governments including in areas of environmental policy (Holden and Jacobson 2006; Arnold and Long 2019). This includes representing their communities on policies beyond their direct control and as such local governments often act as advocates for their communities (Henderson 2019). While common in practice, advocacy continues to be under-recognised, under researched, and rarely formalised in local government legislation. In Australia, local governments increase their policy influence through peak bodies (such as local government associations) which represent their interests in policy engagement. They also form coalitions of local governments at regional levels, some more formalised and stable and others more ad hoc.

Public discourse on local government is rarely centred on their contribution to political engagement instead focusing on accountability to higher levels of government and financial efficiency, including amalgamations (Dollery, Kortt, and Souza 2022).

> The continuing processes of local government reform, and broader governance reform have resulted in structures of metropolitan governance that tend to professionalise, rather than democratise decision-making. Likewise, these have tended, in most cases, to result in a dilution of direct local government roles in new institutions of decision-making
> (Butt et al. 2021, 23)

The success of amalgamations is yet to be determined, "the literature is overwhelmingly pessimistic on the efficacy of amalgamation as a means of improving local government efficiency" (Dollery, Kortt, and Souza 2022, 7). While findings about the financial benefits may be mixed at best, there has been little enquiry into the impacts of amalgamations on important dimensions of local government activity such as governance and citizen participation (Caldas, Dollery, and Marques 2016). Some research indicates that larger local government size has a negative impact on political participation (McDonnell 2018), suggesting that there may be fundamental tensions between efficiency and effectiveness at least on some measures.

Local government has long been understood as a pathway to political engagement with higher levels of government – it is often the first and most frequent point of contact between people and government. In addition, evidence suggests people trust their local governments more than other levels of government (Lawton and Macaulay 2014) and that results in greater trust of the overall political system (Schoburgh and Ryan 2017). Despite this, public debate about the role of local governments in recent decades has been worryingly silent on issues of political engagement and representation. A number of scholars have contributed to building the case for a progressive vision of local government (Beetham 1996; Gaventa 2004; Dollery, Wallis, and Allan 2006; Stoker 2006; Newman 2014; de Vries 2020). Providing ample support for the case that local governments' contribution to democratic quality should be central in discourse about their future.

Participation and deliberation

Local governments have a well-established role in community engagement and are ideally positioned to facilitate engagement for policy responses to climate change and environmental challenges (Fritze, Williamson, and Wiseman 2009; Herriman 2011).

> Community engagement strategies can contribute to improving climate change policy outcomes by; assisting citizens and communities develop informed understandings of climate change ... informing the development and implementation of locally tailored and sustainable structures, support networks and actions; encouraging social innovation and skill sharing, informed by local knowledge and tailored to local conditions ... and, strengthening public support for governments to act on climate change
> (Fritze et al. 2009, 2)

Certain attributes of engagement increase its effectiveness on these measures, including the quality of face-to-face communication (Lingafelter and Leavitt 2012; Buchecker, Menzel, and Home 2013). Deliberation and dialogue are theories which define other attributes of effective community engagement (Craig and Mayo 1995; Westoby and Kaplan 2014). Deliberation can be defined as rational discussions between parties about the merits of and reasons for different courses of action and may require compromise to achieve mutually beneficial outcomes (Dryzek 2011). Definitions of dialogue describe it as something more personal, an establishment of mutual trust and understanding (Westoby and Kaplan 2014), a precursor for effective deliberation. Dialogue, especially 'bridging conversations' are approaches that can increase people's understanding of different viewpoints. This can increase the level of consensus between parties or increase acceptance of decisions that may not have been a first preference (Putnam 2007).

Westoby and others highlight the transformative potential of dialogue which can change hearts and minds – often occurring between small numbers of people where there is trust and mutual respect (Westoby and Dowling 2013). The scale of local government makes them well suited to enabling dialogue and deliberation. For example, they can form genuine and lasting partnerships with local citizens and civil society (Cuthill 2002) to form the basis of 'bridging' conversations. Deliberation has been suggested as a vital tool in achieving the systemic shift that is required to effectively respond to climate change, enabling people to re-assess their pre-conceptions (Hammond 2020; Hatzisavvidou 2020). The extent and quality of engagement between local governments and their citizens continues to vary widely. Research suggests local government community engagement and responsiveness is highly variable with many still failing to effectively engage with their communities due to a range of factors including organisational culture and lack of capacity (Christensen and McQuestin 2019). In Victoria, the *Local Government Act 2020* includes a requirement for councils to embed deliberative approaches into their engagement practices, this has been accompanied by calls for more support for local governments to realise these requirements (Savini and Grant 2020). Factors found to affect the degree of local government community engagement include time, public interest, funding, knowledge and skills of staff, executive leader commitment and degree of councillor support

(Christensen and McQuestin 2019), as well as organisational culture (Herriman 2011). The presence of staff dedicated to community engagement in a local government is a strong indicator that community engagement is well embedded in the organisation (Herriman 2011).

Australian local governments influencing policy change

The degree of local governments' policy influence varies depending on their capacity and attributes. In analysing local government contributions to effective policy formation, it is necessary to make a distinction between local governments' responsiveness to their own citizens and the strength of their voice in vertical advocacy. In ideal cases, these attributes go hand in hand – local governments that are highly engaged with their citizens are able to leverage this legitimacy to influence policy formation that is more responsive to citizens. Local governments have a number of strengths for contributing to collaborative, well-informed and effective policy formation (de Vries 2021a). Local government legitimacy and access to information as a level of government gives them a significant advantage over other non-government organisations in providing representation of community views. While non-government organisations often represent a community of practice, local governments include a diversity of people and therefore can be an effective forum for dialogue, moving a policy conversation towards win-win solutions.

The views and policies of local governments who are well connected to their citizens should influence policy formation at higher levels of government. Yet, policymaking processes are rarely structured to realise their potential contribution. Local governments tend to participate in policymaking at higher levels of government in a similar way to any other external stakeholder or community advocate (KPMG 2015; Department of Agriculture Water and the Environment 2020). Many policies made by state and national governments have significant local impacts and failing to include local governments can compromise policy outcomes. Local governments continue to contribute to environmental policy formation despite contextual factors that often fail to support their role in doing so. The case studies below demonstrate that when local governments are excluded or their input disregarded during policymaking processes, their lack of support for a policy approach can be significant enough for policy change.

Otway ranges environment network, Victoria

The battle to protect the Otway forests had been ongoing since the 1980s, seeking to balance the need for nature conservation with the interests of the forestry industry. A Victorian state government was in power which was sympathetic to the interests of the forestry industry and looking to erode forest protections. A campaign was mobilised between 1999 and 2002 to advocate for the protection of the Otway forests which eventually achieved majority buy-in from potentially impacted communities. Coined the 'water not woodchips' campaign, messages relating to the viability of the local water supply catchments and related impacts on tourism were emphasised (Demetrious 2008).

The involvement of local governments was an important part of the success of the campaign, with several councils passing resolutions in support of the protection of the Otway forests. Majority community support for Otways protection translated into political accountability at the ballot boxes:

> During the 2002 state election campaign, the Victorian Liberal Party supported continued logging in the Otways ... the Liberal Party's Geelong team was decimated. It failed to win every local seat
>
> (Otway Ranges Environment Network Inc 2020 np)

Local government and community support for the protection of the Otway forests influenced electoral outcomes. The community was willing to change their vote on the basis of this issue, favouring state government representatives whose policy position was aligned with their views.

East-West Link, Melbourne

The East-West Link, a proposed tunnel project just North of Melbourne's CBD, was announced by a Victorian Liberal government in 2012. It was a project slated in the 'Eddington report' of 2008, a transport policy document commissioned by Victorian Labor to "connect the last of the 'unconnected' freeways leading towards the city" (Eddington 2008, 129).

Opposition to the project emerged from multiple quarters. Impacted local government, Yarra City Council, took a strong and early stance against the project and established a transport advisory committee to connect key stakeholders to advocate against it, in favour of greater funding for public transport. Yarra and Moreland city councils engaged in physical protests and shared information, resources, and training with their communities and key stakeholders:

> Councillors were instrumental in getting information about what was happening, they had a legitimate position to get information. They first brought it to our attention early on … they're a canary in the coal mine effectively
>
> (anon community quote)

State government was legislatively required to bring the project to an assessment panel, however they restricted access to the business case and did not take up the panel's recommendations.

> The panel made some recommendations of how you could have delivered that project in a much better way … they [state government] really messed up by not listening, by not dealing with the content of the project, and that's the reason why in the end it [the project] collapsed
>
> (anon state government quote)

Advocacy against the project culminated in legal action brought jointly by Yarra and Moreland City Councils. The case was not successful in changing the stance of the incumbent government but was successful in influencing policy change by Labor in opposition. Just weeks before the election, Labor committed to not honouring contracts signed for the project if they were elected. They stayed true to that promise when elected despite costing the Victorian Government $339million to abandon the project (Lucas and Gordon 2015).

Coal seam gas, Northern NSW

Prior to 2010 a number of coal seam gas (CSG) licenses were issued in Northern NSW. As test drilling commenced, community opposition grew. Lismore City Council declared its opposition to the industry early. A community-led campaign also grew, with a prominent strategy 'gas field free' street declarations, which started in the Channon. Residents went door to door on almost every street in the community to collect signatures. These 'street declarations' were presented to Lismore City Council Mayor in a ceremony of community solidarity. The approach spread to other communities across the region (Kia 2012).

Lismore mayor displayed the declarations in her office and advocated for them to members of parliament she met with. Lismore City Council undertook a poll at their local government election which established that 87% of people living in the Lismore municipality were opposed to CSG (Lismore City Council 2018). Other local governments in the region joined forces in opposition to the industry. The state was attempting to exclude local governments from the policymaking process, much to the frustration of local councillors:

> I pointed to the road declarations and I said, these are from the people in our community who do not want CSG, he said, 'they're going to get it anyway' ... I was shocked at his arrogance. I was shocked that he thought this community would just be bulldozed about this
> (anon local government quote)

> The state government will make these arbitrary decisions, not listen, and you've almost got to have a riot on your hands before they'll do something about it. I'd like to see them be a bit more responsive to the needs of the communities, engage with their mayors and their councillors a bit more, find out what's happening on the ground, we're their biggest resource, and I don't think they taking advantage of it ... that gob smacks me, how can you make decisions about our region or an area, if you haven't engaged with the local councils?
> (anon local government quote)

Pressure mounted on NSW government to change their position through street marches, letters to government, meetings with advisors and protestors directly blocking work at drilling sites. As the state government continued to resist, protests blocking work, or 'non-violent direction actions' became a key component of the campaign. This culminated in early 2014 at Bentley where hundreds of people permanently camped on site with thousands more on call to support the blockade when needed – a presence was maintained at Bentley for over 5 months (Shoebridge 2016). The morning a police response was anticipated, instead it was announced that the government was suspending the company's license to operate (Shoebridge 2014). This was followed by a buy-back scheme to resume all the CSG licenses in the Northern Rivers (Roberts 2014). Even though direct action can be credited with the success of the campaign, the support of local government was instrumental. Research found it helped legitimise the voice of the protestors and demonstrate that it was a majority view, providing a counter to the government's continued insistence that it was only a noisy, left-wing minority who opposed the industry (de Vries 2021a).

How local governments influence policy

As demonstrated by these case studies, local governments can and often do play an important role in policy formation in relation to climate change and environmental policy. They do so despite having fewer financial and legislative tools at their disposal in comparison to higher levels of government. Local governments use a range of procedural policy tools such as community engagement, information sharing, and network formation (de Vries 2021b). Some of the more assertive methods used by local governments are similar to approaches used in the non-government sector such as protest, alliance building, and community mobilisation. In these case studies local governments overcame several barriers to influence policy change. They faced considerable pressure not to advocate – and instead align their stance with higher levels of government. This is partly due to the high degree of oversight of local governments in Australia which can be a hindrance to local government responsiveness to local needs (Aulich 2009). It can also foster organisational culture conducive to executing the roles assigned to them by state governments, rather than a culture that is defined by the wishes of local citizens (Crowley 1998). They are dependent on higher levels of government for their funding and responsibilities, and there are few legislative mechanisms to protect their role as advocates. These pressures impact local governments willingness to advocate, "state governments are being challenged to surrender their legislative power over local government in order to facilitate 'real' partnerships with local communities and embrace notions of participatory governance" (Aulich 2009, 57). Henderson (2018) uses the term 'shadow of hierarchy' to describe the ways that state governments influence the activities of local government.

The high degree of influence of local governments in policymaking demonstrated through these case studies is made possible by the authenticity of their relationships with local community members, representatives, and organisations. They strengthen their influence by connecting with and investing in the capacity of their communities, by being agile in responding to community concerns, by networking with allies including non-government organisations, industry, and other local governments, and by advocating for those concerns to higher levels of government. These examples embrace deliberative principles. They demonstrate local governments' contribution to the diversity and availability of information, reasoned arguments and scientific evidence, and opportunities for conversations about the merits of various policy responses, which in turn provides a significant contribution to the legitimacy of resulting policy responses. A strong finding from these case studies is the important role of generative power in compelling policy change. Local government and community actors wrote letters, met with members of parliament and senior public servants, and pushed their message through the media. However, the political influence of views expressed by a majority of the community was essential for these measures to be effective. One interview participant summed up this principle, "don't focus on convincing the government, focus on convincing your neighbours, and the government will follow" (anonymous).

These case studies demonstrate that one of the most powerful ways local governments contribute to policy change is at the early 'problem-framing' stage of the policy cycle. Problem-framing is a powerful stage that influences agenda setting for the rest of the policy development process. It is also a stage when formal engagement processes are often yet to be established. Players who are present in the policymaking arena use their values, ideologies, and methodologies to frame what the problems are and what they see as appropriate solutions. Advocacy by local governments in partnership with communities that influences problem framing can create an important turning point in influencing proposed policy solutions. Community engagement that contributes to problem framing, establishing priorities and community values, is inherently political in nature and cannot be only managed by the bureaucracy or on a project-by-project or industry by industry basis. Thus, local governments emerge as an important conduit of community values, priorities, and strategic plans for their future, that can work with policymakers at higher levels of government to help to pro-actively frame policy conversations. Another important finding is that electoral accountability continues to be an important mechanism for empowering communities and local government voices in policy outcomes. While campaigns of the scale described in this chapter cannot, and will not, be mobilised on every policy issue, they are an important reminder that electoral accountability, while not a panacea, continues to hold decision-makers accountable to evolving community values and priorities.

Tools for local governments

There is the potential to enhance the contribution that local governments make to policy formation at the national and subnational level. Table 4.1 summarises a range of tools or measures that local governments can use to enhance their responsiveness, for example improving

Table 4.1 Democratising local governments

Public sector/administrative dimension	Councillor/political dimension
• Appropriate staff capacity and expertise for example: 　• Dedicated engagement and/or advocacy staff 　• Training and capacity building opportunities 　• Environmental and policy expertise as appropriate • Organisational culture of inclusion, engagement, and respect for difference • Leadership that leads by example	• Councillors who foster relationships with community members and organisations • The presence of local government councillors who are independent of political affiliation • Councillor engagement at a geographic scale that is consistent with community identity, maximising representation of sub-communities (for large local governments, appropriate ward delineations can help manage challenges of scale)
Community identity and civil society	*Council protocols and practices*
• Invest in physical places for community gathering such as town halls, community centres, libraries, squares, marketplaces, gardens, and playgrounds • Maintain a sense of place and local history (in larger LGAs this can be done at a more relatable scale of suburb / ward) • Emphasise active transport and public transport • Invest in civil society through funding, in kind resources and partnerships	• Transparent sharing of information • Council meetings that enable community to participate and submit agenda items • Establish community committees to sustain collaboration and input of expertise • Deliberative community engagement for policy development, long-term strategic planning, and spatial planning

the quality of community engagement. This should be seen as a first and essential step to enhancing local government influence, given that the legitimacy of the local governments policy views is contingent on the foundation of a genuine relationship with its local communities. Table 4.2 lists a range of tools for enhancing local government voice in influencing policy made by national or subnational governments. As demonstrated by the case studies above, these are often complementary, as the legitimacy of local government views contributes to their influence over policy change. These tables present findings from research into approaches used by influential local governments such as those in the case studies in this chapter. Recognising the diversity of local governments, some of these tools include

Table 4.2 Local government voice

- Articulate a positive, community supported vision for the municipality including through Councils' own policies, plans, and infrastructure
- Council motions, declarations, or moratoriums
- Council led community petitions or polls
- Council letters to members of parliament
- In person or verbal discussions between councillors and members of parliament
- Publicly promoting council messages directly, through the media and through protests
- Support community mobilisation including via networking opportunities, training, information provision, and resources
- Networking and alliance building including with NGOs, other local governments, industry and local government peak bodies and other organisations
- Engagement in committees, panels and other forums with national or subnational governments
- Advocacy to increase community protections in relevant legislation
- Council can hold governments accountable to their legislative requirements when needed
- Written feedback on national or subnational governments plans, policies and project proposals, including capacity and resourcing to do so

options for implementation. For example, additional measures for mega-councils to assist in over-coming the challenges of scale for generating community partnerships and conversely networked approaches for smaller local governments.

Tools presented in Table 4.2 will be made more effective by the depth of engagement between local government and their communities including via the tools presented in Table 4.1. This speaks to the importance of genuine relationships between local governments and their communities and the central role of normative change for informing policy change to adequately address environmental challenges such as climate change.

Opportunities for research and practice

There is the opportunity to further develop a comprehensive toolkit for local governments which can equip councils to increase the quality of their engagement with their local communities and increase their policy influence. The tables presented above are proposed as a starting point for such a task. The increased size of local governments that has occurred in recent decades as a result of population growth and local government amalgamations presents a particular challenge for increasing the role of local governments in democratic engagement. Of the examples of highly engaged local governments, none are mega-councils, however none are very small by population. A critical mass seems to be required to give councils sufficient resources, capacity, and political voice; however, this should be balanced by the potential pitfalls of large size in reducing opportunities for engagement and diluting community views.

There are a number of drivers towards larger local governments. They can efficiently manage transport systems and other infrastructure development as city-regions continue to increase in their size and complexity. State governments tend to prefer large local governments as they reduce the number of organisations involved in regional coordination. However, the appearance of a coherent policy narrative may mask diversity beneath it, that mega-councils are less able to accurately represent (Butt et al. 2021). Smaller local governments enable a greater number of community viewpoints to be expressed allowing a more robust contest of ideas at the metropolitan and state policy scales. Recognising and better understanding the tensions between local government efficiency and representation is important for ensuring that diversity and resilience are not being unwittingly eroded. One of the central objectives of liberal democracies is to empower people to collectively influence the policies that impact them (Judge 2014; Katz and Nowak 2017).

Conclusion

The case studies presented in this chapter provide examples where local governments successfully influence environmental policy, often against considerable barriers. They demonstrate the approaches and tools that they use to do so and the opportunities presented by increased local government engagement in the policymaking cycle, particularly for environmental and climate change policy. Further research into local government size, representation, advocacy, and democratic engagement would provide valuable insights to inform future research and reform relating to local government. This can also enhance the rigour and legitimacy of policymaking at higher levels of government. In addition, better understanding how local governments contribute to bottom-up problem-framing and policy formation can inform structural changes to enhance environmental policy outcomes. Local governments in partnership with their communities are in some cases leading the way in their commitment to addressing climate change in Australia.

References

Arnold, G., and Le Anh Nguyen Long. 2019. "Policy Expansion in Local Government Environmental Policy Making." *Public Administration Review* 79 (4): 465–76.

Aulich, Chris. 2009. "From Citizen Participation to Participatory Governance in Australian Local Government." *Commonwealth Journal of Local Governance* January (2): 44–60.

Beetham, David. 1996. "Theorising Democracy and Local Government." In *Rethinking Local Democracy*, edited by D. King and G. Stoker, 28–49. London: Macmillan. https://doi.org/10.1007/978-1-349-24756-1_2

Buchecker, M., S. Menzel, and R. Home. 2013. "How Much Does Participatory Flood Management Contribute to Stakeholders' Social Capacity Building? Empirical Findings Based on a Triangulation of Three Evaluation Approaches." *Natural Hazards and Earth System Sciences* 13 (6): 1427–44. https://doi.org/10.5194/nhess-13-1427-2013

Butt, Andrew, Annette Kroen, Wendy Steele, and Stefanie Dühr. 2021. *Local Government Co-Ordination: Metropolitan Governance in Twenty-First Century Australia. AHURI Final Report*. Australian Housing and Urban Research Institute Limited. https://doi.org/10.18408/AHURI5323001

Caldas, Paulo, Brian Dollery, and Rui Cunha Marques. 2016. "What Really Matters Concerning Local Government Evaluation: Community Sustainability." *Lex Localis – Journal of Local Self-Government* 14 (3): 279–302. https://doi.org/10.4335/14.3.279-302(2016)

Christensen, Helen E., and Dana McQuestin. 2019. "Community Engagement in Australian Local Governments: A Closer Look and Strategic Implications." *Local Government Studies* 45 (4): 453–80. https://doi.org/10.1080/03003930.2018.1541794

Coghill, Ken, Yee-Fui Ng, and Paul Thornton-Smith. 2014. *Enhancing Local Government Democracy: City of Melbourne*. Melbourne: Electoral Regulation Research Network.

Craig, Gary, and Marjorie Mayo. 1995. *Community Empowerment: A Reader in Participation and Development. Experiences of Grassroots Development*. London: Zed Books. https://books.google.com.ec/books?id=oRIL6kHLVgoC&printsec=frontcover&hl=es&source=gbs_ge_summary_r&cad=0#v=onepage&q&f=false

Crowley, Kate. 1998. "'Glocalisation' and Ecological Modernity: Challenges for Local Environmental Governance in Australia." *Local Environment* 3 (1): 91–7. https://doi.org/10.1080/13549839808725549

Cuthill, Michael. 2002. "Exploratory research: citizen participation, local government and sustainable development in Australia." *Sustainable Development* 10 (2): 79–89.

Daniell, Katherine, and Kay Adrian. 2018. *Multi-Level Governance: Conceptual Challenges and Case Studies from Australia*. Canberra: ANU Press.

Demetrious, K. 2008. "New Activism and Communication in Australian Risk Society: A Case Study of the Otway Ranges Environment Network." *Third Sector Review* 14 (2): 113–26.

Department of Agriculture Water and the Environment. 2020. "New South Wales Bilateral Agreement Information." Australian Government. https://www.environment.gov.au/protection/environment-assessments/bilateral-agreements/nsw

Dollery, Brian, Michael A. Kortt, and Simone de Souza. 2015. "Policy Analysis Capacity and Australian Local Government." In H. Brian and C. Kate. *Policy Analysis in Australia*, 105–20. Bristol: Policy Press. https://doi.org/10.46692/9781447310280.011

Dollery, Brian, Joe Wallis, and Percy Allan. 2006. "The Debate That Had to Happen but Never Did: The Changing Role of Australian Local Government." *Australian Journal of Political Science* 41 (4): 553–67. https://doi.org/10.1080/10361140600959775

Dovers, Stephen, and Karen. Hussey. 2013. *Environment and Sustainability: A Policy Handbook*. Sydney: The Federation Press.

Dryzek, John S. 2011. *Foundations and Frontiers of Deliberative Governance. Foundations and Frontiers of Deliberative Governance*. Vol. 9780199562. Oxford: Oxford University Press. https://doi.org/10.1093/acprof:oso/9780199562947.001.0001

Eddington, Rod, Sir. 2008. *Investing in Transport: East West Link Needs Assessment*. Melbourne: Victorian Government.

Fritze, Jess, Lara Williamson, and John Wiseman. 2009. *Community Engagement and Climate Change: Benefits, Challenges and Strategies*. Melbourne. https://library.bsl.org.au/jspui/bitstream/1/1579/1/Community_Engagement_and_Climate_Change.pdf

Gaventa, John. 2004. "Towards Participatory Local Governance: Assessing the Transformative Possibilities." In *Participation: From Tyranny to Transformation*. Manchester.

Hammond, Marit. 2020. "Sustainability as a Cultural Transformation: The Role of Deliberative Democracy." *Environmental Politics* 29 (1): 173–92. https://doi.org/10.1080/09644016.2019.1684731

Hatzisavvidou, Sophia. 2020. "Inventing the Environmental State: Neoliberal Common Sense and the Limits to Transformation." *Environmental Politics* 29 (1): 96–114. https://doi.org/10.1080/09644016.2019.1684732

Henderson, Steven R. 2018. "Advocating within and outside the shadow of hierarchy: local government responses to Melbourne's outer suburb deficits." *Local Government Studies* 44 (5): 649–69.

Henderson, Steven R. 2019. "Framing Regional Scalecraft: Insights into Local Government Advocacy." *Territory, Politics, Governance* 7 (3): 365–85. https://doi.org/10.1080/21622671.2017.1389660

Herriman, J. 2011. Local Government and Community Engagement in Australia. Working Paper No 5. Australian Centre of Excellence for Local Government, University of Technology Sydney, Sydney.

Holden, William N., and R. Daniel Jacobson. 2006. "Mining Amid Decentralization. Local Governments and Mining in the Philippines." *Natural Resources Forum* 30 (3): 188–98. https://doi.org/10.1111/j.1477-8947.2006.00108.x

Judge, D. 2014. *Democratic Incongruities: Representative Democracy in Britain*. London: Palgrave Macmillan.

Katz, Bruce J., and Jeremy Nowak. 2017. *The New Localism: How Cities Can Thrive in the Age of Populism*. New York, NY: Brookings Institution Press.

Kia, Annie. 2012. "How to: Coal Seam Gas Free Communities in Northern Rivers", CSG Free Community Strategy. The Channon.

KPMG. 2015. "Improving Local Governments Role in the Assessment Process for Major Projects in Queensland", Local Government Association of Queensland (LGAQ), Brisbane.

Lawton, Alan, and Michael Macaulay. 2014. "Localism in Practice: Investigating Citizen Participation and Good Governance in Local Government Standards of Conduct." *Public Administration Review* 74 (1): 75–83. https://doi.org/10.1111/puar.12161

Lingafelter, Teresa, and Jacqueline Leavitt. 2012. "Democratic Planning in Seattle: Distributive Outcomes Across Neighborhoods." *ProQuest Dissertations and Theses* 3541: 237. https://search.proquest.com/docview/1115316372?accountid=14541%5Cnhttp://PC6BF4SJ5M.search.serialssolution.com?ctx_ver=Z39.88-2004&ctx_enc=info:ofi/enc:UTF-8&rfr_id=info:sid/ProQuest+Dissertations+%26+Theses+Global&rft_val_fmt=info:ofi/fmt:kev:mtx:dissert

Lismore City Council. 2018. "Council Decisions Relating to Coal Seam Gas Mining, Lismore City Council." March 2018. https://www.lismore.nsw.gov.au/cp_themes/default/page.asp?p=DOC-QDF-04-78-50%3E

Lucas, Clay, and Josh Gordon. 2015. "Victorian Government Settles East West Link Claim for $339m." *The Age*, 2015. https://www.theage.com.au/national/victoria/victorian-government-settles-east-west-link-claim-for-339m-20150415-1ml9bz.html

McDonnell, Joshua. 2018. "The Effect of Municipality Size on Levels of Political Efficacy and Political Participation. A Systematic Review." *Paper Presented to International Political Science Association* 25 (July): 21–5.

Newman, Ines. 2014. *Reclaiming Local Democracy: A Progressive Future for Local Government*. Bristol: Policy Press.

Otway Ranges Environment Network Inc. 2020. "Practical Results to Date: Acheivements of the Otway 'Water Not Woodchips' Campaign." February 2020. oren.org.au/campaign/otway_water.html.

Putnam, Robert. 2007. "E Pluribus Unum: Diversity and Community in the Twenty-First Century." *Scandinavian Political Studies* 30 (2): 137–74.

Roberts, Anthony. 2014. "Metgasco Drilling Approval Suspended" 1. [Media Release] Minister for Resources and Energy, Special Minister of State. NSW Government. https://resourcesandgeoscience.nsw.gov.au/__data/assets/pdf_file/0011/531875/140515-Metgasco-Drilling-Approval-Suspended.pdf

Savini, Emanuela, and Bligh Grant. 2020. "Legislating Deliberative Engagement: Is Local Government in Victoria Willing and Able?" *Australian Journal of Public Administration* 79 (4): 514–30. https://doi.org/10.1111/1467-8500.12420.

Schoburgh, Eric, and Roberta Ryan. 2017. *Handbook of Research on Sub-National Governance and Development*. Hershey, PA: IGI Global.

Shoebridge, Brendon. 2016. *The Bentley Effect*. New York, NY: HSPP Ltd.

Shoebridge, David. 2014. "Crushing Police Force Planned to End Peaceful CSG Blockade." David Shoebridge MLC, Viewed May 2014. https://trove.nla.gov.au/work/250978086?keyword=Crushing%20Police%20Force%20Planned%20to%20End%20Peaceful%20CSG%20Blockade.

Stoker, Gerry. 2006. *Why Politics Matters: Making Democracy Work*. New York, NY: Palgrave Macmillan.

Thomas, I. G. 2010. "Environmental Policy and Local Government in Australia." *Local Environment* 15 (2): 121–36. https://doi.org/10.1080/13549830903527647.

de Vries, Sarah. 2020. "Place Identity and Major Project Deliberation: The Contribution of Local Governments in Australia." *Australian Geographer* 51 (3): 399–419. https://doi.org/10.1080/00049182.2020.1788269.

—. 2021a. "Australian Local Government's Contribution to Good Governance on Major Projects: Increasing Information, Participation and Deliberation." *Commonwealth Journal of Local Governance* June (24) 60–78. https://doi.org/10.5130/cjlg.vi24.7637

—. 2021b. "The Power of Procedural Policy Tools at the Local Level: Australian Local Governments Contributing to Policy Change for Major Projects." *Policy and Society* 40 (3), 414–430 https://doi.org/10.1080/14494035.2021.1955471

Westoby, Peter, and Allan Kaplan. 2014. "Foregrounding Practice-Reaching for a Responsive and Ecological Approach to Community Development: A Conversational Inquiry into the Dialogical and Developmental Frameworks of Community Development." *Community Development Journal* 49 (2): 214–27. https://doi.org/10.1093/cdj/bst037

Westoby, Peter, and Gerard Dowling. 2013. *Theory and Practice of Dialogical Community Development: International Perspectives*. Abingdon, Oxon: Routledge. https://doi.org/10.4324/9780203109946

5 It's just the way we do things around here

How policy worlds influence the implementation of policies

Prudence R. Brown

Introduction

Governments are increasingly recognising that they need new approaches to address complex problems (Brunner 2010, 303). As a result, they are shifting towards new approaches including collaboration, co-production and localised responses (van der Heijden 2013, 4). However, governments are struggling to make the transition. One of the many reasons put forward for this inability to shift is the tensions between old ways and the new norms needed to implement new approaches (Getha-Taylor et al. 2011, i86). Despite this, insufficient attention continues to be paid to the fact that new approaches are not imposed on a blank canvas, but on existing worlds of policy practice, which are both shaped by interactions with policy actors as well as shaping these actors (Shore, Wright, and Però 2011, 3). These complex policy worlds mediate what is achieved and in fact what is achievable through reform efforts.[1] Like many other policy analysis frameworks, the idea of policy worlds helps in understanding how policy actors do the work of policy formulation. One of the important differences is that they take account of both structure and agency within the framework as well as providing a framework for understanding implementation success or failure. Policy worlds consist of an established system of social practices, which can be changed in response to the agency of actors or the agency of the existing policy world (Shore, Wright, and Però 2011). Policy worlds are contingent – practices could be different even though they are seemingly stable and fixed. This means that the existing structure needs to constantly legitimise itself within the power structures (the policy regimes) that are operating. In turn, the policy regime works to structure habits of thought consistent with the existing policy world. The need to shore up the existing regime and the role of existing social practices (or norms) becomes very apparent during processes of reform or disruption.

This chapter explores how understanding the tensions between old and new ways, as well as how and why policy actors fail to engage productively with these tensions, provides a window into why new approaches can be difficult to embed. It uses a case study of the multi-layered policy world of Australian Indigenous policy[2] and how it works to inhibit shifts to a different way of working with Aboriginal and Torres Strait Islander people. It looks at the dominant social logics which are rooted in public administration and constitute the organisational culture or "the way we do things around here" (Jason 2012) and how they support policy actors to resist change. It then looks at the logics which shore up the unusual organisation of work and may be used by policy actors in justifying using the discretion available to them in unproductive ways. It also looks at how the dominant deficit discourse within the Indigenous policy regime works to structure habits of thought, making the shift to new participatory policies even more difficult. But first, the framework to be used for analysis and the case study is outlined.

DOI: 10.4324/9781003368564-5

The Logics of Critical Explanation framework

In this chapter, the Logics of Critical Explanation (LCE) provides the framework for analysing how both policy actors and the policy world exercised their agency in managing the challenges and tensions that emerged in the case study (Glynos and Howarth 2007). The underlying premise of LCE is that policy actors are operating within a system of seemingly stable and fixed practices, but there are gaps in that system that are more apparent at moments when the existing system is challenged. This then allows for analysis of why and how policy actors react during those moments and how acting differently can be mediated by higher level logics which may facilitate, or thwart, new practices. The LCE framework uses three inter-related explanatory logics of practice. *Social logics* are the norms and practices which govern behaviour and so characterise an existing policy world. Social logics include the mindsets, beliefs and traditions of policy actors as they manifest in their everyday activities. Social logics can also be practices which are attempting to be established as new norms, as often occurs during processes of reform. Understanding the operation of *political logics* allows for exploration of the processes that lead to social logics being created, contested or defended, or transformed (Glynos, Klimecki, and Willmott 2015, 395; Glynos et al. 2009, 11–12). *Fantasmatic logics* help analysts to understand why certain practices or ideologies enjoy continuing support even in the face of manifest inadequacy. They operate to manage the contingency of social worlds and allow policy actors to locate themselves comfortably within them and so not critically engage with the discourses and framings which are constructed by that logic (see, for example, Glynos 2011, 383–384).

This chapter focusses on the moments when symbolic and 'real' elements of policy worlds are in conflict, such as when new social logics conflict with existing social logics, or when political and social logics collide (Glynos and Howarth 2007, 110). At these moments it explores how policy actors responded to the need to augment existing social logics with the new logics associated with changed ways of working as well as how the policy world mediated the engagement with new social logics. It does this through a case study of an initiative which sought to reform the approaches of Australian governments to working with remote Aboriginal and Torres Strait Islander communities.

The case study

The case study used in this chapter is the intergovernmental National Partnership Agreement on Remote Service Delivery (NPARSD) (COAG 2009b) and the overarching policy document, the National Indigenous Reform Agreement (NIRA) (COAG 2009a). The core commitment of NPARSD was to change the way governments work with remote Indigenous communities (CGRIS 2011). A new place-based approach was to be operationalised through a "single government interface in each community" which produced publicly available Local Implementation Plans (LIPs) developed in partnership with each community to improve services and infrastructure (CGRIS 2011, iii–v). LIPS were to be developed by regional offices, and officers located in each community, working "across government with local Indigenous people and other stakeholders to develop … [them] and ensure that they are implemented in a timely and accountable way" (COAG 2009b, clause 21(c)). These new commitments were overlaid on an existing policy world, consisting of long-standing traditions, norms and world views. The aim was to introduce new social logics to govern interactions with Aboriginal and Torres Strait Islander peoples and communities. However, as outlined below, the initiative did not pay sufficient attention to the political and fantasmatic logics which worked to support the status quo and resist the need to make space in the existing policy world for the new social logics.

The analysis in this chapter draws on a larger project which examined 24 documents to ensure a full understanding of the logics underpinning the policy world as well as interviews with 19 senior public servants involved in NPARSD at a number of levels of seniority and working with different governments. These interviews explored how the new ways of working were accommodated in the implementation of NPARSD. Further detail on the research method can be found in Brown (2019a). The remainder of the chapter examines in turn the manifestation during implementation of each of the three classes of logics – the social, political and fantasmatic. In particular, each section looks at the implications of these logics for successful shifts to new approaches.

Existing social logics crowd out emerging social logics

Within the implementation of NPARSD, the social logics, or 'the way we do things around here', were characterised by the strongly held administrative traditions of command and control, action orientation and risk aversion. Added to this was a logic of coordination which has become increasing prominent in Indigenous policy since the 1980s (Sullivan 2011, 3). These logics were often in tension with the new approaches that policy actors were asked to implement. As will be explored below, the way this played out during implementation often resulted in a reversion to type rather than a shift to new social logics. One of the prerequisites for effective engagement with Aboriginal and Torres Strait Islander communities is allowing adequate time to build trust and to build local capacity for engagement (Hunt 2013, 13; see also Wilks, Lahausse, and Edwards 2015, ix). In the context of NPARSD, time was also required to allow Aboriginal and Torres Strait Islander people to develop governance arrangements for their engagement with government that they felt were legitimate and which reflected the diversity of the community (Hunt 2013, 11; MacLean et al. 2013). However, moving at a pace dictated by community needs is in conflict with the social logic of action orientation or the practice of wanting to deliver results. Action orientation includes a focus on performance, results and responsiveness to Ministerial direction. The tension was well recognised by policy actors:

> I think that the flexibility [in the NPARSD] was really overshadowed by the push to get [the local plans] done. Cos there wasn't time, even with people who got theirs done really early on ... there wasn't a lot of depth around the outcomes and engagement in a more strategic way. I guess actions was the thing – [plans] were seen as a wish list
>
> (Interview 17)

Policy actors found it difficult to move at the slower speeds the Indigenous communities were comfortable with, as this conflicted with 'the focus of "getting things done"', meaning local decision-making was in tension with the "drive for rapid progress" (Walden 2016, 317). This was further exacerbated by Ministerial impatience and "a media that simplifies complex policy problems" (Stewart and Jarvie 2015, 122). These tensions were visible when policy actors preferred delivering an immediate output rather than substantive engagement early in the policy process. Two policy actors reflected this view: "… yet the pressure to deliver those in such a short time rather than to a standard or a level, meant that the engagement in the original wasn't as good as what it should have been" (Interview14) and "… it's hard to take the time to deeply appreciate this stuff – we talk about taking the time but often reality intervenes and it is very difficult to do it" (Interview 12).

Also, entering into a shared partnership is in conflict with the social logic of command and control, or the practice of keeping a tight rein on the project. Within the implementation of the NPARSD this tension manifested through policy actors showing a preference for expert over local knowledge. For example, in describing a planning exercise which only included superficial engagement, but was delivered in a timely manner, two policy actors were not overly concerned that local priorities were identified without engaging with relevant local stakeholders. Further, they maintained that 'expert knowledge' was sufficient, because:

> ... later on when I sat down and went through [it] with people on a number of occasions, people were saying these are the things that need to change. So I think they partially nailed it probably by accident
>
> (Interview 04)

On top of this, the requirement to share power is in conflict with the social logic of risk aversion. In the implementation of NPARSD, risk aversion manifested through the reluctance to delegate decisions to the local level. For example, one participant identified a situation where local and government priorities were in conflict, and government priorities were the ones that policy actors followed:

> ... we think there's a problem, they don't think it's a problem – how do you determine it? You know, I'll tell you how the nation determines it – it's either a problem or it's not – from [the government's] perspective
>
> (Interview 12)

Further, a number of studies of NPARSD identified the focus 'on results, on getting things done, and on being in control' was experienced by public managers as being in tension with new processes (Stewart and Jarvie 2015, 122). As noted by one Aboriginal community member in that study, "most public servants don't want to change ... they want simplicity ... they want control..." (quoted in Stewart and Jarvie 2015, 122). According to Stewart and Jarvie (2015, 122), the public managers responsible for shaping and managing the programme "had difficulty focusing and conceptualizing what they are to 'do' where there is limited control". Walden's study of NPARSD concluded that "facilitating and enabling participatory processes does not come naturally to bureaucracies and government agencies which are geared to hierarchical decision making processes, that support and allow their work to progress in predictable ways" (2016, 298).

Changing the conception of accountability is in direct conflict with the social logic of command and control. One of the consequences of this tension was conducting consultations with outcomes pre-determined by governments:

> ... most of the things in them were things happening anyway, that's not a very useful place based thing. I don't think it's a place based initiative to say "Oh, let's just gather up all the things we are doing anyway and just call that a place based plan". I'm not saying that that's all the [local plans] were but there were elements of that.
>
> (Interview 13)

In addition, the need to recognise partnerships is in conflict with the social logic of action orientation, or, the practice of wanting to deliver results, to 'tick the boxes'. The tension manifested through a focus on outputs rather than process:

> Maybe it's part of the momentum thing where people just wanted to get on with it. There was certainly a lot of pressure on public servants to show some progress and get [local

plans] signed you know and I think my recollection is that the signing of the ... [local plan] that I went to was kind of – I got the sense that Canberra ... [was] very keen to tick a box that one had been done.

(Interview 05)

Moreover, taking account of the local context requires a culture of evaluative thinking, or questioning assumptions underlying issues. This did not occur in the implementation of NPARSD, as reflected by these two policy actors: "So I just don't think that people really kind of critique their own perceptions and assumptions and judgements. So – yeah – heavy doses of cultural bias and cultural blindness" (Interview 3) and "... we have a lot to learn from international development. It's been a big mistake in Indigenous Affairs to ignore it ... And we haven't learned it and we haven't gotten away from the old model" (Interview 1).

Questioning assumptions is in direct conflict with action orientation. It requires reflection as to whether the goal policy actors working towards is the right one and whether the path taken is the best way to get there. This is the exact reverse of responsiveness to the Minister, where if the Minister asks for something to be done, it is made to happen, and given priority over other actions:

There's a lot of inertia and other priorities. It's just very hard to capture what's going on. So if the Minister is saying I want to know how many kids are going to school then you have to get that

(Interview 12)

The social logic of command and control is implicated in the tendency of policy actors to turn inwards to more familiar bureaucratic processes rather than embrace the uncertainty of working in complex cross-cultural environments (Lea 2008; Sullivan 2008). It is much easier to deliver on concrete actions such as a report or a plan than the more abstract partnership and collaboration that was required under the NPARSD, since providing evidence of activity is seen to be of prime importance: "The deliverable, whatever that is, gets achieved, but the outcome doesn't. So it's kind of a nonsense" (Interview 16). Further, questioning assumptions takes time and stands in the way of delivering outputs. If the questioning suggests a new path is needed, then the proposed course of action may need to be approved, other agencies will need to be won over, and potentially additional funding sought. Such frank and fearless questioning is much more difficult than implementing what has been asked of you, even if you question the assumptions underpinning the approach. In all these ways, it can be seen how a focus on social logics allows for understanding of how existing social logics crowd out the emerging logics that the policy is seeking to embed. How this crowding out is justified can be better understood by examining the operation of political logics.

Political logics legitimise resistance to reform

To neutralise the challenge of the new social norms, political logics came into play. Interestingly, in this case study, logics which might otherwise be thought of as social logics became political, in that they were used to legitimate existing social logics. Political logics establish, defend or contest an existing norm or social logic (or pre-empt the contestation of a norm). If an aspect of current practice is worthy of public contestation, then political logics are the way that the practice is legitimised, particularly in the eyes of policy actors (Glynos and Howarth 2007, 145–146). They facilitate the maintenance of existing social logics, by concealing the radical contingency that is at their heart. Three political logics were evident in the implementation of NPARSD. The first two logics, expert evidence and upward accountability, would usually be thought of as social logics. However, as will be explored below, in the case of the NPARSD they were used to justify actions inconsistent with a shift to the new ways of working. So, evidence was used to justify the sidelining of local knowledge at the expense of mainstream and ideological conceptions of evidence. Similarly, upward accountability was used to justify resistance to participatory approaches. The third political logic of capacity deficit was used to justify thinking of Aboriginal and Torres Strait Islander people in terms of deficit and of risk. It led to a reluctance to acknowledge and attach value to lived experience and local knowledge.

Firstly, the political logic of upward accountability came into play on a number of occasions. Accountability, the "obligation to answer for the performance of duties" (Mulgan 2011, 1), is a fundamental concept in public administration. The aspect of accountability that is often missing, and is required for effective collaboration, is accountability downward, or accountability by government to community members, compared to the more managerial upward accountability to Ministers and higher levels within the bureaucracy. In the implementation of the NPARSD, a lack of accountability to community members was attributed to the pull of upward accountability:

And we've got a government expecting – or a department expecting that this is gonna happen. The expectation is … to make it happen along with all the other work that you've got, without any form of consultation … So, there's just … no rational thinking behind it. And that happened time and time and time and time again

(Interview 7)

In so doing, the political logic of accountability served to justify the lack of devolution which occurred during implementation. Accountability is not usually thought of as a political logic, but in the case of the NPARSD, the way it was used was to legitimise maintaining the status quo:

… this was at the stage with the … government where we as public servants were being pushed extremely hard to deliver, deliver, deliver. And get things moving, so that a lot of the things that people thought were hard didn't get done because we had to show we were doing things so the things that could be demonstrably counted took priority

(Interview 11)

Secondly, to legitimise maintaining existing accountabilities, the political logical of evidence came into play. In the implementation of the NPARSD, evidence-based policy was taken to mean policy informed by expert evidence, so that local knowledge was given a lesser priority and at times actively devalued. This was the case even though policy actors recognised the contestability of evidence, particularly in a cross-cultural space:

So, people are looking at the same sets of data or the same information through the same old prism, and really not kind of seeing what's changed and I think things have changed quite dramatically over the last 30 to 40 years …

(Interview 3)

The lack of value attached to other forms of evidence resulted in privileging expert knowledge over lessons emerging from practical knowledge:

There doesn't seem to be high regard for … the people on the ground, what happens out on community … [w]here do we get – where do we take that experience and learn from it, if not in making policy? But it seems to me that the policy is always done on kind of research rather than reality

(Interview 07)

Thus, the political logic of evidence is used to justify existing power differentials, when the main input that so-called partners can provide (local knowledge) is devalued.

Finally, the emphasis on deficit throughout the documents reinforces a mindset that Aboriginal and Torres Strait Islander people are not capable of improving their own well-being. This is then used to justify intervention – the paternalistic imposition of policies. There is a considerable body of literature that identifies this link: Indigenous policy "couched in deficit terms, with communities being characterised almost solely in terms of dysfunction" (Martin 2006, 5) leads to policy and programme solutions which work against "the prospect of local capability or accountability developing and sustaining – ultimately undermining the possibility of improved outcomes for Indigenous people" (Moran 2016, 195). Policy actors recognised that there was a strong focus on intervention in the implementation of NPARSD. This led to a lack of engagement in general and specifically the substantive engagement which they were asked to move towards. This in turn justifies intervention, as one participant suggested: "So, there's a lot about welfare and well-being and policing and health and that sort of thing, nutrition, fixing people" (Interview 6).

The logic of capacity deficit also reinforced and strengthened the logic of risk avoidance by seeing Aboriginal and Torres Strait Islander culture as a risk that needs to be erased:

[If I could change one thing] I think it would be the fact that governments speak about Aboriginal culture and communities in a deficit approach – that we need to "fix" something. And that I guess for me means that people immediately will make assumptions I guess about the balance of power around any sort of interaction with the community. So if I could fix anything I would fix that government deficit thinking

(Interview 17)

As noted in the quote, the capacity deficit mindset also changes the very nature of interactions with Aboriginal and Torres Strait Islander communities, by reinforcing the supremacy of governments. In this way, it strengthens the already strong logic of command and control. The political logic of capacity deficit supports resisting substantive engagement and the devolution of funding and power. It also supports a mindset that the local context, being dysfunctional, is not a relevant consideration for policy and programme development. By reinforcing strong social logics of command and control and risk avoidance, the political logic of capacity deficit legitimises their retention in the face of the challenge of the social logics required for approaches. In this way, capacity deficit can also be seen as actively working against policy actors engaging constructively with the tensions created by the new ways of working, pushing the exercise of discretion towards the old ways, rather than the new.

In summary, it can be seen that what would normally be thought of as social logics, when used to legitimise the status quo, are better thought of as political logics. This was further reinforced by a logic of capacity deficit. If the role of these political logics in a change process is not recognised and managed, then the tensions between old and new will never be able to be resolved in favour of the new. According to LCE, this capacity to mediate what is achievable is further reinforced by fantasmatic logics.

Fantasmatic logics also mitigate attempts at reform

Fantasmatic logics allow analysts to understand why practices and regimes 'grip' policy actors (Glynos and Howarth 2007, 145). While they provide insights into why certain practices or ideologies enjoy continuing support, they differ from ideology in that they encompass those logics which enable policy actors to navigate seemingly contradictory social worlds with confidence and to avoid critical engagement with the narratives and logics constructed by that fantasy (see, for example, Glynos 2011, 383–384). For example, the underlying deficit discourse of 'Closing the Gap' in remote Australian Indigenous policy is a fantasmatic logic in that it conceals its assimilationist aims and allows policy actors to feel comfortable by appealing to the common sense (from a mainstream perspective at least) of improving education and employment outcomes (see, for example, Brown 2019b).

In the case of NPARSD, two fantasmatic logics can be seen to be operating. Firstly, NPARSD aimed to alleviate disadvantage by implementing the right service mix – to provide the same services as enjoyed by other Australians. On the face of it, this seems to be unquestionably what government is supposed to be doing. This discourse and the broader Closing the Gap agenda help policy actors to feel comfortable implementing policies underpinned by a deficit discourse that is heavily invested in assimilation as they resonate with deeply held (mainstream norms). However, as will be explored below, both of these policy goals also concealed tensions with the new social logics required for new approaches to take hold, which then served to legitimise resistance to change.

On the surface, deficit discourse is not in conflict with new approaches. Policymakers clearly did not think so when they designed a purportedly community development policy framework (the NPARSD) under the umbrella of the deficit-based Closing the Gap policy. However, participants pointed to the way the deficit discourse reinforces a number of logics. For example, it reinforces the political logic of capacity deficit: "And that, I guess for me, means that people immediately will make assumptions I guess about the balance of power around any sort of interaction with the community" (Interview 17). It also reinforces the political logic of evidence, by discounting local lived experience:

[If we moved away from deficit] I think people would, on one level they would look more holistically, I think because they wouldn't see just a big problem but what's there. And I think it would help reconciliation, it would have a big role in that, recognizing the capabilities of locals, the opportunities they represent

(Interview 17)

More generally, policy actors felt that changing the deficit discourse would naturally result in new ways of working that were more consistent with new approaches. This quote is indicative of the views of a number of those interviewed:

It's more about what are the assets, what is working well, what are the factors that mean that is working well and so that you start, so rather than going well what are all the things that are missing, well what are the things that are working well ...

(Interview 8)

These policy actors could see that the dominant overarching discourse reinforces social and political logics that are in conflict with new approaches. They could see that while this was the case, a lack of engagement with new ways of working would continue.

Also, the fantasmatic logic of service improvement taps into the deeply held social logics of command and control, and action. As a result, it reinforces the already strong tendency to discount the value of local knowledge in the design and provision of services. This is entirely logical. If services are to be modelled on the mainstream, with cultural difference only recognised through the need for staff to be culturally competent, then it follows that local knowledge cannot add value. It also leads to a lack of questioning and reflection by policy actors of the underlying premise of the policy. As one participant suggested:

> I realized when I was in [a remote area] that I think we were still engaged in colonization – we hadn't finished up there. We may have finished in other places but we hadn't finished there. And they know it and they will come and tell you that really clearly and that's how they experience it. I tried to have a conversation about that with senior white people in the bureaucracy in some of the bigger government organizations and they were very offended that they could be thought of as colonisers. But we are
>
> (Interview 11)

A comfortable overarching discourse which appeals to strongly held norms allows policy actors to avoid these kinds of critical reflections. The lack of reflection relates directly to a discourse which resonates with deeply held norms and so is readily accepted. This is the role of fantasmatic logics, to conceal the radical contingency of the policy regime.

Conclusions

The implementation of NPARSD demonstrated that an inability to implement new social logics stemmed from difficulties in overcoming the tension between new approaches and established bureaucratic norms and practices (Getha-Taylor et al. 2011). Understanding how and why this occurs then allows for a better understanding of how to facilitate the much-needed shift. Understanding the logics underpinning the existing policy world shines light on aspects which contribute to failure but are often overlooked when the only focus is on the agency of policy actors. Understanding the logics which support existing strongly held norms to resist a shift to new social logics helps in understanding how reform efforts are then undermined. This in turn builds understanding of what is needed to create an environment which is more conducive to reform. Focusing on those moments when the agency of the policy world is exercised highlights that one of the reasons policy actors struggle with the new approaches is their lack of capacity to engage with these tensions and to navigate a middle path which accommodates both the old and new in a meaningful way. This then allows consideration of what kind of capabilities are needed in policy actors who are well placed to manage ambiguity (see, for example, Brown 2017). Moving away from a focus on either structure or agency to consider them both through the policy worlds lens reveals important insights into policy failure. As the case studies shows, if governments are indeed serious about changing the way they work with Aboriginal and Torres Strait Islander communities to address with them the complex issues faced, they will need to move beyond talking about working differently and actively work to construct a policy world which allows it to happen.

Notes

1 That norms can have agency might seem challenging, but as Sayer (2011) argues, "values are about something objective or independent and are capable of being responsive to the things they are about".
2 A note on terminology used in this chapter is needed here. At the time of the case study, governments in Australia tended to refer to 'Indigenous' rather than First Nations or Aboriginal and Torres Strait Islanders. This is shifting, but the tendency is still to refer to 'Indigenous policy'. For this reason, this chapter will refer to 'Indigenous policy' and maintain the terms used at the time when describing the policies. However, when referring to communities or peoples, it will use 'Aboriginal and Torres Strait Islander peoples'.

Further reading

Brown, Prudence R. 2019a. "Understanding Barriers to New Approaches – A Case Study from Australian Remote Indigenous Policy." *Critical Policy Studies*. https://doi.org/10.1080/19460171.2019.1625795

—. 2019b. "Understanding How Deficit Discourses Work against Implementing Participatory Approaches in Australian Indigenous Policy." *Australian Journal of Social Issues* 54 (4): 401–17. https://doi.org/10.1002/ajs4.78

COAG. 2009. "National Partnership Agreement on Remote Service Delivery." *Council of Australian Governments*. Accessed November 10, 2014. https://federalfinancialrelations.gov.au/sites/federalfinancialrelations.gov.au/files/2021-01/remote_service_delivery_np.pdf

Glynos, Jason, and David R. Howarth. 2007. *Logics of Critical Explanation in Social and Political Theory*. Vol. 26. New York, NY: Routledge.

Shore, Cris, Susan Wright, and Davide Però. 2011. *Policy Worlds: Anthropology and the Analysis of Contemporary Power*. New York, NY: Berghahn Books.

References

Brown, Prudence R. 2017. "Attempting to Cultivate More Collaborative Mindsets for Boundary Spanning in Remote Indigenous Policy." *Australian Journal of Public Administration*. https://doi.org/10.1111/1467-8500.12287

—. 2019a. "Understanding Barriers to New Approaches – A Case Study from Australian Remote Indigenous Policy." *Critical Policy Studies*. https://doi.org/10.1080/19460171.2019.1625795

—. 2019b. "Understanding How Deficit Discourses Work against Implementing Participatory Approaches in Australian Indigenous Policy." *Australian Journal of Social Issues* 54 (4): 401–17. https://doi.org/10.1002/ajs4.78

Brunner, Ronald D. 2010. "Adaptive Governance as a Reform Strategy." *Policy Sciences* 43 (4): 301–41.

CGRIS. 2011. *Coordinator General for Remote Indigenous Services, Six Monthly Report September 2010–March 2011*. Canberra: Commonwealth of Australia.

COAG. 2009a. "National Indigenous Reform Agreement (Closing the Gap)." Accessed February 6, 2015. https://trove.nla.gov.au/work/162623638

—. 2009b. "National Partnership Agreement on Remote Service Delivery." Council of Australian Governments. Accessed November 10, 2014. https://federalfinancialrelations.gov.au/agreements/national-partnership-agreement-remote-service-delivery

Getha-Taylor, Heather, Maja Husar Holmes, Willow S. Jacobson, Ricardo S. Morse, and Jessica E. Sowa. 2011. "Focusing the Public Leadership Lens: Research Propositions and Questions in the Minnowbrook Tradition." *Journal of Public Administration Research and Theory* 21 (suppl1): i83–97.

Glynos, Jason. 2011. "On the Ideological and Political Significance of Fantasy in the Organization of Work." *Psychoanalysis, Culture & Society* 16 (4): 373–93. https://doi.org/10.1057/pcs.2010.34

Glynos, Jason, and David R. Howarth. 2007. *Logics of Critical Explanation in Social and Political Theory*. Vol. 26. New York, NY: Routledge.

Glynos, Jason, David Howarth, Aletta Norval, and Ewen Speed. August 2009. *Discourse Analysis: Varieties and Methods: ESRC National Centre for Research Methods Review Paper*. Swindon: Economic and Social Research Council.

Glynos, Jason, Robin Klimecki, and Hugh Willmott. 2015. "Logics in Policy and Practice: A Critical Nodal Analysis of the UK Banking Reform Process." *Critical Policy Studies* 9 (4): 393–415.

Hunt, Janet. 2013. *Engaging with Indigenous Australia – Exploring Conditions for Effective Relationships with Aboriginal and Torres Strait Islander Communities*. Issues paper no 5. Canberra: Closing the Gap Clearinghouse.

Jason, Martin. 2012. ""That's how we do things around here": Organizational culture (and change) in libraries." *In the library with the lead pipe*. https://www.inthelibrarywiththeleadpipe.org/2012/thats-how-we-do-things-around-here/

Lea, Tess. 2008. *Bureaucrats and Bleeding Hearts: Indigenous Health in Northern Australia*. Sydney: University of New South Wales Press.

MacLean, Kirsten, Helen Ross, Michael Cuthill, and Philip Rist. 2013. "Healthy Country, Healthy People: An Australian Aboriginal Organisation's Adaptive Governance to Enhance Its Social-Ecological System." *Geoforum* 45: 94–105. https://doi.org/10.1016/j.geoforum.2012.10.005

Martin, David. 2006. Why the 'new direction' in Federal Indigenous Affairs policy is as likely to 'fail' as the old directions. CAEPR Topical Issue No. 5. Canberra: CAEPR, ANU.

Moran, Mark. 2016. *Serious Whitefella Stuff: When Solutions Became the Problem in Indigenous Affairs*. Carlton, Victoria: Melbourne University Press.

Mulgan, Richard. 2011. "Accountability." In *International Encyclopedia of Political Science*, edited by Bertrand Badie, Dirk Berg-Schlosser and Leonardo Morlino, 1–13. Thousand Oaks, CA: SAGE Publications Inc.

Sayer, Andrew. 2011. *Why Things Matter to People Social Science, Values and Ethical Life*. Cambridge: Cambridge University Press.

Shore, Cris, Susan Wright, and Davide Però. 2011. *Policy Worlds: Anthropology and the Analysis of Contemporary Power*. New York, NY: Berghahn Books.

Stewart, Jenny, and Wendy Jarvie. 2015. "Haven't We Been This Way Before? Evaluation and the Impediments to Policy Learning." *Australian Journal of Public Administration* 74 (2): 114–27.

Sullivan, Patrick. 2008. "Bureaucratic Process as Morris Dance." *Critical Perspectives on International Business* 4 (2/3), 127–141. https://doi.org/10.1108/17422040810869981

—. 2011. *The policy goal of normalization, the National Indigenous Reform Agreement and Indigenous National Partnership Agreements, Desert Knowledge CRC Working Paper Number 76*. (Ninti One Limited, Alice Springs.) http://www.nintione.com.au/resource/NintiOneWorkingPaper_76_PolicyGoalofNormalisation.pdf

van der Heijden, Jeroen. 2013. Looking Forward and Sideways: Trajectories of New Governance Theories. Regulatory Institutions Network (RegNet) and Amsterdam Law School Working Paper. Canberra and Amsterdam: Australian National University and University of Amsterdam.

Walden, Inara. 2016. "*Talking back to policy: Aboriginal participation in policy making.*" PhD thesis, Social Policy Research Centre, UNSW.

Wilks, Sez, Julie Lahausse, and Ben Edwards. 2015. Commonwealth Place-Based Service Delivery Initiatives: Key Learnings project, Research Report No. 32. Melbourne: Australian Institute of Family Studies.

6 The evidence base for policy
Changes in the use of data, information and knowledge within government

Fiona McKenzie

Introduction

In the previous edition of *Beyond the Policy Cycle*, one of the chapters examined information use within government (McKenzie 2006). In Victorian State Government at the time there was a trend towards whole-of-government initiatives and the chapter highlighted the benefits of developing an integrated information base to support the needs of multiple agencies. While public administration papers were extolling the virtues of 'joined up government' at the time (Christensen and Lægreid 2007; VSSA 2007) few, if any, were exploring the ways in which the evidence base might need to be developed to support such inter-agency approaches. The example which formed the focus of the 2006 chapter was the *Regional Matters* atlas (Victorian Government 2002) – a compilation of policy relevant information covering issues of interest to ten state government departments. While this involved the challenge of dealing with many and varied data sources, the central guiding principle was seeking to present, in visual format, "what needs to be known rather than what is easy to map" (McKenzie 2003, 25).

It is interesting to reflect, 20 years on, the degree to which government information use has changed. There have been external changes in the availability and types of data and internal changes within government such as outsourcing and delivery of information online. Such changes have brought opportunities as well as challenges and, while data sources are more plentiful and accessible than ever before, the ability to manage, interpret and apply information for policy purposes is in many ways more challenging for government. In rational models of the policy process such as that presented by Althaus, Bridgman, and Davis (2018, 48–53), information plays an important, although often implicit, role in most stages of the policy process. In particular, the stages of policy analysis, choice of policy options and evaluation have a need for accurate and timely information, however it could be argued that sound information underpins the policy process as a whole, particularly where normative expectations of evidence-based policy are sought (Höchtl, Parycek, and Schöllhammer 2016).

This chapter examines both internal and external changes that have influenced the use of data and information by government. It seeks to determine how such change has enhanced or undermined the production, retention and application of policy knowledge at the current time.

Internal changes in government

Over the past 20 years, key changes in government operations have been noted by local and overseas writers: fiscal constraint, particularly following the global financial crisis, leading to reductions of staff in analytical or research roles (Bristow, Carter, and Martin 2015, 134; Healy 2018, 235; Sasse and Thomas 2022, 31); outsourcing of government services, including IT and research, not only because of financial constraints but also a lack of particular technological skills and capabilities inside government (Giest 2018; Mannheim 2020, 157); staff mobility and turnover leading to a loss of corporate knowledge in government (Sasse and Thomas 2022, 7); and short-term focus of government initiatives (Sasse and Thomas 2022, 5).

Financial constraint

British commentators have noted that the capacity of many government agencies to generate or absorb knowledge for policymaking has been lessened through cuts to research and analysis teams, especially during the period of austerity following the global financial crisis (Bristow et al. 2015, 134; Healy 2018, 235; Sasse and Thomas 2022, 31). Financial constraint can have wide ranging effects, not only in terms of the direct impact of staff cuts or programme closure. In times of financial scarcity, departments or business units can become defensive and may focus more closely on weighing up costs and benefits of any activity. Research, by nature, is an exploratory process and outcomes often uncertain. This creates a problem for funding as the benefits may not be able to be known at the time money is allocated or spent. Research findings may have unexpected outcomes or the benefits may accrue to another agency. In risk averse times, the spending of money on such activities may be curtailed. Alternatively, greater pressure may be placed on researchers to articulate the impact that their research will have. This has become common in funding processes of the Australian Research Council (ARC) and the Research Councils UK (RCUK); however, criticism has arisen that predicting impact contradicts the very purpose of research as an exploratory activity (Chubb and Watermeyer 2017, 2366). Government too has seen a similar trend; the Regional Atlas project mentioned at the start of this chapter was focused on policy concerns of the time, yet the final shape and content of the document was guided by discovery rather than an expectation of findings. An issue like skills shortages was nominated for inclusion precisely because there was little knowledge of the issue or how to address it at the time.

Outsourcing

Increasing outsourcing of government services to the private sector has occurred in recent decades, particularly in relation to IT and web-based systems (Margetts et al. 2003, 2). The trend has attracted both proponents and critics. Cost efficiency is not the only factor increasing outsourcing – the need to access specific expertise, knowledge or tools is a key factor, specifically in relation to managing or analysing big data (Giest 2018, 157). While the use of private sector labour does not necessarily deplete knowledge within the public sector, it can contribute to fragmentation and difficulty in effectively managing the information resources of an organisation. This balance between using external information sources and maintaining in-house analytical capacity in order to effectively access and use information as part of the process of 'knowledge mobilisation' which ensures that evidence can be translated into action (Bristow et al. 2015, 129).

Mobility and turnover

In the UK, it has been recognised that rapid staff turnover among ministers and within the public service has undermined the ability to maintain a knowledge base let alone develop integrated knowledge across government (Sasse and Thomas 2022, 5, 7). In Victoria, public sector mobility has been encouraged in recent years. While only representing a small proportion of overall employees (4.4%), the proportion moving within Victorian Government doubled between

2018–19 and 2019–20 (VPSC 2022). Combined with other trends discussed here, the rapid turnover of staff can undermine the development of a cumulative knowledge base or 'corporate' memory for policymaking.

Short termism

Sasse and Thomas (2022, 9–11) note the contribution of annual funding cycles and ministerial turnover to having a short-term focus. Priority is given to 'quick wins' and 'announceables' and this is further encouraged by the need to feed the demands of a rapid media cycle which "… traps government and media alike in a short-term, reactive hamster-wheel that prioritises sensation over substance" (Spurling 2020, 6). Short-term demands tend to crowd out longer term issues and reduce the space given to strategic thinking.

While fiscal constraint, outsourcing, staff turnover and short-termism clearly have negative impacts on knowledge accumulation and management, we are nevertheless in quite a different world of information where many sources have opened up for government policymakers to use.

External changes affecting government

Two decades ago, the challenge for government in dealing with data was already recognised: "As many policy-makers will attest, a major problem in policy-making is not whether there is enough evidence, but of managing the excess of information …" (Marston and Watts 2003, 146). The situation has certainly not become any easier. Since Marsden and Watts made their observation, the landscape of data and information has undergone considerable change with new and emerging technology offering an even wider array of data sources for government to use (Gray and Lawrence 2019, 4–5). The variety and volume of data now available is unprecedented, creating both opportunities and challenges for government policymakers. The development of data management systems, portals and dashboards enables policymakers to access more data and information, however the technical and absorptive capacity needed to deal with this plethora of data is not always able to keep pace. Höchtl et al. (2016, 147) argue that "the most recent developments in ICT innovation have the potential to influence the internal logic and structure of bureaucratic organizations, thereby changing the process of governance through government." In other words, the technological changes of recent decades have systemic effects on how governments operate and therefore on processes such as policymaking.

The evolution of technology and new data sources has created challenges for knowledge management in large organisations. Data custodians are many, including both private and public entities. And all organisations have had to devote significant resources to creating or updating platforms through which such data can be collated, analysed, interpreted and disseminated. This exercise takes time, money and skill. It is continually challenged by new systems. Custodianship, control and security are key issues to be addressed at the meta scale, while the organisational scale needs to address issues of compatibility, continuity and effective user-interfaces. The key point is that interpretation of the data and its strategic application has tended to be sidelined while such systems are developed and implemented. One result is a growing number of web-based portals which are rich in data but limited in providing meaningful context, guidance or interpretation. The scale of recent data generation, and the technical skills required to manage it, has paradoxically made interpretation (turning the data into information and knowledge) more difficult. The human skills required to manage and manipulate data may be focused on technical aspects (e.g. designing and loading data into dashboards or online platforms) which can result in less attention being given to reflective and strategic interpretation or research. This has important implications for the nature of evidence-based policy into the future.

Data, information knowledge – understanding the difference

The terms knowledge, information and data are often used interchangeably, however, they are distinct concepts (Davenport 1997, 9). Data are neutral elements – they are simply a collection of facts which, until organised and placed in context, do not have any real meaning for the policymaker. Information provides a context for data. It requires skilled people to select, arrange, interpret and translate the data. Knowledge is broader, deeper and richer than data or information. It contains experience, values and contextual understanding. Such knowledge requires time to be accumulated – it is more than expertise on a particular topic but rather a system of knowledge which enables problem solving even in the face of novel challenges like climate change or the COVID pandemic.

Understanding the difference between data, information and knowledge is critical for data management and policy development. This can be seen through the example of open access data provision which has been a trend in recent decades. Providing government data online was seen as improving transparency of government decision-making on the one hand and encouraging citizen participation and innovation through the democratisation of data access on the other. In relation to developing knowledge for policymaking, there are three issues to be highlighted in relation to such data. These relate to user demand for data, government supply of data and dealing with the dispersal of information derived from such data.

Benneworth, Bakker, and Velderman (2018) evaluated the experience of open data access among municipalities in the Netherlands where it was expected that open data might create a virtuous cycle by "allowing public policymakers to harness third-party problem-solving capacity" (Benneworth et al. 2018, 197). Despite these ambitions, however, the authors found that "because they were not able to stimulate use, the benefits were never realised" (Benneworth et al. 2018, 196). This also highlights a problem with web-based systems within government where the internet is sometimes imagined as having a level of agency in terms of teaching power. Combining the 'neutral' or static character of data (as opposed to information) with the internet as a mere platform, it is not surprising that datasets placed online may not magically yield new policy insights.

The selection of datasets to be placed online highlights a second (supply side) issue. The way in which data sources are selected for inclusion requires strategic thought and management, especially where the expectation is the development of policy insights. However, in some cases, data choice may be somewhat ad hoc, reflecting simply the datasets that are available rather than the data that needs to be used. A glance through the contents of DataVic (the Victorian Government's open access data site), for example, shows both significant datasets but also many smaller datasets of questionable value. There is, in fact, a lack of transparency in the processes used to determine which data were placed online. There is an explanation online of the DataVic access policy, but the five key principles outlined are of a technical nature rather than offering strategic guidelines for content:

Principle 1: Government data will be made available unless access is restricted for reasons of privacy, public safety, security and law enforcement, public health, and compliance with the law.
Principle 2: Government data will be made available under flexible licences.
Principle 3: With limited exceptions, government data will be made available at no or minimal cost.
Principle 4: Government data will be easy to find (discoverable) and accessible in formats that promote its reuse.
Principle 5: Government will follow standards and guidelines relating to release of data and agency accountability for that release.

(DataVic 2022)

Furthermore, it is not clear how any benefits arising from use of the data might flow back to government in the form of insights or knowledge that might enhance public policy. In fact, while improving research outcomes is envisaged, the stated benefits of the DataVic access policy are silent on potential use of such findings for future policymaking, stating:

The policy is expected to achieve the following benefits:

- *stimulate economic activity and drive innovation and new services to the community and business*
- *increase productivity and improve personal and business decision making based on improved access to data*
- *improve research outcomes by enabling access to primary data to researchers in a range of disciplines*
- *improve the efficiency and effectiveness of government by encouraging better management practices and use of the data.*

(DataVic 2022)

Another problem with open access data is that, while encouraging citizens to access a wide array of data, it is not necessarily clear how government might then harvest or maintain knowledge of or access to the types of data analysis that are done by those citizens. Unlike platforms like Engage Vic where consultation and collaboration can occur between policymakers and citizens on specific issues, general datasets placed online can be more difficult to create benefit for policymakers. Indeed, if such data are used by private companies, the benefits of data analysis might accrue to particular businesses rather than the general public. The example of open data highlights the potential for information and learning to become quite fragmented and dispersed. The dispersal of information can undermine the ability of a government agency to see and capture the information back, and indeed it would potentially be a huge logistical exercise to try and track the use of data in this way. Data analytics can provide the number of downloads of data from a site such as DataVic, but it cannot tell you how the data have been used or the insights which may have been gained through analysis which would potentially be of public policy interest.

Open data access is only one aspect of the changing nature of government data use. The example is nevertheless useful as it highlights issues which now face modern government in terms of data and information use. A key problem is still one highlighted decades ago – data are not the same as information or knowledge (Davenport 1997). The assumption that more data make for better policy decisions can only be true if we understand the requirement for data to be interpreted – for sense to be made of them and for them to be filtered on the basis of what we really need to know rather than simply what can be compiled into a web portal. While government has long espoused the objective of creating evidence-based policy, the category of 'evidence' may be very broad for policymakers, ranging from data through to research, from experience through to media reports.

Evidence-based policy and policy learning

Undertaking *research* is one way in which new data, information and knowledge can be generated. The relationship between research and policymaking has been the subject of long-running debate. Much of this debate examined the degree to which policymaking has been informed by research (Haux 2019, 7). The concept of 'evidence-based' policy emerged in public policy discussions in the 1990s with the term implying that academic research findings have been applied to create better informed, more rational, policy. However, critics argue that real-world decision-making is often very messy (Boaz et al. 2008, 243). Policymaking is often political rather than systematic, involving the need to balance competing social interests, resolving power conflicts and mediating between different groups with different values. Therefore, there is no simple linear relationship between research and policy (Haux 2019, 14). Caplan (1979) went so far as to describe academics and policymakers as 'two communities' with different values, research reward systems and languages. The two-communities approach suggests that policymakers and academics operate in separate worlds with limited channels of communication between them (Head and Walter 2015, 283; Stead 2016, 453). In academia, research activities require an understanding of current research and scholarship, repeatable methods, rigorous documentation and quality control through the process of peer review. By contrast, policymakers use the term 'research' more loosely to mean an investigation that generates knowledge that is useful for solving a specific problem (McKenzie et al. 2020, 434).

While there is often a stated aim for government to work more closely with academics (Sasse and Thomas 2022, 8), the process of bringing research evidence from academia to government is not always straightforward (Parsons 2002; Boaz et al. 2008; Banks 2018). For example, outputs of academic research may not align well with the types of problems facing policymakers (Nutley 2003, 20; Rowe 2016, 460), and research findings must compete for attention among policymakers with other types of evidence (Boaz et al. 2008, 242). As a result, only a small proportion of academic research finds its way into policy (McKenzie et al. 2020, 433). There is a tension between the need for rapid information gathering for policy and the traditional perception of research as a rigorous but time-consuming exercise. The need for 'evidence-based policy' may be promoted but 'evidence' may not mean research in this traditional academic sense. It may mean datasets or dashboards which can be used for monitoring and reporting. This blurs the definition of evidence-based policy, partly because government has quite distinct purposes for its use of data and information. Whereas reflective and strategic interpretation, knowledge and research are critical for strategic planning and developing new policy, data used for monitoring and reporting is likely to be simpler and delivered in a predictable and repeatable way. The degree of interpretation varies although there is crossover where monitoring data are used to assess potential improvements in policy, programmes or processes (e.g. through MERI[1] frameworks). The application of interpretive skills is required in such situations.

There are two critical aspects of knowledge for government. The first is the need to maintain a knowledge base of relevant material so that policy learnings are preserved and built upon. The second is to enable access to new information and ideas (Dotti and Colombino 2018, 267). A balance is needed between processes of using experience and memory but avoiding path dependence by maintaining access to new ideas and information. Outsourcing and high staff turnover can undermine experience and memory but can create greater opportunity for new information or perspectives to enter the system. This then is a dilemma for government in the 21st century. In seeking new policy learning opportunities, it risks lessening its capacity to benefit from those very opportunities through the dispersal or fragmentation of knowledge. Howlett uses the term 'policy analytical capacity' to refer to knowledge acquisition and use in the policy process. It includes the amount of research a government can undertake or access, its ability to apply statistical methods and modelling techniques to these data and the use of analytical techniques like environmental scanning, trend analysis and forecasting. Importantly, it includes the ability to articulate and communicate its priorities and to integrate information into policy decision-making processes (Howlett 2009, 162–163). As noted earlier, governments are faced with more data and more complex datasets. Challenges of such data include their variety of source, speed of generation, size and uncertainty around their quality (Giest 2018, 153). While government recognises the potential of such data to create more effective and efficient policies, there is limited technical expertise within government to administer or interpret big data. Hence there is an increasing reliance on the knowledge and tools held by private industry. Giest notes (2018, 153) "[t]his ... marks a shift in policy learning."

Outsourcing can disrupt feedback loops required for policy learning (Clarke and Margetts 2014, 395). If part of the data management or research analysis is outsourced, there is separation between those generating knowledge and those applying it to policy problems. Knowledge retention is increased where the entity generating the knowledge is then able to apply, monitor and gather feedback information which enhances the knowledge base further. Continuity of knowledge generation in this way prevents the fragmentation or dispersal of knowledge. This problem can be overcome where close collaborative partnerships are developed for particular projects, yet these rarely continue over long-enough periods of time to enable cumulative benefit from the cycle of research, knowledge generation, policy development, implementation and monitoring which support continuous improvement in policy knowledge.

Ultimately, outsourcing of data, information and research services by government can reduce its own policy capacity and increase the risk that information will not be used effectively in the policymaking process (Clarke and Margetts 2014, 395). In effect, it is relying more on second hand learning via third parties rather than building its own knowledge base (Giest 2018, 156). The outsourcing of IT and data management services reduced digital capacity within the public sector as well as fragmenting data sources. As noted by Clarke and Margetts (2014, 395) this fragmentation "rendered it difficult for government to holistically collect, interpret, and learn from the data it held on citizens in a coordinated fashion." In the era of big data, government potentially has access to very large amounts of data from new sources – from satellites, monitoring devices and the internet of things, among others (Gray and Lawrence 2019, 4–5). It is worth noting that many of these are privately owned and, while private enterprise can leverage their information advantage and channel it into targeted marketing, government is often left with limited access to such data through financial limitations or commercial protections. This is a big change from earlier periods when government had much better access to complex datasets than did businesses or citizens.

In order for government to make use of data, it needs to be interpreted and applied to identified policy problems. This involves a series of skills which may not reside in a single person. The data analyst will require different skills than the policy officer. A technical understanding of data manipulation is far removed from skills of horizon scanning and political assessment. Therefore, relationship development and communication across disciplines is required to form a 'joined up' effort of analysis and research. This highlights the complexity of policy analysis which requires research, analysis, advice, recommendations and mediation (Mayer, Els van Daalen, and Bots 2004, 173; Colombo 2018, 16–18).

Conclusion

Governments and citizens have access to more data than ever before. Yet, even with increasing technological power to collect, maintain and manipulate this data, it remains more challenging than ever to discern what the data may be telling us. In some senses this should not be a surprise – data are simply data. They do not reveal patterns or stories or solutions until humans have interpreted them. This is where the heart of the problem lies for government to effectively use data for policy purposes. While fiscal constraint, outsourcing, mobility and short-term perspectives have all contributed to inefficiencies in the use and application of critical information, it is the misunderstanding of what knowledge really is – how it is created, communicated and applied – that is perhaps a more fundamental problem.

The fragmentation and dispersal of critical intelligence is of concern for policymakers seeking ways to address current issues. But before seeking even more technological solutions, it would be wise to consider *what do we need to know?* rather than *what data are available?* By starting with such a question, a pathway may become clearer, as might the human resources needed to interpret, synthesise and seek novel responses. The data will remain silent on solutions, but the human brain will not.

Note

1 MERI: Monitoring, Evaluation, Reporting and Improvement.

Further reading

Dotti, Nicola Francesco, ed. 2018. *Knowledge, Policymaking and Learning for European Cities and Regions: From Research to Practice*. Cheltenham: Edward Elgar Publishing.

Howlett, Michael. 2009. "Policy Analytical Capacity and Evidence-Based Policymaking: Lessons from Canada." *Canadian Public Administration* 52 (2): 153–75.

Höchtl, Johann, Peter Parycek, and Ralph Schöllhammer. 2016. "Big Data in the Policy Cycle: Policy Decision Making in the Digital Era." *Journal of Organizational Computing and Electronic Commerce* 26 (1–2): 147–69. https://doi.org/10.1080/10919392.2015.1125187.

References

Althaus, Catherine, Peter Bridgman, and Glyn Davis. 2018. *The Australian Policy Handbook: A Practical Guide to the Policy Making Process*. 6th ed. Sydney: Allen and Unwin.

Banks, Gary. 2018. "Whatever happened to 'evidence-based policymaking'?" The Mandarin, November 30, 2018. Accessed September 10, 2022. https://www.themandarin.com.au/102083-whatever-happened-to-evidence-based-policymaking/.

Benneworth, Paul, Inge Bakker, and Willem-Jan Velderman. 2018. "Beyond Big Data, the Open Data Revolution for Research." In *Knowledge, Policymaking and Learning for European Cities and Regions: From Research to Practice*, edited by Nicola Francesco Dotti, 193–205. Cheltenham: Edward Elgar Publishing.

Boaz, Annette, Lesley Grayson, Ruth Levitt, and William Solesbury. 2008. "Does Evidence-Based Policy Work? Learning from the UK Experience." *Evidence and Policy* 4 (2): 233–53.

Bristow, Dan, Lauren Carter, and Steve Martin. 2015. "Using Evidence to Improve Policy and Practice: The UK What Works Centres." *Contemporary Social Science* 10 (2): 126–37. https://doi.org/10.1080/21582041.2015.1061688.

Caplan, Nathan. 1979. "The Two-Communities Theory and Knowledge Utilization." *American Behavioural Scientist* 22 (3): 459–70. https://doi.org/10.1177/000276427902200308.

Christensen, Tom, and Per Lægreid. 2007. "The Whole-Of-Government Approach to Public Sector Reform." *Public Administration Review* 67 (6): 1059–66.

Chubb, Jennifer, and Richard Watermeyer. 2017. "Artifice or Integrity in the Marketization of Research Impact? Investigating the Moral Economy of (Pathways to) Impact Statements within Research Funding Proposals in the UK and Australia." *Studies in Higher Education* 42 (12): 2360–72. https://doi.org/10.1080/03075079.2016.1144182.

Clarke, Amanda, and Helen Margetts. 2014. "Governments and Citizens Getting to Know Each Other? Open, Closed, and Big Data in Public Management Reform." *Policy and Internet* 6 (4): 393–417.

Colombo, Alessandro. 2018. "The Research–Policy Nexus: Boundaries, Bonding and Ten Golden Rules." In *Knowledge, Policymaking and Learning for European Cities and Regions: From Research to Practice*, edited by Nicola Francesco Dotti, 13–26. Cheltenham: Edward Elgar Publishing.

DataVic. 2022. DataVic access policy. Accessed September 12, 2022. https://www.data.vic.gov.au/datavic-access-policy.

Davenport, Thomas H. 1997. *Information Ecology. Mastering the Information and Knowledge Environment*. Oxford and New York: Oxford University Press.

Dotti, Nicola Francesco, and Annalisa Colombino. 2018. "Knowledge for Policymaking: An Evolutionary Perspective to Achieve Policy Resilience." In *Knowledge, Policymaking and Learning for European Cities and Regions: From Research to Practice*, edited by Nicola Francesco Dotti, 13–26. Cheltenham: Edward Elgar Publishing.

Giest, Sarah. 2018. "Policy Learning in Times of Big Data Analytics: The Challenges of Skill-Based Outsourcing." In *Knowledge, Policymaking and Learning for European Cities and Regions: From Research to Practice*, edited by Nicola Francesco Dotti, 153–64. Cheltenham: Edward Elgar Publishing.

Gray, Paul, and Henry Lawrence. 2019. Future Technologies Review. How New Technologies will Shape the Future of the UK's Geospatial Sector, prepared for the UK GeoSpatial Commission by Public, London.

Haux, Tina. 2019. *Dimensions of Impact in the Social Sciences: The Case of Social Policy, Sociology and Political Science Research*. Bristol: ProQuest ebook, Policy Press.

Head, Brian, and James Walter. 2015. "Academic Research and Public Policy." In *Policy Analysis in Australia*, edited by Brian Head and Kate Crowley, 283–301. Bristol: Policy Press.

Healy, Adrian. 2018. "What Role for Policy Studies in a Post-Truth Politics?" In *Knowledge, Policymaking and Learning for European Cities and Regions: From Research to Practice*, edited by Nicola Francesco Dotti, 231–43. Cheltenham: Edward Elgar Publishing.

Höchtl, Johann, Peter Parycek, and Ralph Schöllhammer. 2016. "Big Data in the Policy Cycle: Policy Decision Making in the Digital Era." *Journal of Organizational Computing and Electronic Commerce* 26 (1–2): 147–69. https://doi.org/10.1080/10919392.2015.1125187.

Howlett, Michael. 2009. "Policy Analytical Capacity and Evidence-Based Policymaking: Lessons from Canada." *Canadian Public Administration* 52 (2): 153–75.

Margetts, Helen, Patrick Dunleavy, Simon Bastow, and Jane Tinkler. 2003. Leaders and Followers: E-Government, Policy Innovation and Policy Transfer in the European Union. Accessed September 12, 2022. http://aei.pitt.edu/6549/.

Marston, Greg, and Rob Watts. 2003. "Tampering with the Evidence: A Critical Appraisal of Evidence-Based Policy-Making." *Australian Review of Public Affairs* 3: 143–63.

Mayer, Igor S., C. Els van Daalen, and Pieter W. G. Bots. 2004. "Perspectives on Policy Analyses: A Framework for Understanding and Design." *International Journal of Technology, Policy and Management* 4 (2): 169–91.

Mannheim, Markus. 2020. *Federal Government Spending $5 Billion Per Year on Contractors as Gig Economy Grows Inside Public Service*, ABC News. Accessed September 10, 2022. https://www.abc.net.au/news/2020-09-10/contractors-and-the-public-service-gig-economy/12647956.

McKenzie, Fiona. 2003. "Regional Matters: An Inter-Agency Approach to Understanding Regional Issues." *Australian Journal of Public Administration* 62 (2): 24–32.

—. 2006. "Informing Policy through Integrated Information: An Evaluation of the Victorian Government Regional Atlas Project." In *Beyond the Policy Cycle: The Policy Process in Australia*, edited by Hal Colebatch, 208–27. Sydney: Allen and Unwin.

McKenzie, Fiona, Markku Sotarauta, Jiri Blažek, Andrew Beer, and Sarah Ayres. 2020. "Towards Research Impact: Using Place-Based Policy to Develop New Research Methods for Bridging the Academic/Policy Divide." *Regional Studies, Regional Science* 7 (1): 431–44. https://doi.org/10.1080/21681376.2020.1825117.

Nutley, Sandra. 2003. "Bridging the Policy-Research Divide. Reflections and Lessons from the United Kingdom." *Canberra Bulletin of Public Administration* 108: 19–28.

Parsons, Wayne. 2002. "From Muddling through to Muddling up – Evidence Based Policy Making and the Modernisation of British Government." *Public Policy and Administration* 17 (3): 43–60. https://doi.org/10.1177/095207670201700304.

Rowe, Helen. 2016. "Getting the Relationship between Researchers and Practitioners Working." *Planning Theory and Practice* 17 (3): 459–62. https://doi.org/10.1080/14649357.2016.1190491.

Sasse, Tom, and Alex Thomas. 2022. *Better Policy Making*. London: Institute for Government.

Spurling, Bryden. 2020. *The Peril of Modern Democracy: Short-Term Thinking in a Long-Term World, Alliance 21 Essay*. United States Studies Centre, University of Sydney, Australia. Accessed September 11, 2022. https://www.ussc.edu.au/analysis/the-peril-of-modern-democracy-short-term-thinking-in-a-long-term-world.

Stead, Dominic. 2016. "The Use of Academic Research in Planning Practice: Who, What, Where, When and How?" *Planning Theory and Practice* 17 (3): 453–57. https://doi.org/10.1080/14649357.2016.1190491.

Victorian Government. 2002. *Regional Matters. An Atlas of Regional Victoria*. Melbourne: Victorian Government.

VSSA (Victorian State Services Authority). 2007. *Joined Up Government. A Review of National and International Experiences*. Melbourne: Victorian Government.

VPSC (Victorian Public Sector Commission). 2022. Mobility rates in the Victorian Public Service, non-casual employees. Accessed September 10, 2022. https://vpsc.vic.gov.au/data-and-research/data-facts-visuals-state-of-the-sector/

7 When government is not the only option for setting public performance standards and ensuring compliance

Richard Curtain

Introduction

Australia's Seasonal Workers Programme (SWP) has been set up to regulate and manage the recruitment, employment, living and worker welfare arrangements of short-term workers from the Pacific and Timor-Leste to live and work in Australian horticulture at harvest time. The programme offers valuable insights into the Australian government's approach to managing the risks of low-skill worker vulnerability and potential for employer mistreatment. In operation since 2009 as a pilot and then as a full programme since July 2012, the SWP's longevity means that the Australian government has had the time to identify and address the initial gaps in the programme design and respond to criticism. The SWP, therefore, offers a case study of the strengths and weaknesses of the governance arrangements of a well-established labour market programme of the Australian government. This case study draws on two perspectives. The first lens applied is to draw on a comparative analysis of the similarities and differences between the SWP and New Zealand's seasonal work programme, on which the SWP was modelled. This analysis, making use of previous published work, will provide the wider context to show the origins of the different ways the two programmes have been governed. The comparative assessment of the SWP and New Zealand's Recognised Employer scheme (RSE) has been presented in a series of publications starting in 2016 (see Curtain 2016, 2018; Curtain et al. 2018; Curtain and Howes 2020) and is summarised below.

The main focus of the chapter, however, is to examine in more detail at how the SWP has operated over time, in terms of its governance arrangements and to explore what the key elements of an alternative approach are. The argument presented is that the governance of the SWP has been driven by a Canberra-based government department, using a highly regulated instrument, and top-down, arms-length monitoring to manage risk. The result has been a reactive, 'gotcha' approach to compliance which has often produced a low-trust environment for employers, workers and their country representatives. In the medium term, it is hard to see that this overly complex and highly resource-intensive approach to compliance can survive as a solely government managed and funded programme. A key limitation of both the SWP and the Pacific Labour Scheme (PLS), now merged into the Pacific Labour Mobility (PALM) scheme, is its cost to government. This includes not only the high cost of managing the programmes through the two agencies, it also includes the social cost to government of overseeing a complex domestic programme, with high political visibility and major reputational risks.

The chapter concludes by proposing an alternative, hybrid governance model to apply to the SWP in particular. This is to make much greater use of a market-based model of governance to

DOI: 10.4324/9781003368564-7

complement existing employment laws and compliance mechanisms. In the case of Australian horticulture, it would involve the four leading supermarkets taking co-responsibility for ensuring that their suppliers of fresh produce are applying good agricultural practice which includes complying with labour market regulations. For the SWP specifically, the proposed approach would involve the Australian government removing the highly detailed requirements specified in the Deed of Agreement that SWP approved employers have to accept. In its place, a minimal set of requirements in the form of welfare goals expressed as measurable outcomes should be set. Compliance should be monitored by employer and worker feedback through regular, smart-phone surveys and third-party audits carried out as part of the requirements for the accreditation schemes run by industry. More coordination by lead industry players would also be needed, as happens in New Zealand.

This proposed hybrid approach, it is argued, is much more sustainable in the future than the present set of arrangements governing the SWP. The aim of the proposed alternative arrangements should be, in the words of the Coles Supermarket CEO, Steven Cain, to 'make it easier to do business in Australia by councils, states and governments working together on matters of governance and regulation to ensure workers are paid and trained appropriately, diversity and flexibility are encouraged, and duplication and complexity minimised' (Fullerton 2022).

The design and operation of the SWP

The Pacific Seasonal Worker Pilot Scheme was launched in August 2008 by the Labor government's Minister for Agriculture, Fisheries and Forestry, Tony Burke MP. Despite the sole focus on the sole horticulture industry and the initiating role of the Department of Agriculture, instead the Department of Education, Employment and Workplace Relations was given responsibility as a lead agency for designing and implementing the programme. Five other agencies were also involved: Australian Agency for International Development (AusAid), the Australian Tax Office (ATO), the Department of Foreign Affairs and Trade (DFAT), the Department of Immigration and Citizenship (DIAC), and the Fair Work Ombudsman (FWO) (Reed et al. 2011, 12). The assumption was that these separate agencies would implement the programme through a 'coordinated whole-of-government approach'. But in practice, the lack of coordination between departments has been one cause of the complexity of the governance arrangements, unlike the situation in New Zealand. For New Zealand's RSE, implementation was the lead responsibility of one Ministry (Ministry of Business, Innovation and Employment) that included the agencies of immigration, labour, and business. A separate ministry, responsible for promoting and protecting employment for New Zealanders, was not involved with the operation of the RSE.

The primary object of the Australian SWP pilot and the later programme has been to meet a foreign policy objective: to 'contribute to Australia's economic development objectives in the Pacific region, in particular by enabling workers to contribute to economic development in their home countries through remittances, employment experience and training gained from participating in the Pilot' (Reed et al. 2011, 4). A secondary objective was to help Australian employers engage workers for their locally unmet demand for labour. The same ordering of objectives also applied to the Seasonal Worker Programme. The significance of giving primacy to the foreign policy objective is that the Department of Employment officials administering the SWP saw it as an aid programme, with employers merely playing a subsidiary role. This perception by programme administrators was further reinforced when the Department of Foreign Affairs and Trade (DFAT), which only has a mandate to deliver foreign aid programmes, decided in November 2021 to merge SWP with PLS to inform a 'single, streamlined program' called the Pacific Australia Labour Mobility (PALM) scheme (DFAT 2021).

The Australian Labor government was elected in 2022 with a mandate to implement a new Pacific labour mobility policy. One aspect of its new policy was to 'insource' the domestic operational delivery of the PALM scheme to be delivered by the Department of Employment and Workplace Relations (DEWR 2022, 3). According to a DEWR Discussion Paper on the change, accountability for operational delivery of the PALM scheme was placed within DEWR because it is 'the portfolio responsible for eliminating exploitation, improving workers' pay and conditions and managing employer compliance' (DEWR 2022, 3). The move to an 'insourced' delivery model for PALM operations in Australia reflected the Government's commitment to strengthening the protections and approach to well-being for PALM workers' (DEWR 2022, 3). This move is to ensure that PALM workers 'continue to benefit from the same conditions and wages as Australian workers, a responsibility also within the Employment and Workplace Relations portfolio' (DEWR 2022, 3). This change reverts to the decision of the Rudd ALP government in 2008 to give the lead agency role for the implementation of the SWP to the Department of Employment, later called Department of Jobs and Small Business. This was to placate union concerns about the need to protect jobs for Australian residents first and foremost. The Department, with little experience in conducting a service programme, saw its primary role as manager of a compliance regime and did little to promote the programme to new employers (Hay and Howes 2012).

A key shortcoming of the programme designers and implementers has been the failure to acknowledge that the growth of the SWP (and the PLS) is driven solely by employer demand. Understanding the role of employers in the operation of the SWP is crucial to understanding how the SWP works and how effective the programme is (Curtain and Howes 2020). The programme flaws that flowed from this included not only a lack of promotion of the programme to employers (Hay and Howes 2012). Also missing has been an appreciation of the labour market conditions growers face. A survey of 183 growers in mid-2012 found that only 7 per cent of growers said they had difficulty finding sufficient seasonal workers (Hay and Howes 2012). This is because growers have relied on backpackers. The alternative option of engaging Pacific seasonal workers was not attractive to most growers who were critical of the extensive reporting requirements for approved employers. They also complained about the additional expense of arranging travel and accommodation for seasonal workers compared with the short-term engagement of backpackers as casual workers without any other obligations (Hay and Howes 2012).

In the case of New Zealand's seasonal worker programme, its very name shows the programme's different starting point and emphasis – the Recognised Seasonal Employer (RSE) scheme. The name reflects the fact that the RSE was designed by an industry-led working group and since then its primary focus has been on meeting employer demand for a reliable, experienced workforce. Horticulture New Zealand, the national industry association, represents 21 product associations as well as sector, regional and district groups. Its National Labour Steering Group, supported by Horticulture New Zealand administrative and field staff, organises a network of the regional labour groups and coordinates with both domestic and immigration programmes such as the RSE scheme. Since the beginning of the RSE, Horticulture New Zealand has had a dedicated staff member (who was also a grower) working on the RSE, four days a week. In marked contrast, the SWP operates without any direct relationship to a reference group composed solely of SWP approved employers (growers and labour hire operators) and key industry associations involved in horticulture.

An alternative, market-based approach to governance

It is a common assumption in Australia that it is role of the state to set labour standards and to enforce them through a 'command and control' model of regulation, inspection of compliance and enforcement action carried out by state agencies (Hardy and Howe 2009, 306). In addition, in Australia, trade unions have played a major role in inspecting and enforcing labour standards, as specified in legal instruments known as industrial awards (Hardy and Howe 2009, 306). However, with the decline in union coverage of the workforce from 40 per cent in 1992 to 14 per cent in August 2020, their role as inspectors and enforcers of labour standards has become much less significant (ABS 2022). This applies especially in the agriculture, forestry and fishing sector, where the union presence has been minimal compared to other sectors. In 2020, union members only accounted for 1.9 per cent of the workforce in that sector, down from 3.7 per cent in 2014 (ABS 2022).

Hardy and Howe (2015) propose a strategic approach to addressing employment noncompliance in complex supply chains. Their starting point for a new approach is an acknowledgement of 'an emerging consensus that targeting the direct employer of workers in enforcement action may be both inefficient and ineffective in achieving compliance with employment standards' (Hardy and Howe 2015, 563). They note that changes in employment relationships mean that lead firms in a supply chain now 'hold key regulatory resources and wield considerable influence and bureaucratic control over the compliance behaviour of smaller firms in the sector' (Hardy and Howe 2015, 564). They conclude that a new approach to enforcement is needed because the key drivers of compliance behaviour for an employer are often determined by more powerful firms higher up the supply chain. However, their focus is on innovative enforcement strategies of a state agency – Office of the Fair Work Ombudsman (FWO). The authors have overlooked a role for leading firms in the supply chain in setting standards and monitoring the performance of their suppliers against these standards. This approach, based on supply chains involving vulnerable workers, has been called improving workplace conditions through strategic, sector-based enforcement (Weil and Mallo 2007).

Market or private regulation has become important in supply chains with lead firms that are concerned about their reputations as good corporate citizens. However, evidence from international supply chains shows that private regulation alone is not sufficient to lift labour standards (Locke 2013; Bartley 2018). Also needed is strong and effective labour law enforcement (Amengual and Kuruvilla 2020, 812–815; see also Locke 2013, chap 7; Bartley 2018, chap 7). A conventional government-led compliance approach takes the form of coercive legislative such as criminal penalties for employers who exploit migrant workers. This approach was a key recommendation of the final report of the Migrant Workers Taskforce (2019), commissioned by the Department of Employment. However, this approach depends on migrant workers making formal complaints which are subject to court proceedings which they are often reluctant to do. An alternative approach is needed to combine the bottom-up compliance efforts of suppliers responding to the requirements of the lead firms in a supply chain, with the top-down monitoring by government of compliance with employment law, so that firms are operating within a framework agreed to by both industry and government.

A top-down, government-dominated governance structure

The operating mode of the SWP has been to regulate approved employers through a detailed contractual arrangement specified by the lead government agency called a Deed of Agreement. This agreement with each approved employer has been managed by Canberra-based contract managers, who have enforced compliance through top-down controls. These controls include threats of the enforcement of penalties, on the assumption that at least some approved employers will not meet their obligations (Curtain and Howes 2020, 14–17). The SWP governance report noted that the number of regulatory requirements has increased over time, despite survey results showing that growers were reluctant to take on the role of approved employer because of the red tape involved. To ensure compliance, Canberra-based contract managers, and from October 2020 supplemented by 19 regionally based Pacific Labour Mobility officers, make use of the methods of prevention and deterrence, detection and correction, as spelt in the Assurance Scheme in the Guidelines. Contract managers scrutinise, at arm's length, core documents supplied by approved employers related to worker recruitment, accommodation and welfare and well-being. This scrutiny can include both announced and unannounced monitoring visits, to respond to information such as anonymous complaints and tip offs. The role of the Pacific Labour Mobility officers is to ensure workers are being treated fairly and that their accommodation meets programme standards. They were also expected to assist with processing recruitment, accommodation, welfare and well-being plans, and other required reports (Curtain 2021).

A key lesson from the SWP and RSE comparison

The SWP and RSE comparison shows that a bottom-up, employer-based system of compliance is both possible and is more effective in resolving problems. One indicator of this effectiveness is the relative absence of absconding workers under COVID in New Zealand, fewer than 30 in 2020. In contrast, between March 2020 and December 2022 as many as 4,793 nationals from the PALM sending countries have been recorded as lodging an application for a protection visa in Australia (Department of Home Affairs 2022). A key part of the explanation for this difference between the two programmes in absconding numbers is that New Zealand growers, to provide fruit to export markets, must be GlobalGAP certified. Growers and labour contractors have little incentive to employ workers illegally because the risks are too great to their international accreditation and loss of access to export markets. As Charlotte Bedford (2022) notes, without 'rogue employers' willing to employ RSE workers on their farms outside of the RSE, the incentive for workers to abscond is much weaker. As just noted, this bottom-up compliance approach in New Zealand has been driven by a stronger export market orientation, led by the umbrella industry association, Horticulture New Zealand. In 2012, there were ten times more accredited producers in New Zealand under the GlobalGAP accreditation scheme than in Australia (Curtain et al. 2018, 472). This accreditation system has been adapted to New Zealand conditions in the form of the NZGAP scheme. The latter is described as a comprehensive set of good agricultural practices to provide a 'simplified, cost-effective, and integrated assurance in New Zealand horticulture that is trusted and valued'. NZGAP is owned and operated by Horticulture New Zealand.

Changes in the monitoring role of the major supermarket chains

Australian horticulture in contrast is mostly reliant on the domestic market to purchase its produce. Four supermarket chains control this market accounting for 83 per cent. Based on 2021 figures, Woolworths accounts for 37 per cent market share, and Coles 28 per cent, with these two together accounting for nearly two-thirds (65 per cent) of the domestic market. Aldi Stores and IGA supermarkets account for another 17 per cent of the domestic market (Wallis 2022). This high level of concentration has produced intense price competition, at the expense of suppliers (Letts 2017). As the head of the Australian Competition and Consumer Commission (ACCC), Rod Sims, noted in a keynote speech to the Law Council of Australia:

> Many small businesses and farmers are largely reliant on Coles and Woolworths to access grocery shoppers. As recent history has shown us, this power imbalance places small businesses and farmers in particularly precarious positions with consequent damage to our economy
>
> (Sims 2021)

Changed stance on supermarket responsibility for ethical sourcing

In the recent past, the supermarket chains also shared the common assumption that Australia was a low risk for unethical sourcing due to strength of its legal institutions. In a presentation to a 2016 Australian Senate Inquiry on the exploitation of temporary work visa holders entitled a National Disgrace, a Woolworths Group Manager for corporate responsibility, community and sustainability explained that the company applied its ethical sourcing and audit programme based on a risk assessment of the source country. She explained that Australia was graded as low risk because it was judged to have 'a strong rule of law, an independent judiciary, a good human rights track record and very good and independent enforcement agencies, and the law is enforced' (Senate Inquiry 2016, para 9.76, 284). The Senate Inquiry report noted that Coles Supermarkets also regarded Australia as low risk because of its robust workplace laws. However, the Senate report states that in response to media allegations of breaches of workplace law in relation to migrant workers in June 2015, both Woolworths and Coles took action by writing to their suppliers to remind them of their obligations to observe immigration and workplace laws (Senate Inquiry 2016, 285–286).

The reporting requirements of the Modern Slavery Act 2018

Since that 2016 Senate Inquiry, the supermarket chains have developed explicit codes of conduct related to fair employment practices and other desired practices and implemented audit programmes for their Australian supply chains. The public reporting of these activities, in the form of a modern slavery statement, has become a legal obligation under Australia's Modern Slavery Act 2018. This federal legislation requires companies to report on the risks of worker exploitation in their operations and supply chains and to show what actions they are taking to address those risks. In response to this legislation, the Woolworths Group produces an annual report detailing its assessment of the risks of modern slavery practices in its operations and supply chains, what actions it has taken to address these risks, assess how effective they have been. The Woolworths 2022 Modern Slavery Statement describes its framework for monitoring labour providers to manage third-party labour risks in its operations (Woolworths Group 2022a, 12). Other activities have focused on suppliers and their involvement with labour hire operators (Woolworths Group 2022a, 13–15, 17). Woolworths Group has also developed and implemented from February 2019 a set of requirements for labour providers in its Australian horticulture supply chain (Woolworths Group 2019). In June 2022, Woolworths implemented another set of standards called a 'responsible recruitment addendum: supplier requirements, guidance & remediation protocols' (Woolworths Group 2022b).

The Coles Group also reports on its actions through its Ethical Sourcing Program to assess modern slavery risks within its supply chain (Coles Group 2022a). As part of this programme, Coles introduced in September 2018 and updated in May 2021 a six-page guidance on Ethical Sourcing: Third-Party Labour Providers (Coles 2022b). In November 2019, Coles entered into the Ethical Retail Supply Chain Accord (ERSCA) with three of Australia's largest trade unions. The Accord was re-signed for a further three years in April 2022 (Coles Group 2022a, 38). The aim of the Accord is to improve and protect the rights of all workers regardless of visa or employment status. According to Coles 2021 Modern Slavery Statement, 'members of the Accord meet regularly to discuss opportunities to lift social compliance standards in the Australian supply chain. Horticulture has been a key focus area of the Accord'. The 2022 Modern Slavery Statement provides details of a research project on the accommodation provision for seasonal workers and their agents in horticulture in Devonport, Tasmania and Bundaberg, Queensland. The research findings led to recommended actions for the stakeholder groups involved, including industry, suppliers, government and retailers (Coles Group 2022a, 21). The Coles Group's 2022 Modern Slavery Statement notes that the Group has invested over $1.5m in 2022 to support their Australian suppliers with auditing costs. Audits are conducted by Sedex, Fair Farms Certification Program and SAP Ariba, a third-party risk assessor of suppliers (Coles Group 2022a, 29). The funds were also used to enable Coles to identify trends, build auditor capacity and assess audit quality. This included monitoring suppliers major audit findings so that they are addressed by suppliers within a reasonable time.

The international supermarket chain, Aldi Stores, also makes use of third-party audits in Australia such as Sedex Members Ethical Trade Audit and Growcom's Fair Farms as part of its Australian Fresh Produce Social Monitoring Program (Aldi Stores, 2021, 9–10). Metcash (IGA Supermarkets) asks its fresh food suppliers to join SEDEX which requires a self-assessment questionnaire and conducts independent third-party social audits (Metcash 2022, 35). These responses by the supermarkets are a significant change from their pre-2016 behaviour. This applies especially to the more detailed scrutiny undertaken by Woolworths Group of labour providers in the horticulture supply chain. A major change for the Coles Group is its involvement with three major unions to audit the employment status of all workers. These changes show the potential for large corporates, with a strong interest in keeping their reputation above reproach, to invest in setting standards and in monitoring their implementation.

However, these efforts are limited to each supermarket chain's own supply chain. There is no indication to date from the four leading supermarkets of a coordinated response among themselves to reduce harm in their supply chains or to reward good performers. Such a coordinated response would help to reduce the complexity of different business standards in this sector. In particular, supermarket chains need to address the mixed messages they are sending when they ask suppliers to invest in greater compliance while also demanding price reductions for the produce they are buying (Kuruvilla et al. 2020, 845–846).

Need for a common industry accreditation system

All four leading supermarket chains need to collaborate and agree on common standards for good agriculture practices, including good employment practices. Specific standards for SWP workers need to be developed separately. The four supermarket chains also need to agree on how best to conduct third-party compliance audits flexibly to achieve measurable outcomes such as enhanced worker welfare and productive workplaces. This proposed common approach by the supermarket chains needs to include incentives for suppliers to show that they are compliant. These positive incentives are needed in addition to the obvious disincentives such as not offering further contracts to non-compliant suppliers.

Industry needs to design and implement the good practice standards in such a way that employers will comply substantially with the standard's requirements. This requires clear rules, strong incentives and best practice transfer to improve the chances of adopter compliance (Wijen 2014, 307). However, this will not be easy to do. If the standards are too general or the audit process is too superficial or perfunctory, employers and auditors in a complex setting like horticulture may aim for minimal compliance ('tick the box') at the expense of the achievement of the outcomes sought by the standards. The compliance requirements need to be balanced against a mechanism that achieves outcomes (Wijen 2014, 309; Wijen and Flowers 2022). A more flexible approach to compliance is needed to enable an auditor to work with the employer to 'problem solve' an issue that does not necessarily conform to the letter of the standard but aims to achieve the desired outcome. This approach has been applied successfully in the governance arrangements for New Zealand's RSE in the form of a relationship manager. These relationship managers, who are government employees, operate as trusted 'go betweens' who can sort out problems between the RSE programme administration and employers (Curtain 2019).

Conclusion

An alternative set of governance arrangements for the SWP is needed that responds better to the market conditions horticulture in Australia faces. These arrangements need to be less complex to implement and much less costly to oversee. The extensive effort by the Australian government to deter potential employer misconduct has had and will continue to have several unintended effects limiting the success of the SWP in particular. The regulatory complexity of the programme has discouraged grower involvement and generated a reliance on labour hire firms because they have the resources to meet the programme's requirements. Nevertheless, the high compliance burden and operational inflexibility placed on these approved employers with no rewards for good practice has fostered a low-trust operating environment.

A hybrid system of compliance is needed, based on both the legal employment framework set and monitored by government and the standards of good practice set by industry supply chains. This compliance system needs to be managed by the market actors, operating through an established fresh food supply chain. These actors include the growers, labour hire firms, third-party auditors and produce buyers. Also included must be government at federal, state and regional levels as the regulator and enforcer of minimum employment and accommodation standards. The market actors in particular have the most to lose in terms of their reputation and profitability if the system they are responsible for is not working well. They also have the incentive and resources to build in continuous improvement. Achieving measurable good practice outcomes for workers and growers will require consumers to pay extra for their produce, to ensure that compliance is sustained

References

Aldi Stores. 2021. *Modern Slavery Statement 2021*. June 6, 2022. https://corporate.aldi.com.au/fileadmin/fm-dam/pdf/Corporate_Responsibility/ALDI_Modern-Slavery_Statement_2021.pdf (accessed January 19, 2023).
Australian Bureau of Statistics (ABS). 2022. *Trade union membership, August 2022*. Released December 14, 2022. ABS Website. https://www.abs.gov.au/statistics/labour/earnings-and-working-conditions/trade-union-membership/latest-release (accessed January 19, 2023).
Amengual, Matthew, and Sarosh Kuruvilla. 2020. "Editorial Essay: Introduction to a Special Issue on Improving Private Regulation of Labor in Global Supply Chains: Theory and Evidence." *ILR Review* 73 (4): 809–16. https://doi.org/10.1177/0019793920927693
Bartley, Tim. 2018. *Rules without Rights: Land, Labor and Private Authority in the Global Economy*. Oxford: Oxford University Press.
Bedford, Charlotte. 2022. "Why absconding hasn't been a problem in New Zealand's RSE." Devpolicy Blog, March 18. https://devpolicy.org/why-absconding-hasnt-been-a-problem-in-new-zealands-rse-20220318/ (accessed January 20, 2023).
Coles Group. 2022a. *Our Commitment to Human Rights 2022 Modern Slavery Statement*. https://www.colesgroup.com.au/FormBuilder/_Resource/_module/ir5sKeTxxEOndzdh00hWJw/file/Modern_Slavery_Statement.pdf (accessed January 20, 2023).
—. 2022b. *Ethical Sourcing Third-Party Labour Providers Guidance*. Issued September 2018, current version May 2021. https://tinyurl.com/2ch869oq (accessed January 19, 2023).
—. 2016. NZ's seasonal worker success: lessons for Australia. Devpolicy Blog, March 23. https://devpolicy.org/nzs-seasonal-worker-success-lessons-australia-20160323/ (accessed January 20, 2023).

—. 2018. "Structural changes for SWP: lessons from New Zealand." Devpolicy Blog, October 3. https://devpolicy.org/structural-changes-for-swp-lessons-from-new-zealand-20181004/ (accessed January 20, 2023).

—. 2019. "Go-betweens needed to troubleshoot Pacific labour mobility schemes." Devpolicy Blog, February 6. https://devpolicy.org/go-betweens-needed-troubleshoot-pacific-labour-mobility-schemes-20190206/.

—. 2021. "Solving problems quickly to safeguard the welfare of seasonal workers." Devpolicy Blog, January 29. https://devpolicy.org/solving-problems-quickly-to-safeguard-the-welfare-of-seasonal-workers-20210129-1/ (accessed January 20, 2023).

Curtain, Richard, and Stephen Howes. 2020. *Governance of the Seasonal Worker Programme in Australia and Sending Countries*. Development Policy Centre, Crawford School of Public Policy, ANU College of Asia and the Pacific, The Australian National University, December 8. https://crawford.anu.edu.au/news-events/events/18032/governance-seasonal-worker-programme-australia-and-sending-countries (accessed January 19, 2023).

Curtain, Richard, Matthew Dornan, Stephen Howes, and Henry Sherrell. 2018. "Pacific Seasonal Workers: Learning from the Contrasting Temporary Migration Outcomes in Australian and New Zealand Horticulture." *Asia & the Pacific Policy Studies* 5 (3): 462–80. https://doi.org/10.1002/app5.261.

Department of Employment and Workplace Relations (DEWR). 2022. *Optimising PALM Scheme Delivery in Australia: Discussion Paper*. Australian Government, Canberra, December 1. https://www.dewr.gov.au/pacific-australia-labour-mobility-scheme/resources/optimising-palm-scheme-delivery-australia-discussion-paper

Department of Foreign Affairs and Trade (DFAT). 2021. Streamlining and Strengthening Pacific Labour for a New Era, Joint media release Minister for Foreign Affairs and Minister for International Development and the Pacific, November 23. https://www.foreignminister.gov.au/minister/marise-payne/media-release/streamlining-and-strengthening-pacific-labour-new-era (accessed January 19, 2023).

Department of Home Affairs. 2022. *Monthly Updates: Onshore Protection (Subclass 866) Visa Processing*. Australian Government, Canberra. https://www.homeaffairs.gov.au/research-and-statistics/statistics/visa-statistics/live/humanitarian-program (accessed January 19, 2023).

Fullerton, Ticky. 2022. "The Australian's 2022 CEO Survey: Coles' Steven Cain on the Changing Face of Retail." *The Australian*. December 27. https://tinyurl.com/2m374837 (accessed January 19, 2023).

Hardy, Tess and John Howe. 2009. "Partners in Enforcement? The New Balance Between Government and Trade Union Enforcement of Employment Standards in Australia." *Australian Journal of Labour Law* 23 (3).

Hardy, Tess, and John Howe. 2015. "Chain Reaction: A St'rategic Approach to Addressing Employment Noncompliance in Complex Supply Chains." *Journal of Industrial Relations* 57 (4): 563–84. https://doi.org/10.1177/0022185615582240.

Hay, Danielle, and Stephen Howes. 2012. "Australia's Pacific Seasonal Worker Pilot Scheme: Why Has Take-up Been So Low?" *Development Policy Centre Discussion Paper #17*, Crawford School of Public Policy, The Australian National University, Canberra. https://papers.ssrn.com/sol3/papers.cfm?abstract_id=2041833

Kuruvilla, Sarosh, Mingwei Liu, Chunyun Li, and Wansi Chen. 2020. "Field Opacity and Practice-Outcome Decoupling: Private Regulation of Labor Standards in Global Supply Chains." *ILR Review* 73 (4): 841–72. https://doi.org/10.1177/0019793920903278

Letts, Stephen. 2017. *Wesfarmers Results: Cost Cutting and Food Deflation Slows Coles Sales Growth*. ABC News https://tinyurl.com/2mvyn68r (accessed January 19, 2023).

Locke, Richard. 2013. *The Promise and Limits of Private Power: Promoting Labor Standards in a Global Economy*. New York, NY: Cambridge University Press. Kindle.

Metcash. 2022. *Metcash Annual Report 2022*. https://tinyurl.com/2e5lv69x (accessed January 19, 2023).

Migrant Workers Taskforce. 2019. Department of Employment and Workplace Relations. https://www.dewr.gov.au/migrant-workers-taskforce

Reed, Cheryl, Angela Southwell, Mandy Healy, and Neil Stafford. 2011. *Final Evaluation of the Pacific Seasonal Worker Pilot Scheme*. Prepared for: Department of Education, Employment and Workplace

Relations, Australian Government, Canberra. https://www.palmscheme.gov.au/sites/default/files/2021-08/7b329a_7eb586caf45a45cdb38766df055783f2.pdf (accessed January 19, 2023).

Senate Inquiry. 2016. *A National Disgrace: The Exploitation of Temporary Work Visa Holders*. Report. Parliament of Australia. https://www.aph.gov.au/parliamentary_business/committees/senate/education_and_employment/temporary_work_visa/report (accessed January 19, 2023).

Sims, Rod. 2021. "Protecting and promoting competition in Australia: keynote speech." *Competition and Consumer Workshop 2021, Law Council of Australia*, 27 August, Australian Competition and Consumer Commission. https://www.accc.gov.au/speech/protecting-and-promoting-competition-in-australia-keynote-speech (accessed January 19, 2023).

Wallis, Sophie. 2022. "Supermarket statistics 2022." *Finder website* (accessed January 19, 2023).

Weil David and Carlos Mallo. 2007. "Regulating Labour Standards via Supply Chains: Combining Public/Private Interventions to Improve Workplace Compliance." *British Journal of Industrial Relations* 45 (4), 719–814.

Wijen, Frank. 2014. "Means Versus Ends in Opaque Institutional Fields: Trading off Compliance and Achievement in Sustainability Standard Adoption." *The Academy of Management Review*, July, 39 (3): 302–23. https://doi.org/10.5465/amr.2012.0218

Wijen, Frank, and Mallory Elise Flowers. 2022. "Issue Opacity and Sustainability Standard Effectiveness." *Regulation & Governance*. Published July 18. https://doi.org/10.1111/rego.12485

Woolworths Group. 2019. *Woolworths Group Responsible Sourcing Standards – Addendum Requirements for Labour Providers in our Australian Horticulture Supply Chain*. February 6. https://www.woolworthsgroup.com.au/content/dam/wwg/sustainability/documents/123008_07_Australia%20Horticulture%20Labour%20Hire%20Addendum_A4.pdf

—. 2022a. *Modern Slavery Statement*. August 23. https://www.woolworthsgroup.com.au/content/dam/wwg/investors/reports/2022/full-year/WOW%20MSS%202022%20FINAL.pdf

—. 2022b. *Responsible Recruitment Addendum: Supplier Requirements, Guidance & Remediation Protocols*, June. https://tinyurl.com/ycyy9hct

8 Evaluation as a governing practice
Judging the outcomes of policy and practice

Calista Castles

Introduction

> Evaluation is a critical task in policy-making … It is often assumed, for example, that evaluation is simple, uniformly carried out, and reveals clear-cut and uncontested results that will drive policy reform. In reality, it is not a simple process in most cases.
>
> (Wu et al. 2018)

An old practice within a 'new' discipline, policy evaluation has become a fundamental, but often taken-for-granted, part of contemporary policy work and political scholarship. Today, the practice of evaluating policy is typically understood as the assessment of a policy or programme's design, implementation, and results, which can occur throughout the policymaking process in various forms. In the context of policy studies and scholarship, it is common to hear terms such as policy appraisal, policy evaluation, and policy analysis. Each form of assessment is considered a distinct practice within the dominant authoritative choice model of governing, which invokes policy cycles, occurring at distinct stages in a policy's lifecycle: whether prospective and before implementation of a programme or intervention (ex-ante), during a programme, or retrospective and after implementation (ex-post).

This chapter focuses on the activities that occur in practice after (ex-post) a policy, programme, or intervention is enacted to measure whether the policy achieved its goals, fell short, or missed all together and uses the term 'policy evaluation' to refer to this practice. Other forms of assessment (policy analysis, policy appraisal) that also contribute to policymaking will not be substantially discussed here; nor will the various 'types' of evaluation. The focus is on making sense of policy evaluation as part of how we are governed. Additionally, in this chapter, 'policy' refers to government (the state) policy-texts (e.g., white papers, legislation, national plans and strategies, parliamentary speeches, election platforms) and the interventions, projects, and programmes (e.g., Medicare funded psychology session, work for the dole) that flow from them, used to govern society, and direct the behaviour (or conduct) of the public and government. This chapter helps make sense of policy evaluation as a normative governing practice by drawing on mental health policy to outline some of the various ways policy evaluation is understood and practiced, before considering the broader implications of evaluation as a normative practice, and how this insight could positively reorient social policies in the future. While it is increasingly recognised that policy evaluation is an inherently political activity, this chapter makes a modest contribution towards understanding evaluation as a constitutive practice with normative power.

DOI: 10.4324/9781003368564-8

Making sense of policy evaluation

At its most fundamental level, ex-post policy evaluation has become a practice for judging what makes a policy 'successful' or 'unsuccessful', which in turn leads to questions about what to measure, what to leave out, who needs to be involved, and which methods or processes to use in order to capture any 'success' or 'failure'. For each policy and its evaluation, the questions (problems) and answers (outcomes) (c.f. Bacchi 2009; Rose 2000) are delimited by the stated and/or implicit aims or objectives of a particular policy, the theoretical perspective and analytical approach of the evaluators, the stakeholders involved in the design, conduct and communication of the evaluation, and more broadly the model of governing used to make sense of the practice (see, for example, Bovens, t'Hart, and Kuipers 2008; Cummings 2023). The job of policy participants and observers then becomes how to make sense of and manage this variety in such a way as to render policy 'successes' and 'failures', 'opportunities' and 'challenges' intelligible as policy outcomes that contribute to governing in a meaningful way.

Models of governing help to make sense of policy evaluation as a governing practice, but also place boundaries around what can be known, what activities are carried out, and by whom. The dominant model of governing, the authoritative instrumental choice model (see the introductory chapter for a detailed explanation), constitutes policy as a product of state (government) activity and authoritative decision-making whereby the focus of policy work and evaluation becomes state-centric. The activities associated with policy work, including evaluation, are constituted and reinforced as objective and intentional authoritative instrumental choices in problem-solving (Colebatch 2005, 2006), and policy objectives become, and are treated as, a set of discrete, clear, and consistent set of policy goals that are outside (exogenous) governing practices. The 'success' or 'failure' of policy becomes an indicator of 'government' success or failure to intervene and 'fix' a 'problem', and the evaluation assesses whether the choice of action was 'the best choice' for achieving those objectives and, if not, provides information about what could be a better choice to inform future policy. Alternatively, understanding governing as a continual process of collective management of the problematic directs attention towards the ways multiple policy participants (and observers) make judgements about the worth of governing activities. There is also a focus on the ways policy evaluation – as a practice – structures and manages relationships between stakeholders to initiate and facilitate ongoing collective action. The scope of assessment becomes broader to include the socially produced knowledges (discourses) that are part of governing practices and techniques beyond the state. The nature of policy-as-discourse, how it functions as a mechanism of rule (Williams 2014; Bacchi and Goodwin 2016) also becomes visible and open to critical scrutiny.

Althaus, Bridgman, and Davis (2018, 9) state that public policies are "built on theories of the world". In this way, policy and policy work is implicitly normative and part of a broader technology of governing that sets out how governing ought to take place, by whom, and with what authority. Normativity or normative theory is a form of questioning that seeks to make judgements about 'what ought to be', rather than describe 'what is' (as in positivist or rationalist theory) and highlights the central role of norms, values, beliefs, ontology and epistemology, in shaping governing practices and knowledge production (Pietrzyk-Reeves 2017). Normativity tends to sit in tension with the rationalist approach that has come to dominate policy work and policy evaluation in particular. The rationalist or scientific approach posits that science and scientific (quantitative) methods can provide a complete explanation of the world independent of values and subjective beliefs, whereas a normative approach seeks to positively evaluate the meaning of a valued political focus and/or activity. A normative approach posits that the 'things' thought to exist in the world are constitutive of the world as *it ought to be*; these 'things' only exit because we give them meaning and context, but they could just as easily be called something else and inscribed with different meanings. Thus, the central role of societal norms, political ideology, and values in governing practices and knowledge production are brought into focus (Pietrzyk-Reeves 2017). Through a normative lens, the activities associated with policy work, including evaluation, are constitutive of and reinforce societal norms and ideals. Policy objectives become, and are treated as, signals that are internal to governing practices; policy texts can be understood as productive and normative, and the questions and answers generated as endogenous to the policy and its evaluation. The 'success' or 'failure' of policy becomes an indicator of societies success or failure to govern the conduct of conduct, where "the conduct to be governing may be one's own or that of others" (Dean and Hindess 1998, 2).

While the practice of evaluation outlined in policy textbooks is acknowledged as a normative practice (an ideal to strive for, but that is often unattainable), it is also held up as rationalistic: objective, unbiased, scientifically rigorous, and at arm's length to politics (Davis et al. 2018; Wu et al. 2018). The normative power of evaluation as a constitutive practice remains underexplored. Normative power refers to the ability to diffuse and legitimise norms through society (Manners 2009). Communicating social norms and values via written information (e.g., in policy) has been shown to be sufficient to induce conformity to the communicated desired behaviours, even when it is difficult to detect that conformity is desired (Nolan et al. 2008). Understanding policy evaluation, in the main, as an implicitly normative activity with normative power would broaden the possibilities for balancing different accounts of the problematic and could promote stronger collective commitment to joint activity in the pursuit of mutually agreed objectives.

Evaluation as a policy practice

Most policy textbooks provide detailed histories of policy and policy evaluation, as well as describe the types of evaluation (see, for example, Bovens et al. 2008; Howlett and Ramesh 2013; Davis et al. 2018; Wu et al. 2018; Cummings 2023), so the section is brief. Ex-post policy evaluation has become a fundamental part of contemporary policy work and scholarship, but this was not the case 30 or even 40 years ago. While the analysis and scrutiny of the actions of government and public administrators has existed for centuries, the formal process of ex-post evaluation was only mentioned in policy publications in the 1960s with the development of 'policy cycles' (Howlett and Ramesh 2013). The decades that followed brought (re)conceptualisation and refinement, and by the mid-to-late 1990s, ex-post policy evaluation had become an important part of formal governing practices. Since the 1990s, the field of policy evaluation has grown and cemented itself as a field of knowledge and scholarship: a discourse. Here, the term discourse is used in a Foucauldian-sense to describe bodies of interrelated statements, signs, and practices associated with a particular field of knowledge (policy evaluation) that simultaneously creates the object/s and subject/s it purports to describe (e.g., experts, activities, methods) (Foucault 2002, 54).

The policy cycle, as part of an authoritative instrumental choice model, commonly presented in public policy courses, has played an important role in constituting ex-post evaluation as a practice and a discourse, as well as those who can (legitimately) participate in the activity; so too has the rise of 'governance' as a mode of governing (Kjaer 2010; Colebatch 2014). For example, the literature identifies several actors in policymaking and evaluation, only a few are elevated to the status of 'expert' and the information they provide valued as 'evidence' (O'Dwyer 2004; Head 2010; Davis et al. 2018). Today, notions of 'good governance' which focus on 'accountability' and 'transparency' have heightened citizens' expectations of public administrators over the last decade or so, and arguably citizens have greater means (their vote, social platforms, media) to enforce these demands. Robust assessment of policy can play an important role in holding public administrators to account, curbing sectional interests, and providing a way to compare various stakeholder propositions (if it is freely available and accessible to the public). Holding government (the State) and public administrators to account for their choices and actions has become important for strengthening public trust, enhancing a government's legitimacy to rule, and a means for improving government responsiveness to changing societal needs (Kjaer 2010). Additionally, being able to convincingly prosecute the merit or 'effectiveness' (how and why a policy is or can be successful) and efficiency (are the costs and resources justified) of a particular policy is important for gaining the political and public support required for sustained collective action (Head 2010). Without it, a policy is unlikely to have the desired effects and therefore is unlikely to be considered a 'success'. Policy evaluation as both a discourse and a practice has become a means to these ends.

Forms of evaluation for judging the 'success' (and 'failure') of policy

While Cummings (2023) notes that evaluation serves a mostly utilitarian purpose and is often used as a communication and education tool, ultimately ex-post policy evaluation is about judging policy 'success' (or failure). Judging policy success involves several interrelated questions which, over time, have come to form the field of policy evaluation: questions about what 'success' and 'failure' mean and how to measure them (see Luetjens, Mintrom, and Hart 2019); questions about the process of policy development: was it fair and democratic; questions about whether the programme was adequately and appropriately resourced; questions about planning, fiscal management, and stakeholder relationships; questions about whether public and political support for the policy was sufficient to generate the desired collective action for success. These questions have informed how evaluation is conceptualised, the types of evaluation carried out, and the methods used. And for a policy and its evaluation to have credibility, transparency (clear process) and independence (external to government) are recommended (Davis et al. 2018). Ideally, this means having sufficient 'evidence' to assess the extent to which a policy's outcomes align with its intent, and 'gathered' by a party seen to be at arm's length from politics.

The following sections draw on mental health policy in Australia to highlight important elements and assumption in evaluation practices, some of which have become taken-for-granted.

National mental health policy in Australia

While Australia's provision of 'mental health care' has had a less than optimal past (Krasnostein 2022), the need for national standards of mental health care only arose in the early 1990s during a National Inquiry into the Human Rights of People with Mental Illness (Human Rights and Equal Opportunity Commission 1993), also known as the *Burdekin Report*. The inquiry revealed multiple and recurring human rights abuses within the mental health care system and recommended wide ranging reforms, including the development of the Mental Health Statement of Rights and Responsibilities and a series of national mental health plans. The 1992 national mental health plan was Australia's first attempt to provide national strategic direction and coordinated intervention in the provision of mental health services and preventative activities. Between 1992 and 2022, Australia has had five national policies for improving the mental health of Australians, each spanning a five-year period. At the time of writing, Australia is approaching the end of the five-year cycle of the *Fifth National Mental Health and Suicide Prevention Plan*, hereafter called 'The Fifth Plan' (Department of Health 2017).

Mental health policy, regardless of jurisdiction, sets the overall direction for 'mental health' and 'mental health care' within that jurisdiction by defining a vision, outlining a system of values, principles, and objectives, and establishing the actions required to achieve them and who is responsible (World Health Organisation 2007). In this way, policy itself can be understood as a discourse. Discursive practices are part of sensemaking practices (Weick 1995) as bodies of interrelated statements, signs, and practices associated with particular fields of knowledge which simultaneously create the object/s and subject/s they purport to describe (e.g., policy analyst, ex-post evaluation, input evaluation) (Bacchi and Goodwin 2016). Althaus and colleagues (2018, 9–11) claim that public policies are "an authoritative framework of the government's beliefs and intentions ... built on theories about the world". Theories, norms, ideology, and values all precede policy development; they are constitutive of the objects and subjects within the policy, and policy evaluation perpetuates and reproduces those theories, values, ideology, and norms. In effect, a perpetual, dynamic loop is created between an assemblage of knowledges or discourses that produce the policy, its evaluation, and the practices that sustain them (Miller and Rose 2008). Here in lies the normative power (the ability to diffuse and legitimise norms) of evaluation as a governing practice.

Evaluation of policy as a normative practice

Most practitioners will be familiar with the process of evaluation, which generally involves information collation, stakeholder consultations, data generation, and report production. Common approaches to ex-post evaluation of mental health policy might consider whether the direction of reform has been the right one for achieving the desired outcomes (programmatic approach), or whether the prorgrammes had been satisfactorily resourced and implemented (input/process approach), or could different policy levers or interventions have been utilised to fulfil the policy objective quicker or more effectively (outcomes and impact approach) (Cummings 2023). The outcome of an evaluation, how 'success' or 'failure' is judged, depends on how the policy problematised the issue in the first instance: how the issue was put forward as a problem and what presuppositions underlie the particular problem representation(s) within it (Bacchi 2009; Bacchi and Goodwin 2016).

In the Fifth Plan (Department of Health, 2017), a stated objective is to improve 'mental health' and 'wellbeing', and most policy participants and observers would probably agree this is a worthwhile goal. There are 24 performance indicators (typically quantitative measures used to assess the extent to which a given objective is achieved) outlined in the plan designed to collectively measure the 'health and wellbeing' of Australians and the performance of the mental health system for the life of the Fifth Plan. The indicators of 'good mental health and wellbeing' identified in the Fifth Plan include the prevalence rate of mental illnesses and rates of suicide (Department of Health 2017). The Fifth Plan identifies the criteria for evaluating the prevalence of 'mental illness' as set out in the Australian Bureau of Statistics (ABS, 2020) *National Study of Mental Health and Wellbeing* (NSMHW). The NSMHW draws on the *Diagnostic and Statistical Manual of Mental Disorders, Fourth Edition* (DSM-IV, APA, 1994–2013) and the *WHO International Classification of Diseases, Tenth Revision* (ICD-10, WHO, 1993–2021) to conceptualise 'mental illness' as a 'disorder' and more specifically as:

> a clinically significant behavioral [sic] or psychological syndrome or pattern that ... *must* currently be considered a manifestation of a behavior [sic], psychological, or biological <u>*dysfunction in the individual.*</u>
> (APA, 2000, p. xxxi, emphasis added)

Its use in the context of assessing 'mental health' and 'wellbeing' in the Fifth Plan reinforces an existing binary relationship between 'mental illness' on the one hand and 'mental health' and 'wellbeing' on the other: the presence of one suggesting the absence of the others. However, despite conceptualising mental health as more than the absence of a disorder within the Fifth Plan, the focus remains on diagnostic categories as indicators for use in evaluation of the plan. This flows through the national plan to associated initiatives, such as the national Headspace programme.

In June 2020, KPMG, a private consulting firm, in consortium with the Social Policy Research Centre of the University of NSW and Batyr (a federally supported mental health organisation), undertook an independent evaluation of the national headspace programme on behalf of the Department of Health and Aged Care. Headspace delivers early intervention services designed to strengthen the ability of 'young people' to manage their mental health in an effort to prevent mental illnesses developing or having a significant impact on quality of life (KPMG and the Social Policy Research Centre [SPRC] 2022). The third evaluation of the headspace programme since 2006, it described programme 'success' as indicated by seven key outcomes: increased health literacy; increased early help seeking behaviour; increased access to required services; increased advocacy for and promotion of youth mental health and well-being by young people in their communities; reduced stigma associated with mental illness and help seeking for young people; improved pathways to care for young people; and ensuring young people can access the help they need in an appropriate, accessible, and youth friendly way. Each of these areas had measures for both short-term and medium-term impacts (KPMG and SPRC 2022, 39–41).

All these indicators of success are assumed to contribute to improved mental health and wellbeing: young people's health literacy improves, which leads to better symptom identification, which leads to help-seeking to improve self-regulation and reduce symptoms, which leads to a reduction in mental illness. Young people become advocates and promoters of help-seeking and self-regulation techniques and encourage others to speak out and access support. These indicators or measures of success are made possible by the underlying presupposition that 'mental illness' arises from something 'abnormal' within the individual, something that can be 'fixed' or remediated by improving oneself: one's thoughts, emotions, behaviours need to align with societal norms. But what if people who have been given a diagnosis of a 'mental illness' or a 'disorder' experience 'mental health' or 'wellbeing', but the diagnostic category (i.e., schizophrenia, autism) remains with the person? Where does that leave the 'success' or 'failure' of the policy and what might it mean for policy reform? If the absence or presence of a diagnostic category does not necessarily signify good or poor mental health or well-being (Keyes 2006), this raises significant and important challenges and opportunities for the policy learnings thought to arise from policy evaluation to support a successful policy, or refute and reorient 'failed' or 'unsuccessful' social policy. It also has implications for the termination of programmes or interventions that were of significant benefit to the 'wellbeing' of community members, but did not impact prevalence rates. Importantly, policy evaluation has the power to perpetuate and reinforce particular societal norms and assumptions which delimit the possibilities for policy learnings and policy reform.

Krasnostein (2022, 3) writes that "[s]tigma is a complex social process that excludes or devalues someone on the basis of a particular characteristic" and has been identified in the Fifth Plan, and other inquiries, as a key barrier to support and mental well-being. The dominant understanding of 'mental disorders' or 'mental illness' is linked to specific notions of what is 'normal' or 'abnormal', norms of socially acceptable behaviour and activities, and through evaluation of mental health policy, these norms and assumptions are prescribed and reinforced. How can mental health policy hope to eliminate stigma if it inadvertently perpetuates it? Moreover, if the World Health Organisation (WHO 2021) conceptualises 'mental health' as "a state of mental well-being that enables people to cope with the stresses of life, realize their abilities, learn well and work well, and contribute to their community", is the focus on prevalence rates of 'mental illness' or 'suicide' justified? How do they contribute to advancing the internationally agreed concept of 'mental health'? Additionally, the emerging concept of Aboriginal and Torres Strait Islander Peoples social and emotional well-being situates 'mental health and wellbeing' within a broader context of whole-of-community well-being, which relates to the harmonisation between interrelations relevant and consistent with Aboriginal and Torres Strait Islander understandings of culture, spiritual, environmental, ideological, political, social, economic, mental, and the physical (Gee et al. 2014). This conceptualisation is subjugated by the focus on prevalence rates and this means any learning from an evaluation may not be fully realised or applied in relation to striving for mental health and well-being in a culturally diverse country like Australia.

Things to consider

The questions asked as part of an evaluation are bounded by (implicit or explicit) conceptual dimensions: for example, *positivist, constructivist,* or *transformational* (Bovens et al. 2008; Cummings 2023), which in turn delimit the form an evaluation can take. For example, *Positivist* approaches focus on the use of 'scientific' (rationalistic) methods in pursuit of an objective and rational view of reality, whereas a *constructivist* approach rejects the notion of objective reality and instead emphasises the subjective nature of the world, bringing diverse people together to reach agreement about what is (subjectively) valued (Luetjens et al. 2019; Cummings 2023). While the Headspace evaluation incorporated both quantitative survey data and qualitative focus group and interview (subjective experience) data, the approach was positivist.

Positivist approaches are most common because they tend to suit the common methods of evaluation – *input, output, process, or outcome* – for assessing the success or failure of a particular programme or intervention because questioning if a policy is appropriate (whether the objectives and desired outcomes align with community needs/wants) is considered too political and subjective for an objective and rational process (Fisher 1995; Althaus et al. 2018). It is worth noting here that despite mental health policy promoted greater involvement of consumers of mental health services and carers of those accessing services in design of policy and services (Browne and Hemsley 2008; Department of Health 2017), rarely are those with vested interests in a policy or programme included in the design, conduct, or reporting of the policy or programmes evaluation because of the perception that any outcomes would be subjective and biased. Sanderson (2002) argues, the (over)use of rationalistic methods to produce evidence and knowledge about what works is underpinned by (often contested) assumptions about what kinds of knowledge ought to be valued and how best to use that knowledge in the process of policymaking. The exclusion of lived expertise and those with a stake in policy or programmes based on the notion those views are subjective and biased is a result of privileging particular kinds of knowledge over others. While an evaluator or evaluation team may design or choose various aspects of the evaluation (the kind of survey or types of focus group questions), evaluative indicators or measures are generally built-in to a policy at the point of policy formulation and design (Davis et al. 2018; OECD 2020), either implicitly or explicitly. This is where policy evaluation intersects with, and is delimited by, other processes in policy work such as problematisation (how a particular issue is designated as problematic), how the activity of governing is structured and managed, and who can/does participate.

The following section looks at the impact well-being indicators could have on policy and society.

Measuring what matters to create what matters

The non-government community mental health sector and lived experience advocates have been calling for evaluation of mental health policy and programmes to include well-being criteria that moves away from a focus on the presence or absence of mental illness and include broader subjective experiences (Queensland Alliance for Mental Health [QAMH] 2022). The aim, they say, is to challenge perceptions about mental illness (Keyes 2006) and "fundamentally change the way we fund and position community mental wellbeing services" (QAMH 2022, 7). In Australia, the 2022 Federal Budget included 'wellbeing' objectives based on OECD measures of well-being and social progress (OECD 2011). The government said the inclusion of 'wellbeing' indicators was to "measure what matters" (Commonwealth of Australia 2022) and reorient the narrow focus of economic and fiscal policy away from GDP indicators, which does little to reduce inequality and redistribute wealth. Internationally, there is recognition that public policy and interventions need to account for the complexity of social ecosystems, and there is no reason why evaluation of policy cannot be understood as a contributing part of that complexity.

The inclusion of well-being indicators in government policy is gaining popularity globally as a 'new' way to measure social progress and for transforming the focus of governing (Adler and Fleurbaey 2016; Gaukroger et al. 2022). The argument being that if we change the focus of policy, change what we measure as important, we can also change society but focusing on broader social progress measures. Several countries have utilised well-being indicators to govern society, with some interesting results. For example, Bhutan has had a Gross National Happiness approach since 1972 and has made significant progress towards modernisation while remaining sustainable, emphasising environmental conservation, and ensuring all policies have health and subjective happiness as the core goals (Tobgay et al. 2011). Similarly, the Social Progress Index (SPI) is an initiative tied to the Sustainable Development Goals that systematically and comprehensively gathers worldwide data on key non-economic dimensions of social progress. For example, the SPI measures multiple dimensions of basic human needs, opportunity, and foundations of well-being (Green et al. 2022). While economic development can bring improvements, these improvements do not always accompany social and environmental progress. Proponents of the SPI say having the tools to track social and environmental progress along with economic development can help decision-makers make better policy and investment choices, but also give society a tool for advocating for change and holding governments to account.

Gaukroger and colleagues (2022) argue that despite the hurdles to reorienting public policy, shifting how policy evaluation is understood and used in governing is important to encourage broader collection and use of information and data, where possible, to create theoretical frameworks for reorienting policy objectives. Additionally, the deliberate inclusion of indicators of subjective well-being in fiscal policy to reorient governing suggests that the measures used in policy evaluation are not simply tools for collecting information that is waiting out there in the world to be identified and collected. Evaluative measures can influence the focus of policy and, consequently, governing. In this way, evaluation of policy has normative power because evaluation measures encapsulate *what ought to be* important and are being used to actively (re)structure or (re)orient governing practices, or to (re)enforce and (re)produce old ways of thinking and acting. Measuring well-being is not an end in and of itself, it is a starting point, a tool for embedding and supporting a well-being framework across and within various governing activities.

Conclusion

In conclusion, evaluation as a policy practice is often viewed as 'objective', 'rational', and outside policy. As such, there is a tendency to focus on the 'outcomes' of a particular policy or suite of policy interventions, rather than the various ways evaluation as a practice contributes to the collective *judging* of the problematic and the solutions offered as remedies. This chapter has discussed policy evaluation as a normative practice that is internal to governing, rather than objective and outside it. Thinking about policy evaluation as a normative and internal to how we are governed encourages critical questioning that gives more weight to how particular measures, indicators, and objectives come to be the subject of evaluation than to the numerical representations evaluation produces. To suggest that the evaluation of and for policy is normative is not a radical proposition. Indeed, when Harold Laswell put forward the idea of policy science in the mid-20th century, although his aim was to find ways to reduce unnecessary debate and political delay, his intention was for theory and practice to retain a focus on how policy judgements are made, by whom, when, under what assumptions, and with what effects (Laswell 1958). When policy is evaluated, the framework(s) chosen and the outcomes measured do not simply refer to *what is* in the world, but rather an aspirational vision of what *ought to exist* and what *ought* to be measured. After all, the path from outcomes back to intention (or objectives) is questionable if outcomes are seen only as rational and neutral 'facts' and there is no account of the subjective and constitutive power of those 'facts' and intentions.

Further reading

Adler, Alejandro, and Martin E. P. Seligman. 2016. "Using Wellbeing for Public Policy: Theory, Measurement, and Recommendations." *International Journal of Wellbeing* 6 (1): 1–35. https://doi.org/10.5502/ijw.v6i1.429

Colebatch, Hal K., ed. 2006. "Policy, Models and the Construction of Governing." In *The Work of Policy: An International Survey*, first edn Original, 3–19. Lanham, MD: Lexington Books.

Diener, Ed, Richard Lucas, Ulrich Schimmack, and John F. Helliwell. 2009. *Well-Being for Public Policy*. Oxford: Oxford University Press.

Dolan, Paul, and Mathew P. White. 2007. "How Can Measures of Subjective Well-Being Be Used to Inform Public Policy?" *Perspectives on Psychological Science* 2 (1): 71–85. https://doi.org/10.1111/j.1745-6916.2007.00030.x

Lasswell, Harold D., and Abraham Kaplan. 2014. *Power and Society: A Framework for Political Inquiry*. Piscataway, NJ: Transaction Publishers.

References

Adler, Matthew D., and Marc Fleurbaey, eds. 2016. *The Oxford Handbook of Well-Being and Public Policy, Oxford Handbooks*. Online ed. Oxford: Oxford Academic.

Althaus, Catherine, Peter Bridgman, and Glyn Davis. 2018. *The Australian Policy Handbook: A Practical Guide to the Policy-Making Process*. 6th ed. Abingdon: Taylor & Francis.

American Psychiatric Association. 2000. *Diagnostic and Statistical Manual of Mental Disorders: DSM-IV-TR*. Washington, DC: American Psychiatric Association.

Australian Bureau of Statistics. 2020. "National Study of Mental Health and Wellbeing." *ABS*, 2020–21, https://www.abs.gov.au/statistics/health/mental-health/national-study-mental-health-and-wellbeing/latest-release

Bacchi, Carol. 2009. *Analysing Policy: What's the Problem Represented to Be?* Frenchs Forest: Pearson Education.

Bacchi, Carol, and Susan Goodwin. 2016. *Poststructural Policy Analysis: A Guide to Practice*. Berlin: Springer.

Browne, Graeme, and Martin Hemsley. 2008. "Consumer Participation in Mental Health in Australia: What Progress Is Being Made?" *Australasian Psychiatry* 16 (6): 446–49.

Bovens, Mark, Paul t'Hart, and Sanneke Kuipers. 2008. "The Politics of Policy Evaluation." In *The Oxford Handbook of Public Policy*, edited by Robert Goodin, Michael Moran, and Martin Rein. Online ed., 319–35. Oxford: Oxford Academic. https://doi.org/10.1093/oxfordhb/9780199548453.003.0015

Colebatch, Hal K. 2005. "Policy Analysis, Policy Practice and Political Science." *Australia Journal of Public Administration* 64 (3): 14–23. https://doi.org/10.1111/j.1467-8500.2005.00448.x

—. 2006. "What Work Makes Policy?" *Policy Science* 39: 309–21. https://doi.org/10.1007/s11077-006-9025-4

—. 2014. "Making Sense of Governance." *Policy and Society* 33 (4): 307–16. https://doi.org/10.1016/j.polsoc.2014.10.001

Commonwealth of Australia. 2022. "Measuring what matters: Budget Paper No. 1, Section 4." *Federal Budget October 2022–2023*. https://cdn.theconversation.com/static_files/files/2749/Measuring_What_Matters_October_budget_2022.pdf

Cummings, Rick. 2023. "Policy and Program Evaluation." *Australian Politics and Policy*. Senior ed., edited by Nick Barry, Peter Chen, Yvonne Haigh, Sara C. Motta and Diana Perche. Sydney: Sydney University Press. https://open.sydneyuniversitypress.com.au/9781743328859/9781743328859-policy-and-program-evaluation.html#Chapter51

Dean, Mitchell, and Barry Hindess. 1998. *Governing Australia: Studies in Contemporary Rationalities of Government*. Cambridge: Cambridge University Press.

Department of Health. 2017. *The Fifth Mental Health and Suicide Prevention Plan*. National Mental Health Commission. Publication Number 11926.

Fisher, Frank. 1995. *Evaluating Public Policy*. Wokingham: Nelson-Hall.

Foucault, Michel. 2002. *The Archaeology of Knowledge*. Translated by A. M. Sheridan Smith. London and New York: Routledge Classics.

Gaukroger, Cressida, Akwasi Ampofo, Frances Kitt, Toby Phillips, and Warwick Smith. 2022. *Redefining Progress: A Review of Global Approaches to Wellbeing*. Centre for Policy Development. https://cpd.org.au/wp-content/uploads/2022/08/CPD-Redefining-Progress-FINAL.pdf

Gee, Graham, Pat Dudgeon, Clinton Schultz, Amanda Hart, and Kerrie Kelly. 2014. "Aboriginal and Torres Strait Islander Social and Emotional Wellbeing." *Working Together: Aboriginal and Torres Strait Islander Mental Health and Wellbeing Principles and Practice* 2, edited by Pat Dudgeon, Helen Milroy and Roz Walker, 55–68. Telethon Kids Institute, Kulunga Aboriginal Research Development Unit, Department of the Prime Minister and Cabinet (Australia).

Green, Michael, Jaromir Harmacek, Mohamed Htitich, and Petra Krylova. 2022. *2022 Social Progress Index Report*. Social Progress Imperative. https://www.socialprogress.org/global-index-2022overview/

Head, Brian. 2010. "Evidence-Based Policy: Principles and Requirements." *Productivity Commission 2010, Strengthening Evidence Based Policy in the Australian Federation* 1: 13–26. https://www.pc.gov.au/research/supporting/strengthening-evidence

Howlett, Michael, and Michael Ramesh. 2013. *Studying Public Policy: Policy Cycles and Policy Subsystems*. 2nd ed. Oxford: Oxford University Press.

Human Rights and Equal Opportunity Commission. 1993. *Human Rights and Mental Illness: Report of the National Inquiry Concerning the Human Rights of People with Mental Illness*. Canberra: Commonwealth of Australia.

Keyes, Corey L. M. 2006. "Subjective Well-Being in Mental Health and Human Development Research Worldwide: An Introduction." *Social Indicators Research* 77: 1–10. https://doi.org/10.1007/s11205-005-5550-3

Kjaer, Anne Mette. 2010. *Governance*. Cambridge: Polity Press.

KPMG and the Social Policy Research Centre. 2022. *Evaluation of the national headspace program. Final report*. On Behalf of Department of Health, June 2022. https://www.health.gov.au/resources/publications/evaluation-of-the-national-headspace-program?language=en

Krasnostein, Sarah. 2022. "Not Waving, Drowning: Mental Illness and Vulnerability in Australia." *Quarterly Essay* 85: 1–124. Melbourne: Black Inc Books.

Laswell, Harold. D. 1958. *Politics: Who Gets What, When, How*. New York, NY. Meridian.

Luetjens, Joannah, Michael Mintrom, and Paul t Hart. 2019. *Successful Public Policy: Lessons from Australia and New Zealand*. Canberra: ANU Press.

Manners, Ian. 2009. The Concept of Normative Power in World Politics. Danish Institute for International Studies Brief, 1–5.

Miller, Peter, and Nikolas Rose. 2008. *Governing the Present: Administering Economic, Social, and Personal Life*. Cambridge: Polity.

Nolan, Jessica M., P. Wesley Schultz, Robert B. Cialdini, Noah J. Goldstein, and Vladas Griskevicius. 2008. "Normative Social Influence Is Underdetected." *Personality and Social Psychology Bulletin* 34 (7): 913–23. https://doi.org/10.1177/0146167208316691

O'Dwyer, Lisel. 2004. "A Critical Review of Evidence-Based Policy Making." *AHURI*, Final Report No. 58. Australian Housing and Urban Research Institute, Southern Research Centre.

OECD. 2011. *Compendium of OECD Well-Being Indicators*. OECD Public Governance Reviews. Paris: OECD Publishing. https://www.oecd.org/general/compendiumofoecdwell-beingindicators.htm

—. 2020. *Improving Governance with Policy Evaluation: Lessons from Country Experiences*, OECD Public Governance Reviews. Paris: OECD Publishing, https://doi.org/10.1787/89b1577d-en

Pietrzyk-Reeves, Dorota. 2017. "Normative Political Theory." *Teoria Polityki* 1: 173–185. https://doi.org/10.4467/00000000TP.17.009.6588

Queensland Alliance for Mental Health. 2022. *Wellbeing First*. 2nd ed. November 2022. https://www.qamh.org.au/wellbeing/wellbeing-first/

Rose, Nikolas. 2000. *Powers of Freedom: Reframing Political Thought*. 1st ed. 1999. Cambridge, UK: Cambridge University Press.

Sanderson, Ian. 2002. "Evaluation, Policy Learning and Evidence-Based Policy Making." *Public Administration* 80 (1): 1–22. https://doi.org/10.1111/1467-9299.00292

Tobgay, Tashi, Ugen Dophu, Cristina E Torres, and Kesara Na-Bangchang. 2011. "Health and Gross National Happiness: Review of Current Status in Bhutan." *Journal of Multidisciplinary Healthcare* 4: 293–98. https://doi.org/10.2147/JMDH.S21095

Weick, Karl. 1995. *Sensemaking in Organisations*. Thousand Oaks, CA: SAGE.

Williams, James. 2014. *Understanding Poststructuralism*. Abingdon: Routledge.

World Health Organisation. 2007. "Monitoring and Evaluation of Mental Health Policies and Plans." *Mental Health Policies and Service Guidance Package*. Geneva: WHO

—. 2021. *Comprehensive Mental Health Action Plan 2013–2030*. Geneva: WHO.

Wu, Xun, Martin Ramesh, Michael Howlett, and Scott A. Fritzen. 2018. *The Public Policy Primer: Managing the Policy Process*. Abingdon: Routledge.

9 Contested viewpoints on the management of social problems

The case the Australian Child Support Scheme

Kay Cook

Introduction

This chapter examines Australian child support policy governance as an example of ongoing contest in the collective management of social problems. In the case at hand, the practice of the Australian Child Support Scheme is used to illustrate the iterative, interconnected ways through which interest, evidence and authority come to define policy problems and their technical solutions in ways that reinforce the gendered status quo.

A perennial problem in social policy concerns how to ensure that families can adequately provide for their children. Until children reach an age of maturity and independence, they require significant care and resources. While governments position parents as shouldering the primary responsibility for resourcing children's care through paid employment, governments also support families to either provide care or secure resources through a range of government programmes and services. However, the way that governments have intervened to support families to care or to secure their own means of supporting children has evolved over recent decades in response to the changing nature of Australian families and thus parental capacity to adequately provide sufficient care and resources. In the last 50 years, the way that families have been expected to fund their children's care has evolved, with these changing expectations primarily being placed on mothers, particularly mothers who head separated families.

Prior to 1975, government policy cast women – and particularly mothers – as entirely dependent on their male-breadwinning partner (Castles, 1985), with resources to support children's care expected to be shared within households. Divorce rates and maternal employment were low – primarily as a result of the *Matrimonial Causes Act 1959* that made divorce difficult, and the 'marriage bar' that required many women to give up employment upon marriage. During and following the 1972–75 Henderson Poverty Inquiry, the government introduced a range of benefits to support mothers' care work, such as the Supporting Mother's Benefit (1973) which provided income to unmarried and separated mothers who did not qualify for a Widows' Pension, the Family Allowance (1976) and Family Income Supplement (1983). These payments saw governments play an increasing role in financing the support of children, particularly when the unified family 'team' broke down. The introduction of no-fault divorce in 1975 saw the number of single parent households significantly increase. Financing children's care when a family unit could no longer be assumed thus became a pressing policy concern.

To ensure that the balance of financial responsibility for children remained with parents even after separation, the government also introduced programmes that sought to: (a) increase mothers' earning capacity; and (b) compel fathers' provision of funds to children living elsewhere. Programmes and subsidies to support women's entry into the labour market included the funding of childcare service and the provision of childcare rebates (Mitchell 1999; Mahon,

DOI: 10.4324/9781003368564-9

Bergqvist, and Brennan 2016), and the introduction of the Jobs, Education and Training Scheme (Australian Institute of Family Studies, 2011). While the courts offered separated mothers a means of pursuing maintenance payments from the children's previous breadwinner, the cost, delays and lack of compliance associated with the existing legal remedy required governments to intervene. As a result, in 1988–89, the government introduced the Child Support Scheme.

Child support is private money paid by a non-resident parent to a resident parent for the purpose of supporting children following parental separation. The provision of a child support service meets Australia's obligation under the Convention on the Rights of the Child (United Nations, 1989, Article 27) that states should "take all appropriate measures to secure the recovery of maintenance for the child from the parents or other persons having financial responsibility for the child".

Since its inception, child support has been highly contested, and significant reviews and reforms have ensued. Payers, approximately 85 per cent of whom are fathers, have an interest in reducing their child support liabilities and avoiding ordered payments, where possible. Research suggests that payers use a range of illegal and legal means to reduce their taxable incomes and thus child support liabilities, such as working cash-in-hand, diverting personal income into business accounts or family trusts, or not lodging tax returns (Shephard 2005; Natalier 2018). The role that the state plays in the private transfer of funds is to calculate the amount of money to be provided given varying parental incomes and the sharing of care between households, and to provide a service to collect and transfer parental payments. But, the state's role – and I would argue, conflicted interest – in child support extends beyond the calculation and transfer of payments. When recipient parents are eligible for Family Tax Benefit (FTB) payments, use of the state-calculated child support payment amount is mandatory, as child support is regarded as income for the purpose of calculating FTB Part A payments. For the 15 per cent of parents whose incomes place them above the eligibility threshold for FTB payments (House of Representatives Standing Committee on Social Policy and Legal Affairs 2015; Department of Social Services 2022a), payment amounts can be decided privately between parents, or they can choose to use the government payment calculation. As such, the state plays a role in governing the private financial transfers made between some parents in separated families, but not those on high incomes.

To make sense of the ongoing personal and political contests that have besieged the child support programme since its enactment in 1988/89, the chapter draws on Jamrozik and Nocella's (1998) framework for evaluating organisation performance from the perspectives of politicians, administrators, front-line workers and child support policy targets. Given the complexity and competing interests of the actors involved in child support policy, it has been a site of ongoing contest. Part of this contest stems from different views of what problems governments have sought to address (Bacchi 1999, 2009), and the misalignment between policy solutions and the interests of policy targets (Cook and Natalier 2013, 2014, 2016; Cook and Skinner 2019, 2020).

While researchers have previously examined the mismatch between state policy responses and parents' expectations, no study has examined the how child support policy evolution speaks to or reflects the interests of a wider array of actors within this administrative ecosystem. In response, this chapter sets out the political, administrative and operational interests that exist within the child support policy ecosystem and maps these onto the history of child support policy reform. In doing so, the chapter identifies child support as a governmental tool that has been used over recent decades to manage the boundary between the governing and the governed, seeking to depoliticise and minimise ongoing political contest. However, in managing this boundary, child support reform has increasingly aligned the interests of the state with those of unwilling child support payers and away from the original purpose of the Scheme. However, a new government in mid-2022 – elected in part on the basis of discontent with the gender-hostility of the previous government (Biddle and Gray 2022; Browne 2022) – has re-opened the door for sweeping child support change, this time centring gender.

To examine the evolution of child support as a technical device to manage the boundary between the governing and the governed, the chapter begins by setting out Jamrozik and Nocella's (1998) framework. An overview of the Child Support Scheme over recent decades is then provided, before applying the interests and insights that Jamrozik and Nocella's framework represents onto this history of child support policy development. An overview of the major points of reform Scheme follows. Here, Tania Li's (2007) work on the contradictory positions of governmental practice is used to examine the way in which interest, evidence and authority align to reinforce the boundary between the governed and governing.

Governing contested social truths

Governing the resourcing of children's care when they are living in a single-parent families entails the management of a complex suite of competing interests, as states must manage parents' moral and social obligations to provide for their children (Eekelaar 1991; Cook and Skinner 2020), containing government expenditure, and the social ramifications of the opportunity costs of care being inequitably distributed between separated parents. As Head and Alford (2015, 711–712) note, "government organizations are good at implementing policies and delivering services that are relatively standardized, routine, and high volume", but are less effective at complex, unpredictable, open-ended and intractable issues, described as 'wicked problems', most commonly ascribed to social problems (Rittel and Webber 1973). For example, Jamrozik and Nocella (1998, 5) provide an analysis of how 'wicked problems' are managed, referring to such problems as the "so called pathological conditions that are commonly referred to as social problems – such as poverty, unemployment, family dislocation and so on".

Policy scientists have contended that it is the social complexity of a problem that make it particularly challenging (Stone 1989; Hancock 2006), as it is competing values rather than incomplete knowledge that structures their possible remedy. As a result of this, albeit artificial, division authors have suggested that "if it were possible to make a wicked problem more technical, possible 'solutions' might be obtainable" (Newman and Head 2017, 417). However, such technical solutions first rely on social problems being defined in a way that enables technical "corrective measures to produce desirable results" (Li 2007, 123). As such, by rendering complex social problems technical, the sites of contest merely expand to include the definition of the problem, the nature of technical measures and the desirability of the results. But, rather than allowing for a proliferation in the sites of possible contest, greater political and governmental management is required. Here, the government's view of the problem, its causes and management thus come to define the nature of the problem, its causes and suitable technical solutions, which relies on the implementing government being positioned as a "neutral vessel dedicated to the improvement of 'the people'" (Li 2007, 134). As such, in devising, implementing and reforming technical solutions to complex social issues, such as the Australian Child Support Scheme, governments must manage the boundaries between themselves and those they seek to govern.

While different views of the problem will be held by different social actors, be they politicians, administrators, front-line workers or policy targets, governments require a means of transforming these possible sites of contest into a state of 'nonpolitics' (Li 2007). Before setting out how nonpolitics was achieved by centring the seemingly 'neutral' and 'objective' interests

Actor	Programmatic interests			
	Manifest	Assumed	Extant	Requisite
Political	X			X
Administrative	X	X		
Operational		X	X	
Recipient			X	X

Figure 9.1 Divergent views on the technical management of social problems

Adapted from Jamrozik and Nocella (1997, p. 52)

of the state, the chapter first sets out the different – and fundamentally misaligned – perspectives of the social actors engaged in the child support programme.

Jamrozik and Nocella (1997) contend that there are four distinct levels of activity involved in interventions into social problems, namely: (1) policy making and resource allocation; (2) administration; (3) service delivery; and (4) service receipt. When policies are proposed and legislated, enacted, implemented and received, the actors involved in each of these levels perform different activities and also bring different lenses to the problem at hand. As Jamrozik and Nocella (1997, 52) describe, each of the aforementioned policy actor's views of the programme performance reflect a distinct perception of social reality, reflecting manifest, assumed, extant and requisite understanding of the nature of the intervention (Figure 9.1).

According to Jamrozik and Nocella (1997), a 'manifest' perspective foregrounds the officially approved and publicly propagated account of programme performance that foregrounds the programme's intent, summarised here as 'what the program is'. The 'assumed' version, by contrast, reflects a subjective account of practice wisdom regarding what works and how, focusing on 'how the program does'. From an 'extant' perspective, the focus is on the objective performance and implementation of the programme, or 'what the program does'. Finally, a requisite perspective foregrounds the desired – but perhaps unfulfilled – outcomes of the programme, or 'what the programme should'. However, these perspectives do not exist in isolation. Rather, Jamrozik and Nocella (1997) contend that the different actors approach policy problems, and the interventions designed to address them, from distinct orientations that encompass a duality of perspectives.

First, politicians are interested in and present the manifest version of the programme, espousing an official account of the programme's aims and objectives. But, at the same, politicians may draw on the requisite accounts to foreground the desired objectives which may have been hampered or unfulfilled due to technical or political problems. Second, programme administrators will also espouse official, manifest accounts of social programmes, such as on official documentation and communications. However, administrators will also rely on and promulgate assumed accounts of how the programme operates in practice and where its administration could be improved or redesigned. Third, front-line programme administrators will also draw readily on assumed knowledge about how the programme works, but they also hold knowledge about and can draw on examples of what impact the programme has in reality. Finally, programme recipients have insight into the programme's extant impact as well as having insight into whether this reality aligns with their requisite perspective regarding what the programme ought to achieve.

Returning to the technical management of wicked problems, ongoing efforts are required to ensure that the politically palatable version of the programme simultaneously demonstrates the alignment of the programme with recipients' needs while also rendering potentially contradictory user perspectives invisible and irrelevant to programme evaluation and reform. In managing the boundary between the governing and the governed, through the construction of evidence and programme evaluation, the interests of the powerful come to stand in for the interests of policy targets. As a result, the purported beneficiaries of child support policy – namely single mothers with majority care for children following parental separation – were transformed from those requiring state support into those requiring governance. The political need to frame the results of the inevitably lacking technical intervention as desirable meant that any failures had to be recast as technical setbacks or, even further, resulting from the personal inadequacies of programme beneficiaries.

Child support insights and interests

Applying Jamrozik and Nocella's (1998) framework for mapping the perspectives of different policy actors to child support reveals a range of interests in the functioning of the Child Support Scheme. Drawing on policy documents contemporaneous to key events in the technical evolution of the Scheme, various interests are evident.

To provide a brief summary of each position, which will be unpacked in more detail shortly, for politicians, their interest in child support lies in the purpose of the programme and whether it delivers on its objectives. Like politicians, child support programme administrators are also interested in the purpose of the Scheme. But rather than having insight into whether the programme delivers on its objectives, programme administers' interests lie more in how the project will achieve its objectives through regulatory mechanisms and system design. Front-line workers also have insight into and an interest in what the Child Support Scheme can and cannot do, as set out in the programme's rules and regulation. But, front-line workers also engage with the practice of the scheme and as such have insight into how outcomes are achieved through administrative tools and interfaces. Finally, child support programme participants have experience using – or trying to use – the Scheme's administrative tools and interfaces and combine the insights gained from programme participation with their evaluation of whether these tools deliver on what they feel that the Child Support Scheme ought to do. Unlike other social programmes, the recipients' view of child support is highly polarised, with paying parents having a fundamentally different perspective on what the Scheme ought to achieve compared to recipient parents.

Given parents' fundamental contest over the 'success' of the Scheme – and the alignment between recipients' interest in programme evaluation with politicians' interests in ensuring public confidence – parents' concerns have fuelled ongoing reviews and reforms to the Scheme since its inception. However, as I have described elsewhere (Cook and Natalier 2013, 2014, 2016; Cook 2019; Cook and Skinner 2019, 2021), it is not recipients' evaluations of programme failure, but rather it has consistently been the voices of paying parents who have instigated and dominated child support reform processes. While a review of these reform processes has been conducted previously, and is beyond the scope of this chapter, what this research identifies is that there has been a gendered alignment between the concerns of paying fathers (who comprise approximately 85 per cent of payers) and the interests of neoliberal politicians seeking to reduce government costs and individualise responsibility for social problems over previous decades. Rather than re-prosecuting these issues, this chapter instead sets out how the alignment of interests of various policy actors, and the obscuring of insights from 'unhelpful' perspectives, has worked to depoliticise child support over recent decades. However, Australia has entered a newfound era of feminist, or at least more socially just, policy reform, as illustrated by the remit of the Women's Economic Equality Taskforce (Australian Government 2022) and the Economic Inclusion Advisory Committee (Chalmers and Rishworth 2022), and the foregrounding of gender and financial abuse in the 2022–2032 National Plan to End Violence Against Women and Children (Department of Social Services 2022b) and the work of the Joint Select Committee on Australia's Family Law System (2021a, b), which the government has largely endorsed (Australian Government 2023). As such, the Child Support Scheme finds itself in a situation where previous attempts to depoliticise and manage a 'wicked' social problem have been called into question and are once again open for significant reform.

Programme introduction

In the decades leading up to the introduction of the Child Support Scheme in 1988/89, Australia was experiencing high rates of single parent poverty and pressure to increase state payments (McClelland 2000; Edwards 2019). At the same time, child support administered via the courts was ineffective with low payment values and rates of compliance. Politically, a privately funded, but publicly operated, scheme to transfer payments from non-resident parents to resident parents provided a solution. Using Jamrozik and Nocella's (1997) framing, politicians' manifest and requisite interests lay in what the new Child Support Scheme was and what financial benefit it would achieve for impoverished single mothers and their children, respectively. Departmental administrators, labelled 'femocrats' (Edwards 1986; Edwards, Howard, and Miller 2001), took up the Hawke government's manifest framing of what the Scheme was, adding technical detail of how mothers' caring labour would be calculated and costed via the child support formula. In addition, and perhaps most importantly to the government that was facing burgeoning state expenditure, the original design of the Child Support Scheme resulted in the reduction of single mothers' other benefits, as child support has always been counted as income in the calculation of family payments made to mothers (Edwards 2019). As such, administrators' design of how the Child Support Scheme would work did not fully realise mothers' interests in improving their material living conditions. Rather, the state's requisite interest in reducing welfare expenditure was prioritised.

In terms of the operation of the new Scheme, a primary consideration was how parents were entered into the programme and who collected and transferred the money. Prior to the Scheme's introduction, parents could either negotiate and transfer child support payments privately or seek a court-ordered amount which would then also return to parents for enactment. For single mothers who received a state payment, which was – and continues to be – the majority given Australia's generously means-tested family payments (Joint Select Committee on Certain Family Law Issues 1994; Department of Social Services 2022a) and low rates of maternal employment at the time (Cook 2019), it was compulsory to have a child support order calculated so as to limit the state's family payment outlays (Child Support Evaluation Advisory Group 1992). Payments calculated by the Department of Social Security would then be collected and transferred by the Tax Office (Edwards 2019), with 56 per cent of liabilities paid to the Tax Office through involuntary wage-withholding (Joint Select Committee on Certain Family Law Issues 1994, 603). From programme participants' perspectives of what the programme 'ought' to achieve, the Scheme was heralded as a win by mothers, with collection rates vastly improving on court-ordered payments (Hancock 1998). For fathers, however, the compulsory and state-operationalised nature of the Scheme was viewed as an overreach (Child Support Consultative Group 1992; Edwards 2019; Joint Select Committee on Certain Family Law Issues, Neal dissenting report).

However, it has been fathers' ongoing frustration with the operation of the Scheme that has fuelled ongoing political contest and reform (Cook and Natalier 2013, 2014, 2016). While fathers have been frustrated by the scheme's enforcement of their breadwinning role beyond the nuclear family, and without women being forced to uphold their end of the gender-contract (Cook 2019; Cook and Skinner 2019), it is men's requisite interest in 'financial autonomy' and 'personal responsibility' that fathers share with politicians that I argue has fuelled over three decades of unhelpful child support policy reform (Edwards 2019).

Early pushback

Since its inception, child support has been highly contested (Child Support Evaluation Advisory Group 1992; Joint Select Committee on Certain Family Law Issues 1994; Alexander 1995; Hancock 1998). Payers, approximately 85 per cent of whom are fathers, have an interest in reducing their child support liabilities and avoiding ordered payments, where possible.

Within six years of the Scheme's inception, a Joint Select Committee on Certain Family Law Issues (1994) was established to review the child support programme's operation and effectiveness – recommending that collections be made private rather than transferred through the Child Support Agency. Politically, the review suggested that private agreements could reduce government intervention into parents' private affairs, and the administration costs to government. However, while it was noted that Private collections would likely negatively impact low-income single mothers who are already subject to state surveillance. Research from 1994 shows that 66 per cent of custodial parents received no child support due to the lack of agreements or non-payment, with ineffective collection being a key issue. Only 56 per cent of liabilities were paid on time, with almost half being paid through involuntary wage-withholding. Despite efforts to change community attitudes and improve voluntary payments, evidence of increasing compliance was not found. Overall, the child support programme's effectiveness in supporting low-income single mothers and ensuring fathers' financial responsibilities was questioned.

Ongoing operational reform

In response to pressure from non-resident, paying parents, a House of Representatives Standing Committee on Family and Community Affairs (2003) undertook a significant review of the child support programme, with a 2005 Ministerial Taskforce designing a new child support formula as a result. The reforms recommended by the 2003 Committee – and formula operationalised by the Taskforce – were implemented in 2006–07 and 2008, respectively. However, research has shown that there are a range of issues that have persisted. Departmental data, for example, shows that approximately a third of parents have payment liabilities between $0 and $500 per year (House of Representatives Standing Committee on Social Policy and Legal Affairs 2015; Department of Social Services 2022a) while only 24 per cent of payers receive income support payments. At the same time, only 20 per cent of the child support payer caseload have orders set at the minimum annual rate, which at the time of writing was $457.60 annually (Department of Social Services 2022a). Research suggests that payers use a range of illegal and legal means to reduce their taxable incomes and thus child support liabilities, such as working cash-in-hand, diverting personal income into business accounts or family trusts, or not lodging tax returns (Shephard 2005; Australian Law Reform Commission 2013; Cook 2013). In addition, child support liabilities can be reduced by having greater over-night care of children, as the current formula references the relative share of each parents' income as well as their relative share of the costs of children, operationalised as the share of overnight care. Minority-share parents with low taxable incomes are able to reduce their child support liability to zero if they have overnight care of children 14 per cent of nights in the year, down from 30 per cent in the previous formula (Smyth and Henman 2010). Finally, liable parents have an interest in avoiding making payments, if consequences to themselves, their children or their relationship with their ex-partner will be minimal. There are no penalties imposed by the state on non-compliant payers, although payers may be prevented from leaving the country if their arrears are significant and reported to the Department. Some payers may not wish to cause financial distress to children as a result of non-payment, although research from Australia and abroad suggests that fathers instead regard either mothers, the state or a new partner (Municio 2013; Cook and Skinner 2019) as responsible for ensuring children's financial well-being. The relationship with their ex-partner can also inform payers' compliance behaviour. Withholding payments might inflame parental hostilities, resulting in such consequences as renewed family law disputes, mothers' withholding of child contact, or non-compliance being reported to the Department for administrative action. How state policies and administrative procedures existing within child support – and at the intersection with others systems, such as taxation, family law and welfare – recognise, respond to or prevent child support minimisation and avoidance has not been fully examined, although continual reviews, inquires and academic research have highlighted ongoing concerns.

Receiving parents, typically low-income single mothers, have a complex set of interests vis-à-vis the assessment, ordering and payment of child support and its interaction with government benefits. While a simplistic, behavioural economic account would suggest that women have an interest in maximising the value of their child support orders, high-value orders may reduce the likelihood of payment, encourage liable parents to minimise their incomes or provoke renewed family law or other disputes. Rather than operating on purely economic terms, women's interest in child support is highly relational, although their engagement with the system is compelled on an economic basis. A recent review of single mothers' financial and personal safety found that one in six had left a violent relationship (Summers 2022). In the context of ongoing family violence, women can be exempt from seeking child support while maintaining their FTB entitlements, however, the statistics reveal that less than only 14 per cent receive such an exemption (Department of Social Services 2022a). Qualitative research has found that women either do not know about the exemption or are urged to proceed with a child support order, regardless (Cook 2021). Many women report signing up for a 'Private Collect' child support order and not pursuing its payment as a way of appeasing both the state's and their ex-partners' demands (Cook 2021). When women do seek payments, underpayments may or not be pursued, as – like for payers – women calculate the consequences of their actions with respect to bureaucratic, relational and financial outcomes, which can include the possibility of FTB overpayments and subsequent future debts to the state, renewed family law or child support action, ex-partners minimising their liabilities, increasing the risk of physical or psychological violence, reducing fathers' likelihood of taking up child contact. How the Child Support Scheme supports women to "secure the recovery of maintenance for the child from the parents or other persons having financial responsibility for the child" (United Nations, 1989, Article 27(4)), while keeping them financially, psychologically and physically safe is a poorly understood yet critical concern.

The government, as the third party involved in the private transfer of child support, has an interest in maximising liabilities, as their value reduces state FTB Part A (FTBA) outlays by 50 cents for every dollar of child support above a very modest annual threshold. For more than half of the child support caseload, payments do not even need to be received to reduce state FTBA outlays, as the expected amount is used in payment calculations. As such, while the state has an interest in determining child support liabilities, this interest is not necessarily extended to collecting and transferring payments. As a result of their calculative interest, the government has spent a considerable amount of time revising how child support can be collected, and refining the child support formula, with major reforms introduced in 2006-08 that sought to add technical detail to the calculation of child support liabilities (House of Representatives Standing Committee on Family and Community Affairs 2003; Ministerial Taskforce on Child Support 2005; HRSCSPLA 2015).

Conclusions

Given the complexity and competing interests of the actors involved in child support policy, it has been a site of ongoing contest. Part of this contest stems from different views of what problems governments have sought to address (Bacchi 1999, 2009), and the misalignment between political, policy and administrative solutions and the interests of policy targets (Cook and Natalier 2013, 2014; Cook and Skinner 2020). The political, administrative and operational interests that exist within the child support policy ecosystem identify child support as a governmental tool that manages the boundary between the governing and the governed, seeking to depoliticise and minimise ongoing political contest through the use of administrative formula, privatising the operation and conduct of the scheme, and holding ongoing rounds of review. However, in managing this boundary, child support reform has increasingly aligned the interests of the state with those of child support payers and away from the purported original purpose of the Scheme. In light of the new era in Australian politics that seeks to foreground gender equality and women's safety (Department of Social Services 2022b; Australian Government 2023), the purpose, function and operation of child support and the Scheme are likely to once again become sites of contest over how social problems are best managed.

References

Alexander, L. 1995. "Australia's Child Support Scheme: Much Promised, Little Delivered?" *Family Matters* 42: 6–11.
Australian Government. 2022. *Women's Economic Equality Taskforce. Commonwealth of Australia.* Retrieved February 27, 2023 from https://www.pmc.gov.au/office-women/womens-economic-equality/womens-economic-equality-taskforce.
———. 2023. *Australian Government Response to the Inquiry of the Joint Select Committee on Australia's Family Law System.* Attorney-General's Department. Retrieved February 18, 2023 from https://www.ag.gov.au/system/files/2023-01/government-response-to-the-JSC-reports.pdf.
Australian Institute of Family Studies. 2011. *Lone and Couple Mothers in the Australian Labour Market: Exploring Differences in Employment Transitions.* Research Paper No. 48, Melbourne: AIFS.
Australian Law Reform Commission. 2013. *Family Violence and Commonwealth Laws— Improving Legal Frameworks, Final Report.* Canberra: Australian Government.
Bacchi, C. 1999. *Women, Policy and Politics: The Construction of Policy Problems.* London: SAGE Publications.
———. 2009. *Analysing Policy: What's the Problem Represented to Be?* London: Pearson.
Biddle, N., and M. Gray. 2022. *Australians' Views on Gender Equity and the Political Parties.* Canberra: ANU Centre for Social Research and Methods.
Browne, B. 2022. *Polling – Voting Behaviour and Gender – July 2022 – Key Results.* Canberra: The Australia Institute. Retrieved February 27, 2023, from https://policycommons.net/artifacts/2611706/polling/3634261/
Castles, F. 1985. *The Working Class and Welfare: Reflections on the Political Development of the Welfare State in Australia and New Zealand 1890–1980.* Wellington: Allen & Unwin.
Chalmers, J., and A. Rishworth. 2022. *Members Appointed to Economic Inclusion Advisory Committee.* Commonwealth of Australia. Retrieved January 13, 2023 from https://ministers.treasury.gov.au/ministers/jim-chalmers-2022/media-releases/members-appointed-economic-inclusion-advisory-committee
Child Support Evaluation Advisory Group. 1992. *Child Support in Australia: Final Report of the Evaluation. Volume One – Main Report.* Canberra: Australian Government Publication Service.
Cook, K. 2013. "Child support compliance and tax return non-filing: A feminist analysis." *Australian Review of Public Affairs* 11 (2): 43–64.
Cook, K. 2019. "Gender, Social Security and Poverty." In *Revisiting Henderson: Poverty, Social Security and Basic Income*, edited by P. Saunders, 250–67. Carlton: Melbourne University Press.
———. 2021. "State Tactics of Welfare Benefit Minimisation: The Power of Governing Documents." *Critical Social Policy.* https://doi.org/10.1177/02610183211003474
Cook, K., and K. Natalier. 2013. "The Gendered Framing of Australia's Child Support Reforms." *International Journal of Law, Policy and the Family* 27 (1): 28–50.

———. 2014. "Selective Hearing: The Gendered Construction and Reception of Inquiry Evidence." *Critical Social Policy* 34 (4): 515–37.

———. 2016. Gender and Evidence in Family Law Reform: A Case Study of Quantification and Anecdote in Framing and Legitimising the 'Problems' with Child Support in Australia. *Feminist Legal Studies* 24 (2): 147–67.

Cook, K., and C. Skinner. 2019. "Gender Equality in Child Support Policy: Fathers' Rhetoric of "Fairness" in a Parliamentary Inquiry." *Social Politics* 26 (1): 164–87.

———. 2020. "Technical Fixes as Challenges to State Legitimacy: Australian Separated Fathers' Suggestions for Child Support Policy Reform." *Social Politics* 28 (2): 501–20.

Department of Social Services. 2022a. *Services Australia Child Support Extract Data 2022. Child Support Program Fact Sheet – September Quarter 2022*. Retrieved February 16, 2023 from https://data.gov.au/data/dataset/6379b974-e547-4303-a361-6edebbb52550/resource/6b8cb72e-3fff-4a23-b1e1-61123518132d/download/child-support-a3-fact-sheet-september-qtr-2022-finalr1-pdf-09.12.22.pdf

———. 2022b. *National Plan to End Violence Against Women and Children 2022–2032*. https://www.dss.gov.au/sites/default/files/documents/10_2022/national_plan_accessible_version_for_website.pdf

Edwards, M. 1986. "Child Support: Assessment, Collection and Enforcement Issues and Possible Directions for Reform." *Windsor Yearbook of Access to Justice* 6: 93–140.

———. 2019. "Child Support." In *Successful Public Policy: Lessons from Australia and New Zealand*, edited by J. Luetjens, M. Mintrom and P. 'd Hart, 139–64. Canberra: ANU Press.

Edwards, M., C. Howard, and R. Miller. 2001. *Social Policy, Public Policy: From Problem to Practice*. Crows Nest, NSW: Allen & Unwin.

Eekelaar, John. 1991. Are Parents Morally Obliged to Care for Their Children? *Journal of Legal Studies* 11: 340–53.

Hancock, L. 1998. "Reforming the Child Support Agenda? Who Benefits?" *Just Policy* 12: 20–31.

———. 2006. "Bringing in the Community Sector: Partnerships and Advocacy." In *Beyond the Policy Cycle*, edited by H. K. Colebatch, 42–65. Crows Nest: Routledge.

Head, B. W., and J. Alford. 2015. "Wicked Problems: Implications for Public Policy and Management." *Administration & Society* 47 (6): 711–39. https://doi.org/10.1177/0095399713481601

House of Representatives Standing Committee on Family and Community Affairs. 2003. *Every Picture Tells a Story: Report on the Inquiry into Child Custody Arrangements in the Event of Family Separation*. Canberra: Australian Government.

House of Representatives Standing Committee on Social Policy and Legal Affairs. 2015. *From Conflict to Cooperation: Inquiry into the Child Support Program*. Canberra: Australian Government.

Jamrozik, A., and L. Nocella. 1998. *The Sociology of Social Problems: Theoretical Perspectives and Methods of Intervention*. Cambridge: Cambridge University Press.

Joint Select Committee on Australia's Family Law System. 2021a. *Third Interim Report: Australia's Child Support Scheme*. Canberra: Commonwealth of Australia.

———. 2021b. Final Report. Canberra: Commonwealth of Australia.

Joint Select Committee on Certain Family Law Issues. 1994. *Child Support Scheme: An Examination of the Operation and Effectiveness of the Scheme Canberra*. Canberra: Australian Government.

Li, T. M. 2007. *The Will to Improve: Governmentality, Development and the Practice of Politics*. Durham: Duke University Press.

Mahon, R., C. Bergqvist, and D. Brennan. 2016. Social Policy Change: Work–family Tensions in Sweden, Australia and Canada. *Social Policy & Administration* 50 (2): 165–82.

McClelland, A. 2000. *'No Child ...' Child Poverty in Australia*. Brunswick, VIC: Brotherhood of St Laurence.

Ministerial Taskforce on Child Support. 2005. *In the Best Interests of Children—Reforming the Child Support Scheme*. Canberra: Australian Government.

Mitchell, D. 1999. Family Policy and the State. In *Women, Public Policy and the State*, edited by L. Pocock, 73–84. Melbourne: Macmillan Education Australia.

Municio, I. 2013. *Matriarchal Families and Interchangeable Fathers: How Discourses on Parenting Allocate Positions to Women and Men in Post-Divorce Families*. Working Paper, Södertörn University.

Natalier, K. 2018. "State Facilitated Economic Abuse: A Structural Analysis of Men Deliberately Withholding Child Support." *Feminist Legal Studies* 26 (2): 121–40.

Newman, J., and B. W. Head. 2017. "Wicked Tendencies in Policy Problems: Rethinking the Distinction between Social and Technical Problems." *Policy and Society* 36 (3): 414–42. https://doi.org/10.1080/14494035.2017.1361635

Rittel, H. W. J., and M. M. Webber. 1973. "Dilemmas in a General Theory of Planning." *Policy Sciences* 4: 155–69.

Shephard, A. 2005. "The Australian Child Support Agency." *Family Court Review* 43 (3): 387–401.

Smyth, B., and P. Henman. 2010. "The Distributional and Financial Impacts of the New Australian Child Support Scheme: A 'before and day-after reform' Comparison of Assessed Liability." *Journal of Family Studies* 16 (1): 5–32.

Stone, D. A. 1989. "Causal Stories and the Formation of Policy Agendas." *Political Science Quarterly* 104 (2): 281–300.

Summers, A. 2022. *The Choice: Violence or Poverty*. Sydney: University of Technology Sydney.

United Nations. 1989. *Convention on the Rights of the Child*. UNICEF.

10 Performing the policy cycle

Cosmo Howard

Introduction

This chapter addresses a puzzle: although it is widely accepted that the policy cycle is not a reliable description of how policymaking occurs in practice, the framework remains popular among students and practitioners of public policy (Jann and Wegrich 2006). The *Australian Policy Handbook* text, which uses the policy cycle model as its core conceptual hook, is now in its sixth edition and has sold more than 30,000 copies (Althaus, Bridgman, and Davis 2018). This paper seeks to explain why the policy cycle remains so popular among policymakers, despite its descriptive limitations. Existing defences of the policy cycle have focused on its role as a normative ideal to aspire to, or a pragmatic heuristic tool that can be adopted, modified or discarded as necessary (Jann and Wegrich 2006; Cairney 2019). This chapter highlights another important utility of the policy cycle: it can function as a performative script that helps policy actors to frame their work in ways that are intelligible and acceptable to key audiences. While this dramaturgical function of the policy cycle is useful in helping policymakers to communicate their complex work to wider publics, this chapter shows that the policy cycle script can also be misused to create misleading impressions about policy processes. Furthermore, the chapter suggests that the *Australian Policy Handbook* is also useful to practitioners because it provides a set of 'heroic' identities that policy actors can adopt, which motivate policy work and help individuals and organisations to manage the role and value conflicts inherent in policymaking. However, drawing on the work of Carl Jung, the chapter shows that internalisation and expression of these heroic identities by policy actors can produce problems for individuals and systems, with potentially serious consequences for policy effectiveness and democratic accountability.

The chapter begins by briefly summarising existing debates about the utility of the policy cycle model. It then presents a dramaturgical perspective on the policy cycle to show how it helps policymakers to present their work publicly and manage stakeholder impressions. After this, it addresses how the *Australian Policy Handbook* furnishes a set of heroic identities for policy workers to adopt. The next section addresses the potential for misuse of the policy cycle script and shows how heroic character archetypes can encourage individual and organisational actors to underestimate and deny the ignoble aspects of policy work.

Contextualising the policy cycle

Much of the debate in recent decades surrounding the policy cycle model has concerned its strengths and weaknesses in describing policymaking in practice (Jann and Wegrich 2006; Cairney 2019). Some critics see the policy cycle as a new incarnation of the 'rational comprehensive' approach to policymaking associated with the rise of the policy analysis discipline in the decades after World War Two, with its 'high modern' emphasis on applying reason and technology to solve collective problems and progress towards a better society (Everett 2003; Cairney 2019, 57). Like the rational paradigm, the policy cycle is organised around a logical sequence of discrete stages, progressing from identifying the policy issue/problem, through prioritising policy objectives and the systematic consideration of alternatives, followed by an authoritative decision, implementation and formal evaluation using rigorous and objective analytical techniques. The model has been presented in different guises and variations since the 1970s, with subtle differences in how the stages are labelled, but a broad consensus on the content and ordering of the stages (see for example ; May and Wildavsky 1978; Jann and Wegrich 2006; Howlett, Ramesh, and Perl 2009; Althaus, Bridgman, and Davis 2018; Cairney 2019).

Equating the policy cycle with the post-war rational-comprehensive paradigm and high-modern faith in scientific rationality and linear human progress downplays several distinctive features of the policy cycle model (Howard 2005). Instead, the policy cycle is better understood as an attempt to adapt rational policy analysis to the different social, political and policy context of late modernity. To do so, the policy cycle departs from earlier linear models of policymaking in at least three ways. Firstly, the policy cycle accepts that policy initiatives don't solve problems, but instead create different problems that need to be addressed, necessitating ongoing rounds of policy intervention. This is consistent with the late modern idea of 'reflexive modernity', meaning that the major problems confronting contemporary societies are human-made and often the result of earlier policy efforts to solve problems (Beck, Giddens, and Lash 1994). Secondly, while the policy cycle retains the idea that there is a unified authoritative decision-maker in charge of the policy process, the model represents a conscious effort to open the policy process to outside participants. It reflects what Radin (2000) calls the move 'beyond Machiavelli' in policy analysis, because the traditional small coterie of elite policy professionals no longer enjoys a monopoly on the supply of advice to decision-makers. There is now much greater competition and contestability in the provision of advice, as well as public scrutiny of that advice. Furthermore, conflicts over policy have become more complex, as the range of intersecting social interests, values and identities that are impacted by policy have multiplied significantly. Thirdly, proponents of the policy cycle approach are usually quite relaxed about the extent to which their models really describe reality. The authors of the *Australian Policy Handbook*, for example, acknowledge the limitations of their policy cycle model as a direct description of policymaking, but suggest it is still useful for several reasons. It is a normative ideal to strive towards, even if policymaking doesn't always follow the ideal path of taking sufficient time and doing things in the correct order. The authors also suggest that the model performs a heuristic function. It provides a broad 'map' of policymaking, and even if the policy cycle map doesn't contain all the details of the terrain it is supposed to chart, it is better to have a basic map than none at all (Althaus, Bridgman, and Davis 2018, 216). On this note, the authors suggest the policy cycle is likely to be something that policy actors move beyond once they encounter the real world of policymaking: '*The Australian Policy Handbook* starts with the tradition of rational authoritative choice recognizing that this lens provides an entry to a complex, nuanced reality; having digested the material, one can move beyond the cycle and throw away the script' (Althaus, Bridgman, and Davis 2018, 216).

The next sections take up this idea that the policy cycle is a script, but suggest it is not one that policymakers throw away; rather, they actively use the script to make their policy work intelligible and acceptable to key audiences. They can also use the *Australian Policy Handbook* to make sense of their professional identity and purpose, along with the challenges they face as policy actors.

The policy cycle as a performance

The increasing demands on the policy process and policy workers have created dilemmas for policy actors. While there remains a strong expectation that governments should act decisively and not be beholden to special interests in civil society or (even worse) government departments, policymakers also attract criticism if they neglect to consult with and consider the needs and views of affected groups and agencies. Policy workers should be nimble, responsive and pragmatic, embracing opportunities for reform and addressing problems as they arise; at the same time, we expect them to pursue a coherent vision without getting side-tracked by transient issues and political chatter. Adding to the complications and tensions of contemporary policymaking are the growing numbers of players and steps involved. In addition to the proliferation of external voices and interests, there are many more internal actors and systems that must be engaged to implement policy ideas. Joining conventional ministerial departments are new quasi-autonomous bodies operating under a diverse range of missions, and complex relationships to parliament and the political executive. Furthermore, political advisers have become more prominent in Westminster systems. In presidential systems, political appointments are finding their way deeper into the bureaucratic machinery. Those appointments cannot be dismissed as mere apparatchiks, as they often work in close collaboration with policy experts inside agencies to channel advice to decision-makers (Eichbaum and Shaw 2008).

A consequence of this complex and pluralistic assemblage of policy actors is that the practice of policymaking is often highly decentred, where multiple players seek to frame policy issues so as to embed their own interests and interpretations in the discussion (Cairney 2019). The result is that modern policymaking is invariably messier than the policy cycle model suggests. But this creates problems for communicating policy work to the public and to critical audiences such as legislatures and the media. It creates challenges for 'credit claiming', where politicians use policymaking to demonstrate their substantive commitment to solving policy problems and delivering on promises. More fundamentally, the messiness is problematic because policy work risks being unintelligible to outside observers. It means policymaking lacks a coherent narrative to help observers make sense of what was done, how, why and by whom.

In this context, the policy cycle can act as a tool of impression management, to help policy actors tell a story about their work that is intelligible and acceptable to key audiences. To explain this perspective, I adopt the dramaturgical or performative approach to social relations (Goffman 1959; Hajer 2009). This approach focuses on how social and political actors use interactions to try to shape how others interpret and evaluate their actions and competencies, in order to appear credible and secure trust, cooperation and authority. Because much of what social actors do is opaque to observers, these actors must consciously create impressions during the brief encounters they have with audiences. To assist with creating impressions, actors can select from several elements. These include *roles* – the limited range of socially normalised identities and behaviours that individuals and groups can adopt. They also include *scripts*, which are the narratives actors consciously choose, rehearse and perform to explain their intentions, actions and interactions, and the consequences for themselves and others. Such scripts often reference 'stock' story structures, such as the Aristotelean tripartite sequence of opening/exposition, complication/conflict/crisis and climax/resolution (in which the protagonist triumphs or fails, and the 'moral' or lesson of the story is revealed) (Evans 1986). These narrative structures are powerful because they contain familiar cultural tropes that resonate with audiences.

Roles and scripts require considerable development and refinement. Actors need to shift into and out of 'character' while away from view, so the coherence of their role presentations is not compromised. They also need to hide facts that complicate or contradict the presented script.

This is especially true when a team of actors shares responsibility for a performance, because any open disagreements within the team could undermine the whole performance (Goffman 1959). To explain how these role shifts and narrative concealments work, dramaturgical scholars use the theatrical metaphors of backstages and frontstages. On the backstage, conflicts and negotiation between competing members of the performing team are worked through, and actors get into character. Once these preparatory steps have been completed, the actors emerge onto the frontstage, where the key imperatives are keeping in character and sticking to the script. The point of dramaturgical analysis is not that these 'performances' are deliberate manipulations or fabrications of social reality (although there is always an element of deception); instead, they reflect the point that observers need to be able to make sense of what they see, and this process is helped if widely recognised roles and norms are emphasised (Fawkes 2015, 677).

Rather than a script policy actors learn and then forget, the policy cycle supplies a narrative that can help audiences make sense of complex and messy policy endeavours, thereby enhancing the legitimacy of policy work. The cycle script invokes the familiar tripartite narrative structure, with an opening phase that sets the scene and defines the problem/quest. This is then complicated by the need to consider alternative paths that the policy actor could take, in the form of assessment of policy alternatives. In this middle act, the policy actor may also experience conflict with other actors who have different interests and agendas. Resistance must be overcome, and antagonists reconciled. The third act of the story begins with the climax of the policy cycle narrative via a decision to adopt a specific policy. This is followed by implementation, representing the triumph of the policy actor over adversity and adversaries, and lastly the moral of the story, in the form of the lessons learnt from the policy experience through programme evaluation. To be sure, these impression management strategies are rarely completely successful. Policy actors face threatening situations when their capacity to manage impressions is impeded by unforeseen events, by exposure of the activities of the backstage to public view, or by the unwillingness of some or all actors to continue playing the roles they have adopted or been assigned. These problems are revisited in the concluding section.

So far, this chapter has explored how the policy cycle invokes a common story structure to help policy professionals narrate their work to audiences. The next section looks at the roles or characters associated with the policy cycle in the *Australian Policy Handbook* and shows how these form part of the public expression of policy work. It is suggested that these roles help policy professionals to find a sense of purpose and persevere in the face of obstacles and resistance.

Characters of the policy cycle narrative

While academic debate about and teaching of the policy cycle focuses overwhelmingly on the cyclical sequence of stages, the types of actors involved in and implied by the policy cycle have not received significant attention. Yet, every story needs characters. These include a protagonist, the main actor around which the story revolves, and whose goals and struggles form the major intrigue of the drama. Narratives almost always also include one or more antagonists, who stand in the way of the protagonist achieving their objectives. These ideas are not new to policy theory. For example, the Narrative Policy Framework (NPF) emphasises how actors frame policy issues as conflicts between 'heroes' and 'villains' (Jones and McBeth 2010). In this section of the paper, I extend the NPF by showing that the categories of protagonist/hero and antagonist/villain can assume multiple archetypal forms, and that distinctions between heroes and villains play an important role not only for managing audience impressions, but also in the psychology of policy actors. To address these points, it is useful to draw on Carl Jung's (1933) work on the persona and archetypes. Jung, like Erving Goffman, argued that individuals fashion their conduct in order to conform to idealised behavioural norms. Jung argued people assume 'personas', or outward facing identities designed to 'impress and conceal', in order to align with dominant norms, and hide desires, motivations and beliefs that are socially unacceptable (Fawkes 2015). Although Goffman saw dramaturgy as a largely deliberate and conscious act, Jung attributes a strong role to the unconscious psyche in the adoption of personas, in at least two senses.

Firstly, the individual does not invent personas from scratch; nor are these outward expressions of identity tailored responses to specific social contexts as suggested by dramaturgical sociology; instead, personas are drawn from a core, universal set of stable archetypal images or characters in the collective human unconscious, that are common to all cultures and have persisted throughout human history (Carr 2002; Brown, McDonald, and Smith 2013). Jung's discussion of archetypes was complex and exploratory, and as such he did not settle on a single exhaustive list of archetypes (Shelburne 1988). For Jung, archetypes could have positive, idealised or 'light' qualities, as well as less socially and ethically desirable traits, which Jung referred to as the 'shadow' archetypes. Table 10.1 presents a list of commonly identified Jungian archetypes and their shadows (Jung 1959).

The second important difference with Goffman's approach is that Jung does not believe individuals can step outside of these archetypal characters simply by going 'backstage' (Fawkes 2015). This is because the adoption of personas and their continuous performance in social interaction involves a degree of psychological denial or repression. Specifically, the adoption of the positive character archetypes involves the work of denying, both to the external world and internally within the psyche, the desires and actions of the corresponding shadow traits. For example, when adopting the persona of the hero, an actor must avoid the possibility of becoming a bully – a problem explored in the concept of the 'antihero', whose mix of selfless and selfish motives and actions results in moral ambiguity. Jung argues that most individuals are not able to fully reconcile these contradictions at the conscious level.

Further, the more the conscious mind or 'ego' strives to live up to the approved traits, the more the unconscious mind will adapt to and compensate for this (Fawkes 2015). Jung argues one of the key psychic adaptations to this problem is 'splitting', where actors come to see light and shadow traits as separate, and then deny their own shadow qualities by projecting these on to others (Jung 1933, 1959). Jung argued that such splitting serves an important coping function in individuals and collectives who experience a psychic conflict between the public persona – that which is expected of them in society – and the desires, motivations and behaviours they experience but cannot reconcile with prevailing norms.

Table 10.1 Jungian archetypes and traits

Archetype	Shadow
Hero: pursues a higher purpose selflessly	**Bully:** achieves own goals at the expense of others' needs
Warrior: bravely confronts and overcomes resistance	**Aggressor:** dominates opponents using power and force
Mother: nurtures and loves all equally and unconditionally	**Siren/temptress:** lures others under false pretences of love and care, to appease their vanity
Father: imposes benevolent authority and resolves conflict	**Tyrant:** fails to hear others' voices and concerns
Sage: possesses wisdom, learns from experience and shares expertise	**Trickster/sorcerer:** uses special knowledge to deceive lay people

While Jung's ideas have not been applied systematically to public policy to date, they have been discussed in relation to professionals working in other contexts. Some organisational studies scholars have explored how archetypes and splitting are experienced and used by organisations, their employees and external stakeholders. Brown, McDonald and Smith's (2013) research on social entrepreneurs in Scotland looked at the multiple archetypes that entrepreneurs adopt, how they often split the aggressive business elements from the caring social reform dimension and how few managed to successfully integrate both traits. Carr's (2002) work on organisational reform uncovered 'hallmarks of splitting – generalization, dichotomizing, distortion, concealment, manipulation, exaggeration of difference, and demonisation of the "other"' within the organisations in his study. Fawkes (2015, 678), writing about the public relations profession, uses Jung to address the divergences between the public 'face' that PR professionals must present and the hidden aspects of their work. Fawkes notes that these aspects are not just hidden from the public, on the backstage, but are often 'excised from the collective consciousness of the organisation'. This in turn enables a practice of projecting the negative aspects of identity onto other actors, such as competitors.

The Australian Policy Handbook draws on Jungian archetypes and practices of splitting and projection, and its use of these psychological constructs helps explain its enduring popularity with policy workers. The handbook invokes archetypal images and separates the light and shadow archetypes, associating the former with heroic unelected officials, and the latter with villainous politicians and special interests. This form of splitting is psychologically useful to policy professionals who might otherwise be demoralised by the gap between their individual and organisational personas and the less noble elements of their policy work. What follows is an outline of how the *Australian Policy Handbook* adapts the archetypes for policy work and splits light and shadow traits in policymaking.

The hero and the warrior

The hero is the dominant positive archetype of the policy cycle. The heroic policy professional is an administrator who is unwavering in their selfless, passionate pursuit of a higher mission or purpose, beyond their own career advancement. These traits are found in the handbook's discussion of the professional ethos of public servants. For the authors, a key trait of effective policymaking is how policymakers work 'in the interests of others' (Althaus, Bridgman, and Davis 2018, 224). The policymaker has a 'sense of public spirit' (Althaus, Bridgman, and Davis 2018, 224). The passion of the heroic public servant is also emphasised: this 'includes determination and desire as well as intelligence and creativity' (Althaus, Bridgman, and Davis 2018, 242). The second archetype, the warrior, is less obvious in this policy cycle narrative, where there is an aversion to 'heated confrontation' (Althaus, Bridgman, and Davis 2018, 223). Yet the warrior qualities of 'persistence and guile' are seen as necessary to good policymaking (Althaus, Bridgman, and Davis 2018, 223), as is the emphasis on discipline and the development of tactics and strategy to secure good policy decisions, especially in the face of cynical political opposition (discussed further below).

Parental archetypes

The two parental archetypes (mother and father) are also in evidence in the policy cycle. The mother is the figure of care and inclusion, who helps the inexperienced to grow and succeed, and who listens and embraces all equally. The mother archetype stands for universal love and inclusion, representing the policy actor who seeks to embrace the diversity of interests and voices through stakeholder consultation, and does not favour one over another. In the policy cycle narrative, good bureaucratic policymakers take on this motherly empowering role in relation to ministers, who are portrayed as hapless and child-like: 'When the latest reshuffle brings a disappointing appointment [of a new minister], policy staff use their skills to work in creative ways to make up for a perceived deficit, and explore ways to find a minister's strengths' (Althaus, Bridgman, and Davis 2018, 233). The mother archetype is also found in the deliberate efforts at inclusiveness by unelected officials: 'Through initiatives such as participatory governance, community engagement, deliberative democracy and e-democracy, public servants are contributing to the development of democracy within communities' (Althaus, Bridgman, and Davis 2018, 222–223). The father archetype enters the policy cycle to resolve conflicts and use his benevolent authority to impose a decision in the best interests of everyone. While the policy cycle recognises that there are many different perspectives that potentially conflict with one another, it is the role of the father figure to overcome these differences. In the policy cycle, '[g]ood policy process avoids this difficulty by insisting on coordination' (Althaus, Bridgman, and Davis 2018, 224). It resolves 'the potential clash between technical expertise and political imperative' (Althaus, Bridgman, and Davis 2018, 224). This is especially important as '[t]he demands on policymakers are intense, multi-layered and sometimes paradoxical' (Althaus, Bridgman, and Davis 2018, 221). The father character is often played by policy actors in central agencies, who apply 'whole of government objectives' and thus reduce the possibility of 'professional bias' (Althaus, Bridgman, and Davis 2018, 224).

The sage

Finally, the *Australian Policy Handbook* stresses the sage figure, in the form of the expert who has a high degree of specialist knowledge and uses this to inform policymaking. Effective policy actors possess 'special knowledge and skills in a widely recognised body of learning derived from education, training and knowledge at a high level' (Althaus, Bridgman, and Davis 2018, 224). The sage character also appears in the closing act when the policy is evaluated. The sage uses their wisdom to learn from the policymaking exercise. The sage then informs the hero of the outcome of their policy quest and tells the hero of new quests the latter must undertake in their never-ending commitment to helping others. In this way the policy cycle is reborn over and over through the heroic efforts of policy actors to strain against obstacles, show equal care for all and seek a higher purpose that transcends individual interests, through the application of knowledge and authority.

The shadows

From a Jungian perspective, each of these idealised archetypes has a shadow or a dark side. The *Australian Policy Handbook* tends to attribute these shadow traits to politicians and special interests. The hero's shadow, the bully, insists on getting their way and uses fear and uncertainty to overrule opponents. The warrior's shadow, the aggressor, uses their superior strength to prevail. The authors of the Australian policy cycle warn about these two overly assertive shadow characters: '[c]lever operators get proposals into cabinet without appropriate scrutiny, citing urgency or pressing political concerns, or sometimes simply asserting seniority' (Althaus, Bridgman, and Davis 2018, 218). The virtuous mother figure is shadowed by the siren or temptress, with obvious and problematic gendered connotations, who is vain, and seduces and co-opts the vulnerable for her own ends, or who is herself seduced and co-opted by other darker forces. The authors warn against capture by interest groups and stakeholders as well as the dangers of the political desire for electoral popularity. They attribute this shadow character largely to elected politicians, and quote a journalist who describes politicians' vanity: 'The first year you take the risks. The second year you bed down your risks. And the third year you give away all the money you saved in the first two years. It's suck simple, it's just pathetic really' (Kingston in Althaus, Bridgman, and Davis 2018, 225). Furthermore, 'Ministers typically engage in unceasing media and image management in order to stay on top in the popularity stakes' (Althaus, Bridgman, and Davis 2018, 225). This leaves the poor public servants 'rushing' between the shifting whims and priorities of their conceited superiors, and as a result '"[u]rgent" takes precedence over "important"'(Althaus, Bridgman, and Davis 2018, 225).

The father's shadow is the tyrant, who like the bully imposes his will despite the legitimate needs and views of others, but also displays rigidity and lack of responsiveness. Flexibility and responsiveness are lost when tyrannical characters dominate policymaking: 'If public servants are heavily committed on pre-planned projects, there will be little capacity to respond to emerging issues without other priorities falling behind. A culture of responsiveness is also important' (Althaus, Bridgman, and Davis 2018, 238). Finally, the sage archetype is shadowed by the trickster or sorcerer, who uses their expertise to deceive others for their own self-serving ends. The trickster is reminiscent of contemporary anxieties about policy experts who exploit their superior knowledge to trick politicians and the public into adopting policies that align with the experts' personal interests and professional agendas. The *Australian Policy Handbook* is largely silent on this risk, attributing it to pressures outside of the public service, in the form of 'capture' by vested interests: 'Timely advice usually requires specialist and detailed knowledge. Capturing that knowledge without being captured by interest groups and stakeholders is a challenge' (Althaus, Bridgman, and Davis 2018, 238). Thus, the *Australian Policy Handbook* addresses the challenge of expertise being mobilised to trick the public and political representatives but sees the source of this deception primarily in special interests, rather than the public service itself.

Misuse of scripts and archetypes

Performative techniques and psychological archetypes may have benefits for policymaking, but they can also be misused. This section looks at how to distinguish constructive uses of performances and personas in policymaking from harmful examples. A key factor is whether performances and personas *facilitate collective sense-making* in relation to policy work. Scripted performances of the kind described by Goffman and subsequent dramaturgical theorists can help with sense-making by organising the messy complexity of policy work into discrete activities (the 'stages' of the policy cycle framework). The narrative approach can also assist in linking specific policy issues and proposals to larger contextual factors, which helps stakeholders and the broader public to understand the need for and implications of policy action. Yet, performative scripts can also be used to give false impressions about policy work. Where a policy process reverses the sequence of steps outlined in the cycle narrative – such as in cases where governments or government agencies decide on a policy and then go in search of a justification – the use of the cycle narrative risks misleading observers about the true motivations behind the policy. This has real-world implications for policy effectiveness and the lives of those subjected to policy interventions.

For example, the Iraq War of 2003–11 was publicly justified by the US, Australian and UK governments as a necessary and urgent response to Iraq's possession of weapons of mass destruction (WMDs) in the context of the War on Terror. In reality, the invasion was primarily driven by a desire on the part of several powerful domestic actors in the US for regime change in Iraq, which had existed prior to the War on Terror (MSNBC 2013), along with US allies' eagerness to demonstrate enthusiastic support for American military initiatives (Dobell 2020). These policy goals were either politically unacceptable or inadequate on their own, so policymakers highlighted the WMD problem, despite serious flaws in the supporting intelligence. The result was a poorly planned invasion that made grossly insufficient provision for post-war governance and precipitated decades of regional instability, with enormous human and financial cost. The official narrative, which presented the war as a logical, timely and proportionate response to the WMD problem, culminating in policy success with President Bush's announcement of 'mission accomplished' in May 2003, did not help stakeholders and broader publics make sense of the policy intervention, but instead distracted them from the real implications and limitations of the invasion.

The adoption of archetypal personas by individuals and organisations involved in policy work can help these actors and the broader public make sense of their place and role in policymaking. When actors encounter difficulties in the form of resistance to their efforts to improve public policy, they can use the shadow archetypes to understand how and why opponents stand in their way. Furthermore, by emphasising the positive, heroic archetypes in their own self-talk and public personas, they can derive psychic comfort, strengthen their emotional resolve to overcome obstacles and persuade others to support their causes. At the same time, archetypes and personas can work to undermine sense-making in public policy. While 'splitting' positive character traits from their undesirable shadows and projecting these onto external objects is an important psychological coping mechanism in many professional situations, the script of the heroic policy worker battling dark forces of reaction and deception hides the ethical ambiguity of much policymaking. To be successful in getting policies adopted and implemented, policy champions routinely need to pull rank and exert power over opponents; they use expertise tactically to sway lay audiences to support policies; and they strategically tailor their messaging to emphasise points that resonate with stakeholders. These behaviours are associated with the shadow personality traits, but they are still important for effective policy work. In this context, excessive splitting and projection of shadow traits onto external parties can harm self-awareness about personal and policy limitations. For example, George W. Bush's public assertion that the War on Terror was being waged against an 'Axis of Evil' (Bush 2002) and that 'Every nation in every region now has a decision to make: Either you are with us or you are with the terrorists' (Bush 2001), unhelpfully split the countries of the world into good and bad, implying that the US and its allies could do no wrong and had nothing to learn from their critics.

Conclusion

This chapter set out to explain the enduring appeal of the policy cycle framework. It argued that, in addition to its function as a heuristic and normative ideal, the policy cycle is also useful because it helps policy actors craft narratives about policy work that are intelligible and acceptable to external audiences. The policy cycle allows policy actors to conceal the complexity and messiness of the policy process through a simple story arc that shows policymakers grappling with difficult problems, resolving political conflicts and working to improve society. In addition to this 'external' performative function of the policy cycle, the *Australian Policy Handbook* serves an important 'internal' function for the individuals and organisations engaged in policy work. It furnishes policy actors with a set of archetypal roles that help them make sense of their motivations and identities, as well as the difficulties they encounter with other policy actors in their work. The handbook does this by presenting a heroic image of the bureaucratic policy professional, who valiantly struggles against the dark forces of vested interest and political opportunism to progress good public policy.

When individuals, organisations and governments only acknowledge positive traits, their members are denied the space to recognise and discuss contradictions between outward personas and internal experiences and emotions (Carr 2002; Fawkes 2015). According to Jung, the psychological costs and risks of splitting can be addressed through individual and collective efforts to increase consciousness of the role of archetypes in shaping behaviour. This includes an acceptance that everyone is driven by negative archetypes as well as idealised images. As the Jungian writer Robert Bly (2009) puts it, we must 'eat the shadow' to better understand our own actions and address the undesirable elements of our feelings and behaviours. While recourse to public personas and psychological splitting are inevitable and valuable elements of sense-making for policy professionals, it is hoped that raising consciousness about the role of archetypes in policymaking, as this chapter does, can create a more realistic account of policy actors' intentions, strategies, achievements and shortcomings.

References

Althaus, Catherine, Peter Bridgman, and Glyn Davis. 2018. *The Australian Policy Handbook: A Practical Guide to the Policy-Making Process*. 6th ed. Abingdon: Taylor & Francis.
Beck, Ulrich, Anthony Giddens, and Scott Lash. 1994. *Reflexive Modernization: Politics, Tradition and Aesthetics in the Modern Social Order*. Stanford, CA: Stanford University Press.
Bly, Robert. 2009. *A Little Book on the Human Shadow*. New York, NY: Harper Collins.
Brown, Mary Louise, Seonaidh McDonald, and Fiona Smith. 2013. "Jungian Archetypes and Dreams of Social Enterprise." *Journal of Organizational Change Management* 26 (4): 670–88. https://doi.org/10.1108/JOCM-Sep-2012-0146
Bush, George W. 2001. "Text: President Bush Addresses the Nation." *Washington Post*, September 20, 2001. https://www.washingtonpost.com/wp-srv/nation/specials/attacked/transcripts/bushaddress_092001.html
———. 2002. "Text of President Bush's 2002 State of the Union Address." *Washington Post*, January 29, 2002. https://www.washingtonpost.com/wp-srv/onpolitics/transcripts/sou012902.htm
Cairney, Paul. 2019. *Understanding Public Policy: Theories and Issues*. London: Bloomsbury Publishing.
Carr, Adrian. 2002. "Jung, Archetypes and Mirroring in Organizational Change Management: Lessons from a Longitudinal Case Study." *Journal of Organizational Change Management* 15 (5): 477–89. https://doi.org/10.1108/09534810210440388
Dobell, Graeme. 2020. "Cabinet Papers Reveal Australia Was on Path to War in Iraq in 1998." Australia Strategic Policy Institute. https://www.aspistrategist.org.au/cabinet-papers-reveal-australia-was-on-path-to-war-in-iraq-in-1998/ (Accessed December 7).
Eichbaum, Chris, and Richard Shaw. 2008. "Revisiting Politicization: Political Advisers and Public Servants in Westminster Systems." *Governance* 21 (3): 337–63.
Evans, Jonathan D. 1986. "Episodes in Analysis of Medieval Narrative." *Style*: 126–41.
Everett, Sophia. 2003. "The Policy Cycle: Democratic Process or Rational Paradigm Revisited?" *Australian Journal of Public Administration* 62 (2): 65–70.
Fawkes, Johanna. 2015. "Performance and Persona: Goffman and Jung's Approaches to Professional Identity Applied to Public Relations." *Public Relations Review* 41 (5): 675–80.
Goffman, Erving. 1959. *The Presentation of Self in Everyday Life*. New York, NY: Anchor.
Hajer, Maarten A. 2009. *Authoritative Governance: Policy Making in the Age of Mediatization*. Oxford: Oxford University Press.
Howard, Cosmo. 2005. "The Policy Cycle: A Model of Post-Machiavellian Policy Making?" *Australian Journal of Public Administration* 64 (3): 3–13.
Howlett, Michael, Michael Ramesh, and Anthony Perl. 2009. *Studying Public Policy: Policy Cycles and Policy Subsystems*. Vol. 3. Oxford: Oxford University Press.
Jann, Werner, and Kai Wegrich. 2006. "Theories of the Policy Cycle." In *Handbook of Public Policy Analysis: Theory, Politics, and Method*, edited by Frank Fischer and Gerald J. Miller, 43–62. Boca Raton, FL: CRC Press.

Jones, Michael D. and McBeth, Mark K. 2010. "A Narrative Policy Framework: Clear Enough to be Wrong?" *Policy Studies Journal* 38(2), 329–353.

Jung, Carl Gustav. 1933. *Modern Man in Search of a Soul*. London: Kegan Paul.

———. 1959. *The Archetypes and the Collective Unconscious*. New York, NY: Bollingen Foundation.

May, Judith V., and Aaron B. Wildavsky, eds. 1978. *The Policy Cycle*. Beverly Hills, CA: Sage.

MSNBC. 2013. "'Building momentum for regime change': Rumsfeld's secret memos." MSNBC (Accessed December 7).

Radin, Beryl A. 2000. *Beyond Machiavelli: Policy Analysis comes of Age*. Washington, DC: Georgetown University Press.

Shelburne, Walter A. 1988. *Mythos and Logos in the Thought of Carl Jung: The Theory of the Collective Unconscious in Scientific Perspective*. Albany, NY: Suny Press.

11 Public value and complex problems in pluralistic settings and the *Meriba Omasker Kaziw Kazipa* (for Our Children's Children) Act 2020

Prudence R. Brown and Sarah Warner

What is public value?

Public value (PV) is an attractive concept for governments and practitioners, particularly in the context of developing new narratives in support of reform (O'Flynn 2021, 867). Indeed, terms such as PV, public interest and public good are commonly assumed to underpin public policies and programmes. While there are differences in meaning, all of these terms relate to assumptions about what is seen to be valuable and are seldom subject to deep questioning. Indeed, the term 'public value' is often used as if it is "unproblematic and uncontested" and is often simply interpreted as meaning "what the public wants" (Hartley et al. 2017, 867). The formalisation of PV as an idea which underpins public sector thought and action owes much to the work of Mark Moore (1982). His aim was to facilitate a shift in thinking away from public administration, where 'efficient' programmes deliver well-defined policy goals, to recognise that policy actors are also inextricably involved in goal setting and political management. He was primarily concerned with challenging the uncritical incorporation of private sector practices into public management. So rather than shareholder value animating policy action, policy goals are, in Moore's conception, conceptualised as achieving a "substantive purpose" (Moore 1983, 21), which then crystallised as PV.

This shift in thinking relies on defining a 'public', which is called into being for the issue under consideration (Moore 2014). Recent research draws on critical conceptions of the public which consider it to be plural rather than singular (Prebble 2018). Implicit in this approach is the importance of seeing PV as not only as an activity of government but also as an activity of citizens and community members – where PV is conceptually located within the broader activity of democratic theory (Bryson, Crosby, and Bloomberg 2014, 447). A shift towards PV also requires a focus on what the value is. How policy actors and scholars approach these questions will inevitably depend on their ontology and epistemology. Cluley and Radnor (2020) have mapped the philosophical underpinnings of different conceptions of PV (see Table 11.1). Positivists see PV as pre-defined and quantifiable (and so able to be measured) whereas constructivists see it as context dependent and post-structuralists see PV as discursively created and context dependent. These latter underpinnings are better able to embrace complexity and contingency as they take into account that PV is both context dependent (Meynhardt 2009) and value frame dependent (Bozeman 2007). More broadly, Benington (2011) sees PV as a "contested democratic practice".

If the focus is on recognising when PV is created, then attention turns to examine the processes of collaborative negotiation especially between government officials and other stakeholders, which have the aim of resolving social problems and achieving shared goals or purposes (Head 2019). This inevitably turns attention to how much value is created and issues of how, what, when and where PV can be measured, especially in empirical research (Brown, Cherney, and Warner 2021). Working towards PV also relies on defining and balancing the preferences of the public

DOI: 10.4324/9781003368564-11

Table 11.1 Philosophical underpinnings of value

Positivism	Structuralism	Constructivism	Post-structuralism	Post-modernism
Value is definable and quantifiable. Value can be measured. Value cannot be created, it exists before creation	Value exists because of the underlying structural systems that produce it	Value will be different depending on the social circumstance and time. Value is created through social interaction	Value is fluid and changeable and is affected by discourse. It is discursively created through text, social norms and social interaction	Value is something that can change over time depending on the dominant discourses

Source: Cluley and Radnor (2020, 214, Table 11.1).

about what is valuable. How this defining and balancing occurs, particularly in complex and pluralistic settings, is not necessarily straightforward. It will depend on the forms of thought that policy actors use to define and legitimate the principles, actions and priorities underpinning their actions (Brown 2021). These difficulties animate many of the current debates in PV research. As Moore (2021, 1605) states "we do not know who the proper arbiter of public value is".

This chapter argues that differences as to how PV is defined, attained and legitimated have led to three main schools of thought, which overlap in many aspects, but have fundamental differences in some critical ways of thinking about public and values. While recognising the difficulties of categories to represent complex ideas, the differences between the three schools are nonetheless summarised in Table 11.2.

Table 11.2 Differences between public value, responsive and public values approaches

	Public value creation approach	*Responsive public value approach*	*Democratic public values approach*
Approach to value/s	Dynamic	Pre-existing but can be dynamic (depending on the public)	Pre-existing
Location of agency	At the level of public managers/government	At the level of public managers/government	Occurring in multiple sites
Process of deliberation	From the inside out	From the outside in	From the outside in
Need for the public to be involved in these processes	Preferable, but not required	Required	Required
Location of value	With the public (what they perceive to be of value) "What does the public most value?"	With public individuals "Public value is what the public values"	In the public realm (what is valuable to do) "What adds value to the public sphere?"
Conception of the public	Aggregation of individual preferences	Aggregation of individual preferences	Broader ideas beyond the aggregation of individual preferences (and the State)
Influence of less privileged publics	At the will of policy actors	At the will of policy actors, but more chance of direct influence	More chance of direct influence, but may be dominated by the majority

Source: Drawn from Warner, Brown, and Cherney (2021, 858) and extended.

The following sections explore each of these schools and some of the current debates that are animating them.

Public value creation approach

The first school is termed the 'public value creation approach'. This view sees PV as created by public sector agencies or related entities. The outcome of this process is not just about achieving a policy goal or benefiting stakeholders; these outcomes must, in some sense, be seen as valuable by the broader public. The preferences are articulated through processes determined by government. Often this is through some form of networked governance (Stoker 2006), usually during agenda setting, but can also occur through other processes, such as bureaucratic activity, usually during policy formulation (Talbot 2011, 31). Regardless, the assessment of individual public preferences into an aggregate assessment of what can be considered of value is done by policy actors who arbitrate on disputes between competing publics and values to make this final decision (Moore 1995). The model is summarised in Figure 11.1. The interests of different publics may be reflected in the final decision, but their views only inform, not decide, the final verdict.

This conception is most aligned to Moore's original ideas and has animated a large body of research. O'Flynn (2021) provides a broad ranging review of how PV has developed, the debates and future directions. Two areas of contestation figure heavily in the literature in this field. The first relates to the measuring PV creation and the second to PV destruction (or dis/value). Moore was adamant that the assessment of the value of governmental activity must go beyond outcomes to also take into account whether the government has acted fairly and justly (Moore 2014, 472). Scholars who focus on measurement (positivists) see PV creation as an inherent attribute of the delivery of intended policies and therefore recognition can occur through measurement of performance and outcomes. Those who see PV as recognised by the public through its creation, through observation of policy effects in a social and political context (constructivists and others), are less interested in measurement.

Cui and Osborne (2022, 4) identify three sources of PV destruction. First, where citizen groups are excluded, or their interests sacrificed, in the interest of creating value for the broader society. The examples they provide are travellers or asylum seekers, but this could equally include Indigenous peoples in settler-colonial societies. Second, where public services are captured by certain individuals or groups with limited access for the general population. An example of this is government subsidy of private education. Third, where there is disagreement between stakeholder groups about what is valuable. An example of this might be mining projects in the era of climate change.

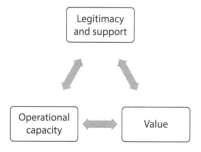

Figure 11.1 The strategic triangle

Democratic public values approach

The second school is termed a 'democratic public values approach'. This school adopts a more expansive conception which sees PV located in the public sphere, which is broader than what the State values and what individuals value: the focus shifts to thinking about "what adds value to the public sphere?" (Benington 2009, 233). Here PV is seen as a "contested democratic practice" which takes into account both what the public sees as valuable and what it is that adds value to the public sphere (Hartley et al. 2019). Implicit in this approach is the conceptual location of PV in democratic theory (Bryson, Crosby, and Bloomberg 2014, 447). This conception has received less scholarly attention, although this is shifting. A prominent debate focusses on arbitrating between competing claims and deliberative approaches, including co-design.

A fundamental part of the process of deciding on what is valuable is arbitrating between competing claims. In their review of key issues for public leadership research, Getha-Taylor et al. suggest that further research is needed on the "forces influencing how leaders balance competing values" (Getha-Taylor 2011, i92). This has always been problematic in pluralistic settings, but Hartley and Benington (2021, 1612) argue that the current "global crisis of conflict and uncertainty" means that consensus is no longer achievable and that PV creation will require "a tough dialectical process of negotiating some basic foundational values between competing factions". Further, Prebble (2021, 1649) argues that the reliance on collective choice processes allow us to arbitrate between values is flawed because it assumes that we can "overcome the issues associated with heterogeneity".

In all of these approaches, there is usually a process of reconciling differing views. However, it is not always possible to reach agreement on issues and balance tensions. Sometimes, solutions need to be found that preserve, rather than compromise, core value positions (Warner, Brown, and Cherney 2021).

Responsive public value approach

The term 'responsive public value approach' is used to describe the third school. This approach is reflected in Meynhardt's ideas of PV from the 'outside-in', but is also consistent with the approach in Cluley, Parker, and Radnor (2021), which argues that current approaches do not reflect the reality of the "intrinsic complexity of public services and their users" (p. 657). In this approach, policy actors need to become responsive to "societal needs" (Meynhardt and Bäro 2019, 104). This allows them to reorient their focus towards, and engage with, the 'publics' associated with the issue. In this way, PV is of less interest as a stand-alone concept, than as its role as "a useful compass in search of purpose and meaning in doing business" (Meynhardt and Bäro 2019, 104). This echoes back to Moore's original ideas which saw public managers as entrepreneurs with a "restless, value-creating imagination" (Benington and Moore 2011, 3). The value of the concept is seen as a guide to action to contribute to societal well-being, rather than a means unto itself.

Case study – *Meriba Omasker Kaziw Kazipa* or for Our Children's Children traditional adoptions

The case study explores the concept of PV through the recent introduction of legislation by the Queensland Parliament to acknowledge Torres Strait Islander traditional adoption practices. The legislation, the *Meriba Omasker Kaziw Kazipa*, which translates as for Our Children's Children, is a significant piece of legislation because it is the first piece of legislation in Australia which accepts traditional "lore into law" (Committee 2020, 3). This case study provides a good example of the operation of PV because it is possible to see issues which emerge in relation to multiple publics and multiple values, some of which appear in conflict. The analysis draws from policy documents in the public domain including the Hansard record and the reports and papers of the Parliamentary Committee of Health, Communities, Disability Services and Domestic and Family Violence Prevention as well as newspaper reports and the publications made available through the Office of the Commissioner – *Meriba Omasker Kaziw Kazipa*.

In September 2020 the *Meriba Omasker Kaziw Kazipa* Act was passed unanimously by the Queensland Parliament. It was a significant piece of legislation because it allowed Torres Strait Islander traditional child-rearing practices to be recognised by Queensland or Western law. Torres Strait Islanders are a significant group of First Nations people in Australia (ABS 2022). Torres Strait Islander people have cultural practices and traditions which go back thousands of years. The practice of traditional adoptions, known as *Ailan Kastom*, allows children to be raised outside their biological family, where the child's birth parents and the cultural parents agree that the rights and responsibilities for the child are permanently transferred to the cultural parents (Office of the Commissioner 2022). Moreover *Ailan Kastom* is connected to other aspects of customary law "which gives a sense of stability and social order of Torres Strait islander societies" (Office of the Commissioner 2022). In this way the legislative change is as much honouring Torres Strait islander culture as it is about the issues it resolves for adoptive children.

On presenting the Bill to the house Cynthia Lui, a Torres Strait Islander and Member of the Queensland Parliament, described the purpose of the bill as providing:

> … legal recognition of an ancient, sacred and enduring child-rearing practice, an integral part of Torres Strait Islander cultural fabric since time immemorial. This practice sits on the foundations of Torres Strait Islander culture and cultural decision-making processes in Torres Strait Islander community and family life. It promotes inclusiveness by allowing children the ability to grow into their full potential without doubt or questions about their identity
>
> (Lui 2020)

The failure of Western law to recognise traditional adoption practices has produced numerous difficulties for Torres Strait islanders in their interactions with mainstream law and society. Some examples include not having a birth certificate that reflects their adopted family, not having a driver's licence or passport, as well as the more distressing experiences when Torres Strait Islanders might inadvertently learn of their adoption through having to produce inaccurate birth certificates, for example when enrolling in school (Committee 2020, 10). As Cynthia Lui said on the passage of the legislation "It enables people to apply for a birth certificate that reflects their lived identity, and opens easy access to government services such as financial support and school enrolment" (Palaszczuk 2022). These obstacles have not hindered the practice, only interfered with the adopted children's experiences with western society and legal systems (Committee 2020, 114).

Arguably the lack of recognition could be constructed as the creation of disvalue in PV as described by Cluley, Parker, and Radnor (2021) above, where a particular group has been underacknowledged. Further, the significance of the Act is in the way it allows the recognition and therefore continuation of cultural adoption. It does not regulate the traditional practice, that remains "private and sacred" (Committee 2020, 3). It also allows "Torres Strait Islander cultural rights including the right to practise their own laws, customs and traditions, and the right to self-determine their own identity" (Lui 2020).

Context

Before considering the operation of PV in this policy, it is first useful to provide further context to the policy. The practice of *Ailan Kastom* is indigenous to Torres Strait Islander people and has been ongoing for many years. The commitment to support recognition of *Ailan Kastom* in legislation was made during the 2017 election campaign (Office of the Commissioner 2022). Two particular aspects of context are important, first the ongoing relationship between First Nations people in Queensland and second the current desire of the Queensland government to 'reframe' that relationship.

Relations between First Nations people and the mainstream in Australia are characterised by the ongoing spectre of colonialism often described as settler colonialism (Strakosch 2015). Child rearing has been a significant area of contestation between the two groups, with colonial regimes consistently interfering with Indigenous people's access to their own children. This is most notably characterised through the Stolen Generations policies which forcibly removed Indigenous children from their families (Wilson 1997). However, it remains the case that Indigenous children are overrepresented in out of home care environments (Chamberlain et al. 2022). Consequently, the area of child rearing is an opportune site for the Queensland Government to 'reframe' their relationship with Torres Strait Islanders.

Recognition of this traditional practice has been advocated for by Torres Strait Islanders since the 1980s. In 1988, Torres Strait Islanders first described their customary practice to a non-islander audience at a conference on adoption (Ban 1993). A subsequent change of government in Queensland put this issue on the political agenda in its review of adoption legislation at that time. However, ultimately no special provisions were made to acknowledge Torres Strait Islander cultural adoptions in that review, and it has remained an area of advocacy for Torres Strait Islander people by the *Kupai Omasker* Working Party. Finally, in 2017 the Queensland Government made an election commitment to introduce laws to recognise the practice this commitment was delivered upon in 2020 when the legislation was passed unanimously by the Queensland Parliament (Crawford 2020).

Two publics

PV in this example is complicated by the existence of multiple publics. Torres Strait Islanders, a group often marginalised, have brought this issue to the fore. This piece of legislation, emerging as it does from Torres Strait Islanders desiring to advance their ownership of their connection to culture, allows Torres Strait Islanders to engage as a separate public. The value of the *Ailan Kastom* only effects Torres Strait islander people and the issues which emerge from conflicts with mainstream law are felt most keenly by Torres Strait islander people alone. Moreover, in many ways the Torres Strait Islander community as a distinct First Nations group with their own cultural traditions which pre-date colonisation, can be considered a separate public. So, the primary public that is 'called into being', to use Moore's terminology, is that of Torres Strait Islanders (Moore 2014).

However, the motivation to reframe the relationship with First Nations Queenslanders calls into being another public. This is supported by the language used by the Minister for Aboriginal and Torres Strait Islander Partnerships on the passage of the Bill:

> The bill marks a historic and significant milestone in bringing together island custom with Queensland law, delivering on our commitment to reframe the relationship with First Nation Queenslanders and move forward with mutual respect and recognition of a Torres Strait Islander cultural practice that deepens and enriches the lives of our Queensland communities
>
> (Crawford 2020)

Public value and complex problems 109

So, a secondary public is also relevant for considering PV processes. The analysis that follows considers the issue predominantly from the perspective of the primary public, but also note where there are differences in the consideration of the issues for the secondary public.

Analysis

This section considers how PV in relation to the *Meriba Omasker Kaziw Kazipa (for Our Children's Children) Act 2020* operates. It considers the legislation against the categories set out in Table 11.2.

An analysis of PV and the legislation is in Table 11.3. It uses the categorisation of PV approaches described in this chapter to show how PV in this complex policy environment is locatable. It is important to note that there are complexities to the categorisations supplied here and the circumstances which make it difficult to map directly against the legislation and so Table 11.3 is offered an indicative guide.

First, where **agency** is located for PV is considered. It is clear in this example that Torres Strait islanders as a distinct community or public are the ones who benefit from the legislation because it helps solve issues which members of their community experience in their interactions with mainstream law. However, there is also PV for the public managers and the government who benefit from the introduction of the legislation as a way of delivering on their broader commitment to reframe the relationship with First Nations people.

The connection between the legislation and the broader PV is visible in the following statement by the Minister for Aboriginal and Torres Strait islander Partnerships:

Legal recognition of Torres Strait Islander traditional child rearing practice is among the strongest acts of reconciliation in our state's history as we progress a Path to Treaty in Queensland, and demonstrates culture can be protected through legislation

(Crawford 2021)

Here the Minister is explicitly connecting recognition of the cultural practice in child rearing with reconciliation, which inevitably involves both publics.

However, despite the Minister wishing to make the connection between reconciliation and the new legislation, it remains the case that agency to change the legislation was always in the hands of the mainstream public managers. This is what makes it possible to consider as an act of reconciliation and why an act of reconciliation is necessary. So, even though the policy change benefitted the Torres Strait Islander public, public managers within the mainstream system were

Table 11.3 Public value and the *Meriba Omasker Kaziw Kazipa* legislation

	Public creation value approach	Responsive PV approach	Democratic PV approach
Approach to value/s		✓	✓
Location of agency			✓
Process of deliberation		✓	✓
Need for the public to be involved in these processes		✓	✓
Location of value		✓	
Conception of the public	✓	✓	
Influence of less privileged publics		✓	

the ones who did the work of assessing how the policy would work, and though they consulted Torres Strait Islanders and even worked closely with them, it is the public managers who ultimately had the agency to change the legislation. Therefore, the location of PV agency is tentatively assessed as in keeping with the democratic public values approach which allows for agency in more than one site. This is made clear as the direct benefits of the legislation accrue to both Torres Strait Islander communities and to public managers wanting to reframe the relationship with them and ultimately holding the authority to change legislation.

The second element is the **process of deliberation**. The different approaches to PV characterise the process of deliberation as either occurring from the inside out (public creation value approach) or the outside in (responsive public value and democratic public value approaches). Ultimately, the process of deliberation for this example is unsurprisingly from the outside in – it is the Torres Strait Islander communities who have continued to advocate for this issue and it is from these efforts that it was placed on the public managers' agenda. However, it should be noted that there are also elements of inside out deliberation, as the motivation for proceeding came from the Government's desire to reframe relationships with First Nations Queenslanders. Nonetheless, the legislation would not have occurred without Torres Strait Islander advocacy, as the Government had, for many years, been unable or unwilling to find a legislative solution, leaving Torres Strait Islanders to manage the complexities of the clash of legal systems.

The third element is the **need for the public to be involved** in these processes. The case study sits clearly with the responsive public value and democratic PV approaches. The process adopted appears to be consistent with that advocated by Stoker (2006), in that it involved a deliberative process where PV was collectively built, involving elected and appointed government officials and key stakeholders. However, the way the legislation has been developed to remove others from decisions relating to traditional adoption suggests that this is actually not a negotiation of PV between these different parties. The issue is the purview only of Torres Strait Islanders, as a distinct public and so there is no capacity to reconcile different views in a deliberative process. As the involvement of Torres Strait Islanders was critical for the processes, we assess the example as sitting most comfortably with the responsive public value and democratic public value approach. The fourth element is where **PV is seen to be located**. The primary place that PV is located is with Torres Strait Islanders. For this reason it is located in the responsive public value approach which sees PV in terms of 'public value is what the public values'. The Torres Strait Islander community value this change and advocated with public managers for this to occur.

There are significant differences in cultural practices of child rearing between Torres Strait Islanders and mainstream Queensland. These are not just value differences but ontological differences arising from different understandings of how individuals fit within the world. Therefore, the location of value could only have ever emerged from the 'outside in', to use Meynhardt's terminology, because the mainstream could not have valued this kind of different approach to child rearing. Moreover, child-rearing policy has been weaponised in the public administration of colonisation where it was used to force assimilation and sever connections to culture, for First Nations people, the state has consistently embedded mainstream values of child rearing in policy and practice. It has taken consistent pressure and tenacity from First Nations people to make possible a situation where a policy instrument which manages ontological differences in child-rearing approaches could have come to fruition. This example is again complicated by the secondary public and aim of delivering reconciliation between First Nations people and the mainstream society. In this case the location of PV is consistent with the democratic public value approach – which considers what adds value to the public sphere. However, because the location of value is advocated for by Torres Strait Islanders and the legislation primarily effects them, the location of PV is assessed as more clearly with the responsive PV approach.

The fifth element is the **conception of the public** – either it is seen as consisting of an aggregate of individual preferences or as broader ideas beyond aggregation of the individual within the state. In this case study, the conception of the public is another way in which a primary and secondary public is visible. The two publics show that the conception of the public is that it is more than an aggregation of individual preferences. Indeed, this is something that is particular about this legislation because it seeks to acknowledge and support a distinct public, Torres Strait Islanders in their cultural practice, rather than treating them as individuals who are subject to the legislation which governs other adoption practices in Queensland. This is an example of two publics operating simultaneously with different laws applying to them, as exemplified by the phrase used to describe the legislation as 'lore into law'.

The final element of PV **acknowledging less privileged publics** is perhaps the most straightforward assessment to be made. In the original conception of PV proposed by Moore, it is at the will of policy actors. Although there is some sense here in which the public managers are ultimately the only ones which are able to progress the issues onto the public agenda, there is an appreciation of the role of the Torres Strait islander advocates in progressing this issue onto the public agenda, reflecting a responsive public value approach. Assessing how PV can be identified in the example of this legislation has highlighted that the term is challenged when different publics and different values are involved. Moore's original approach to PV from the perspective of public managers could not have allowed for the ideas of two publics which are visible in this example. Nor are the discussions about whether PV is knowable able to be effectively assessed in this example where the PV accrued to Torres Strait Islanders through the recognition of their traditional practices is unknowable to non-islanders, but is still valuable. This example demonstrates that while the idea of PV resonates in ways which are important to the exercise of public policy, it continues to require extension and reassessment as more and more novel sites of public policy in pluralistic societies emerge.

Conclusion

As O'Flynn (2021) notes, PV is still developing as a concept. Nonetheless, the concept has developed considerably through this healthy contestation. As Moore (2019, 370) noted, the original "narrow vocational project" has "blossomed into a larger humanitarian project focussed on building the capacities of democratic governance, and the pursuit of the good and the just". Meynhardt (2009, 215) suggests that PV research is most useful where it sharpens "our understanding of the evolving nature of political, social, and juridical obligations on one hand and co-production of values in societies searching for coordination, legitimization, and meaning at the other". However, achieving a coherent framing to guide policy and practice consistent with these broader aims is still a work in progress.

This chapter has reviewed the main schools of PV research and discussed some of the contestation. It then used some of the distinguishing factors between the different schools to explore a case study where the ideas of value and the public are complicated and at times in tension. The case study highlights that simple appeals to 'public value' are difficult when dealing with ontological differences and the need to navigate between cultures.

These difficulties do not diminish the value of PV considerations in policy and practice. Indeed, Meynhardt and Fröhlich (2019, 31) suggest the need for more attention being paid to "value awareness", or competence to recognise the relevance of PV to the work of public managers, and "value emphasis", or the relative weight put on differing values in public manager deliberations. The analysis of the case study supports that incorporating these practices will enable public managers to better recognise the trade-offs that are necessarily employed in complex and pluralistic settings

Further reading

Ban, Paul. 1993. "The Quest for Legal Recognition of Torres Strait Islander Customary Adoption Practice." *Aboriginal Law Bulletin* 2 (60): 1–4.
Brown, Prudence R., Lorraine Cherney, and Sarah Warner. 2021. "Understanding Public Value – Why Does It Matter?" *International Journal of Public Administration* 44 (10): 803–07. https://doi.org/10.1080/01900692.2021.1929558.
Meynhardt, Timo, and Andreas Fröhlich. 2019. "More Value Awareness for More (Public) Value: Recognizing How and for Whom Value Is Truly Created." In *Public Value: Deepening, Enriching, and Broadening the Theory and Practice*, edited by Adam Lindgreen, Nicole Koenig-Lewis, Martin Kitchener, John D. Brewer, Mark H. Moore and Timo Meynhardt, 23–39. Abingdon: Routledge.
Moore, Mark 2019. "Reflections on the Public Value Project." In *Public Value: Deepening, Enriching, and Broadening the Theory and Practice*, edited by M. R. Rutgers, A. Lindgreen, N. Koenig-Lewis, M. Kitchener, J. D. Brewer, M. H. Moore and T. Meynhardt, 351–71. Abingdon: Routledge.
O'Flynn, Janine. 2021. "Public Value: Where Have We Been and Where Are We Going?" *International Journal of Public Administration*. https://doi.org/10.1080/01900692.2021.1884696

References

ABS. 2022. "Aboriginal and Torres Strait Isalnder Peoples." Australian Bureau of Statistics, accessed August 8. https://www.abs.gov.au/statistics/people/aboriginal-and-torres-strait-islander-peoples
Ban, Paul. 1993. "The Quest for Legal Recognition of Torres Strait Islander Customary Adoption Practice." *Aboriginal Law Bulletin* 2 (60): 1–4.
Benington, John 2009. "Creating the Public in Order to Create Public Value?" *International Journal of Public Administration* 32 (3-4): 232–49. https://doi.org/10.1080/01900690902749578
———. 2011. "From Private Choice to Public Value?" In *Public Value: Theory and Practice*, edited by John Benington and Mark H. Moore, 31–49. Basingstoke: Macmillan.
Benington, John, and Mark Moore. 2011. "Public Value in Complex and Changing Times." In *Public Value: Theory and Practice*, edited by J. Benington and M. Moore, 1–20. Basingstoke: Palgrave Macmillan.
Bozeman, Barry. 2007. *Public Values and Public Interest: Counterbalancing Economic Individualism*. Washington, DC: Georgetown University Press.
Brown, Prudence R. 2021. "Public Value Measurement vs. Public Value Creating Imagination – the Constraining Influence of Old and New Public Management Paradigms." *International Journal of Public Administration* 44 (10): 808–17. https://doi.org/10.1080/01900692.2021.1903498
Brown, Prudence R., Lorraine Cherney, and Sarah Warner. 2021. "Understanding Public Value – Why Does It Matter?" *International Journal of Public Administration* 44 (10): 803–07. https://doi.org/10.1080/01900692.2021.1929558
Bryson, John M., Barbara C. Crosby, and Laura Bloomberg. 2014. "Public Value Governance: Moving Beyond Traditional Public Administration and the New Public Management." *Public Administration Review* 74 (4): 445–56.
Chamberlain, Catherine et al. 2022. "Supporting Aboriginal and Torres Strait Islander Families to Stay Together from the Start (SAFeST Start): Urgent Call to Action to Address Crisis in Infant Removals." *Australian Journal of Social Issues* 57 (2): 252–73. https://doi.org/10.1002/ajs4.200
Cluley, Victoria, Steven Parker, and Zoe Radnor. 2021. "New Development: Expanding Public Service Value to Include Dis/value." *Public Money & Management* 41 (8): 656–59. https://doi.org/10.1080/09540962.2020.1737392
Cluley, Victoria, and Zoe Radnor. 2020. "Progressing the Conceptualization of Value Co-creation in Public Service Organizations." *Perspectives on Public Management and Governance* 3 (3): 211–21. https://doi.org/10.1093/ppmgov/gvz024
Committee, Parliamentary. 2020. Meriba Omasker Kaziw Kazipa (Torres Strait Islander Traditional Child Rearing Practice) Bill 2020 – for our children's children Report No. 40, 56th Parliament August 2020, edited by Communities Health, Disability Services and Domestic and Family Violence Prevention Committee, Queensland Parliament.

Crawford, Craig. 2020. Meriba Kaziw Kazipa (Torres Strait Islander Child Rearing Practice) Bill Second Reading. In *Hansard – 8 September 2020*. Brisbane: Queensland Parliament.

———. 2021. *Media Statement: Torres Strait Islander Tradition Recognised in World-First Achievement*. Queensland Government. https://statements.qld.gov.au/statements/93943.

Cui, Tie, and Stephen Osborne. 2022. "Unpacking Value Destruction at the Intersection between Public and Private Value." *Public Administration (London)*. https://doi.org/10.1111/padm.12850

Getha-Taylor, Heather, Maja Husar Holmes, Willow S. Jacobson, Ricardo S. Morse, and Jessica E. Sowa. 2011. "Focusing the Public Leadership Lens: Research Propositions and Questions in the Minnowbrook Tradition." *Journal of Public Administration Research and Theory* 21 (suppl1): i83–97.

Hartley, Jean, John Alford, Eva Knies, and Scott Douglas. 2017. "Towards an Empirical Research Agenda for Public Value Theory." *Public Management Review* 19 (5): 670–85.

Hartley, Jean, and John Benington. 2021. "The Cloud of Unknowing: Time for Value-ing Gerunds." *Administration & Society* 53 (10): 1610–23. https://doi.org/10.1177/00953997211053508

Hartley, John, Alessandro Sancino, Mark Bennister, and Sandra L. Resodihardjo. 2019. "Leadership for Public Value: Political Astuteness as a Conceptual Link: Symposium Introduction." *Public Administration*. https://doi.org/10.1111/padm.12597.

Head, Brian. 2019. "What Is Public Value and Why Does It Matter?" *Public Value Workshop*, University of Queensland, July 11, 2019.

Lui, Cynthia. 2020. Private Member's Bill – Meriba Omasker Kaziw Kazipa (Torres Strait Islander Traditional Child Rearing Practice) Bill. In *Hansard – Queensland Parliament*: Brisbane: Queensland Parliament.

Meynhardt, Timo. 2009. "Public Value Inside: What Is Public Value Creation?" *International Journal of Public Administration* 32 (3–4): 192–219. https://doi.org/10.1080/01900690902732632

Meynhardt, Timo, and Anne Bäro. 2019. "Public Value Reporting: Adding Value to (non-) Financial Reporting." In *Public Value: Deepening, Enriching, and Broadening the Theory and Practice*, edited by Adam Lindgreen, Nicole Koenig-Lewis, Martin Kitchener, John D. Brewer, Mark H. Moore and Timo Meynhardt, 87–108. Abingdon: Routledge.

Meynhardt, Timo, and Andreas Fröhlich. 2019. "More Value Awareness for More (Public) Value: Recognizing How and for Whom Value Is Truly Created." In *Public Value: Deepening, Enriching, and Broadening the Theory and Practice*, edited by Adam Lindgreen, Nicole Koenig-Lewis, Martin Kitchener, John D. Brewer, Mark H. Moore and Timo Meynhardt, 23–39. Abingdon: Routledge.

Moore, Mark. 1982. "Notes on the Design of a Curriculum in Public Management." https://j.mp/3a1Wejb

———. 1983. "A Conception of Public Management." https://j.mp/2DyolL0

———. 1995. *Creating Public Value: Strategic Management in Government*. Cambridge, MA: Harvard University Press.

———. 2014. "Public Value Accounting: Establishing the Philosophical Basis." *Public Administration Review* 74 (4): 465–77. https://doi.org/10.1111/puar.12198

———. 2019. "Reflections on the Public Value Project." In *Public Value: Deepening, Enriching, and Broadening the Theory and Practice*, edited by M. R. Rutgers, A. Lindgreen, N. Koenig-Lewis, M. Kitchener, J. D. Brewer, M. H. Moore and T. Meynhardt, 351–71. Abingdon: Routledge.

———. 2021. "Commentaries on "Public Value Is Unknowable": Valuing the Dimensions of Public Choices." *Administration & Society* 53 (10): 1603–09. https://doi.org/10.1177/00953997211052596

Office of the Commissioner. 2022. "*Office of the Commissioner (Meriba Omasker Kaiw Kazipa).*" Quensland Government, accessed August 8. https://www.ocmokk.qld.gov.au/our-journey

O'Flynn, Janine. 2021. "Public Value: Where Have We Been and Where Are We Going?" *International Journal of Public Administration*. https://doi.org/10.1080/01900692.2021.1884696

Palaszczuk, Annastacia. 2022. Palaszczuk Government Passes Meriba Omasker Kaziw Kazipa Act 2020. In *Media Statements*. Brisbane: Queensland Government.

Prebble, Mark. 2018. "Is "We" Singular? The Nature of Public Value." *The American Review of Public Administration* 48 (2): 103–18. https://doi.org/10.1177/0275074016671427

———. 2021. "Response to Commentaries: Public Authority: Paradox, Process, and Palindrome." *Administration & Society* 53 (10): 1643–54. https://doi.org/10.1177/00953997211053487

Stoker, Gerry. 2006. "Public Value Management: A New Narrative for Networked Governance?" *The American Review of Public Administration* 36 (1): 41–57. https://doi.org/10.1177/0275074005282583

Strakosch, Elizabeth. 2015. *Neoliberal Indigenous Policy: Settler Colonialism and the 'Post-Welfare' State*. London: Palgrave Macmillan.

Talbot, Colin. 2011. "Paradoxes and Prospects of 'Public Value'." *Public Money & Management* 31 (1): 27–34. https://doi.org/10.1080/09540962.2011.545544

Warner, Sarah, Prudence R. Brown, and Lorraine Cherney. 2021. "Public Values in Pluralistic and Complex Settings – Are Agonistic Ideas the Answer?" *International Journal of Public Administration* 44 (10): 803–07. https://doi.org/10.1080/01900692.2021.1909620

Wilson, Ronald. 1997. *Bringing them home: report of the National Inquiry into the Separation of Aboriginal and Torres Strait Islander Children from their Families*, edited by Rights Australia. Human and Commission Equal Opportunity, *Report of the National Inquiry into the Separation of Aboriginal and Torres Strait Islander Children from their Families*. Sydney: Human Rights and Equal Opportunity Commission.

12 Stocktake and future agenda

H.K. Colebatch and Calista Castles

This book arose from a suggestion by the publisher that there would be interest in a new edition of *Beyond the Policy Cycle*, a collection edited by Colebatch, published in 2005. It reflected the discontent among social scientists teaching and researching policy about the analytic frameworks in use, and this book continues the work of analytic development. So, the reader might ask first, 'where has this taken us?', in what way does 'policy' help us understand governing in the 21st century? and second 'were do we go from here'? And the editors have divided the work between them: Colebatch writing on how the analysis has developed, Castles on where we go from here.

The challenges for analysis

Beyond the Policy Cycle arose from the frustration of policy scholars who felt that they were compelled to talk (and teach) about the policy process in a way that made no sense – but from which it was difficult to escape. It seemed that we had to begin the conversation in the language of authoritative instrumental choice (AIC), even though it was at variance with empirical experience, and experienced policy practitioners tended to slide over these contradictions with cryptic allusions to 'in theory … in practice'. Bridgman and Davis recognised the problem and offered several putative accommodations of their own: one, that AIC was a normative ideal which practitioners could aim for but might never reach, or another, that the 'policy cycle' was a simple model which newcomers would find helpful in making sense of the policy process, but in time, they could discard it in the light of their experience (though it was not clear what analytic framework would replace it). We wanted an analytic approach which did not need such escape hatches. As we worked on developing one, *Beyond the Policy Cycle*, its successor *Policy as Practice: making sense of governing* took shape.

The core of our approach is that 'policy' is a way of making sense of what people do that brings about governing – which does not mean that all of them are trying to accomplish this outcome or that some of them can be seen as 'policy makers'. We asked not 'what made policy' but what was it that people did – what practices, what processes, what institutional context – which led to an outcome that might be understood, and referred to, as policy. This took us back into understandings of the social world: what situations were seen as normal, and which were seen (for some reason) as problematic, and calling for attention, and possibly some form of governing: we saw the analysis of policy as starting with the process of 'problematisation' and we recognised that what was seen as needing to be governed varied over time and place.

But what is seen as 'normal' or 'problematic' (and in need of better governing) seems to depend on who is being asked: there may be opinions, but which ones can command attention? And this raises questions about institutional arrangements – both the formal structures of government and other forms of social organisation – and widens the scope of the inquiry into policy. We are asking 'in what way are social practices governed, and what part (direct or indirect) does public authority ('the government') play in this governing?' Rather than starting with 'the government' and seeing 'policy' as the instruments through which it rules, we start with the existence of order and ask how it came to be, how it is accomplished, and what part authority plays in this.

Here, the chapters by H.K. Colebatch (Chapter 2) and Sarah Warner (Chapter 3) on caring for children and assessing the quality of schools show us a great deal about the way governing grows. Schools had been in existence for a long time before governments showed any interest in assessing them. Parents were much more interested in assessment, not simply as a measure of their own child's growth (is he/she/they making good progress?), but well before that point, in the choice of a school, and that choice may relate more to questions of identity (is this school appropriate more for someone of my social class/religion/values?) than to measures of performance, though it was widely believed that students at 'elite' schools performed better at the final examination. It was this parental interest (closely linked to the tendency for access to high-paid careers to be linked to high scores in this exam), which drove various institutions to collect data on the exam performance of students from every school (which enabled the mass media to construct 'league tables' and identify the 'top schools'). While this was seen as an indication of 'school performance', research showed that differences between schools were related much more to the characteristics of the students than the work of the school (which the private schools confirmed by offering scholarships) (i.e. fee discounts) to students from the state schools who were likely to score highly at the final exam.

This 'assessment through ranking' then gained an international dimension from the OECD's Program for International Student Assessment (PISA), which collected data through a range of tests at a number of points in the student's progress, enabling international comparisons of aggregate achievement and brought the Australian government (which runs no schools) into the assessment game. And the assessment became the policy objective: to achieve a higher ranking in the PISA table. The more schools focus on the improving the variables measured by PISA, the more 'successful' they are. Variables not measured by the PISA testing – such as 'capacity to innovate' or 'reliability', which are commonly seen as aspirations for schooling – cannot be considered as evidence of policy success. So, the criteria for success depend on who is doing the assessment, and different assessors may have different views of the nature of the problem and the sort of responses that might be considered.

This is why researchers of policy have given more attention to the way we think about the process from which 'policy' emerges. It is recognised that there are many participants jostling for a place at the table, and many concerns seeking official attention. While the AIC account saw 'policy-makers' making 'decisions', which led to 'implementation' by subordinates, an alternative account saw the process as a continuing collective managing of the problematic (CMP), in which participants interacted to produce a mutually acceptable outcome, which could then be 'enacted' by authoritative action. These two accounts operate in conjunction: the 'stakeholders' (as the participants were labelled) want to devise an order which all could follow, and the authorities want to be able to announce a decision, knowing that the most vocal participants had been involved in framing it. Participants may have different reasons for involvement, but want to be able to agree on what was to be done without having to reach agreement on the nature of the 'problem'.

What the AIC account did was give them labels for their action: they were 'researching the problem', 'framing options', or 'evaluating the effectiveness of existing policy settings'. This 'made sense' of what they were doing, to themselves and to others, and validated the outcome:

'the way we do things here'. As Cosmo Howard points out in his chapter (Chapter 10), this shows the participants as contributing to governing, and 'policy work' came to be recognised as an ensemble of practices for generating coordination through a combination of collaboration and authority. The labels used are drawn from the AIC account: problem specification, measurement of need and provision, indicators of goals and measurement of progress. Advocacy is still possible, but it needs to be expressed in bureaucratic, instrumental terms. But policy practitioners also know that they need to think about their work in terms of the alternative account – the CMP – and ask 'what are the forces which bear on the situation we are dealing with, what are their concerns, and to what extent could they be mobilised in response to the problem that we have identified?' This calls for policy to be located within a broader world of governing, rather than simply superimposed on an unknown (and presumed to be 'ungoverned') world. As a practitioner might put it, 'there's what you have to do to get agreement' (back-stage, as Goffman would put it) 'and how you talk about it when the mike's on' (i.e., front-stage).

The complexity of multiple claimants and concerns gives rise to a process we have called *structuring*: participants ask 'what sort of claim is this, and who normally manages such claims?' This calls for attention to the multiple sources of social order and asks if the attention of authority (and the coercion that this implies) is required if the situation is to be adequately governed. Policy research has focused attention on the multiplicity of participants, the diversity of their organisational bases, and the variable relationships they have with 'the government'. They are interested in the same situation, but not for the same reasons, or with the same objectives. But they are likely to be known to one another and used to negotiating collective action. They may be seen as a single entity (e.g. a 'policy community'), but are really a framework for interaction.

There are many voices in the policy conversation, and both analysts and participants need ways to ascertain which are the most significant ones. Analysts in the AIC tradition tend to start with 'the government' and ask 'what sort of problem is this, and who can be expected to deal with it?'. Governing in Australia has a colonial inheritance of technical bureaucracies, each with its own concern – roads, schools, health care, water supply, etc. – and repertoire of knowledge and practice. There may be several claimants from within government, with distinct perspectives on problem and response, and 'official' bodies may have strong links to 'outside' interests – e.g., a health agency and the medical profession or the pharmaceutical industry.

In the AIC account, this can be regarded as 'capture' of the agency by the outside interests; the CMP account may distinguish between 'insiders', who maintain (and adapt) the current practice, and 'outsiders': advocates for change, but both are seen as parts of the maintenance of the 'negotiated order' of that field of practice. The participants can be seen as a specific, focused network – e.g., 'the vaccination policy community'. Prudence R. Brown (Chapter 5) discusses the way in which this makes for distinct 'policy worlds', with their own understandings of the world and what they are trying to do, and of the ways in which they try to engage with those in other policy worlds. And Sarah de Vries (Chapter 4) illustrates the difficulty of the task facing policy workers trying to focus policy attention on locality and envisage the possibility of local variation, when all the attention has been focused on function (and the only question was which function should lead the conversation) and assumed central control and universal response.

But while *structuring* simplifies the process of governing a little by generating some sort of hierarchy among the claims, there is still a need for *managing* these claims: there may be a number of competing claims; potential participants may be reluctant, or hindered by official demands or lack of resources. How much do these claims warrant collective attention? Resources? Regulation? If there are parallel, perhaps competing, courses of action available, is there any attempt to relate them to one another? And which claims warrant being attended to now, which will be recognised but action deferred, and which will be kept at bay. In the AIC account, managing is seen in constitutional terms: any overlap or ambiguity can be resolved by cabinet decision. But practitioners find that political leaders are reluctant to engage in conflicts with their peers (and potential allies) and expect that officials can 'sort it out'. This means that a lot of policy work is negotiation between officials to develop a pattern of action, and a way of describing it, which can be presented as a positive achievement by all the interested parties. There may be many of these, some recognised as 'stakeholders', and known to each other: 'camped permanently around each source of problems' (Davies 1964). In the AIC account, these are seen as 'applicants', hoping for a decision by government. In the CMP account, they are more likely to be seen as co-creators of the order, sometimes as essential collaborators, whose opposition would make any official action ineffective. And where there is contest between stakeholders, there needs to be negotiation, tolerance of overlap and redundancy, and acceptance of ambiguity about the outcome. And for the participants, it is important to maintain the commitment to a negotiated order – and for each of them, their place at the table: this is probably more important than any specific issue in dispute.

And this, of course, has its impact on the final part of the 'policy cycle': *assessing* the success of policy. Who is to judge its success, and in what way? Are those who carried out the policy qualified to assess its success? Or those who were said to be its beneficiaries? Are there independent data sources with reliable indicators? There are many claims of success, but many questions about their validity. In the AIC account, it is expected that the objectives of the policy will be specified at the beginning, preferably with a clear measure of the desired outcome (e.g., 'to reduce the rate of non-completions by 50%'). This has encouraged the emergence of 'policy evaluation' as a distinct field of social science and official practice, in which participants have to work out their own ways of handling the multiplicity of aspirations and the paucity of measures. The CMP account is more focused on process and perception: 'is this matter now seen as being appropriately managed – i.e., by the right people in the right way?' But evaluation is not just about success or failure to manage a 'problem', as Castles (Chapter 8) highlights, it is also a form of political thought but is rarely treated as such.

But what is the *relationship of models of policy to what we know about the practice*? Any model is, after all, an abstraction. In what way does it relate to practice? We can see a number of different ways in use.

a The model can be seen as a descriptive generalisation of practice: 'this is what most practice is like'. It may be built by examining instances of what is taken to be policy, and extracting the features that they all share (and, presumably, that other forms of governing do not) to build a picture of the 'characteristic features' of policy.
b This can be extended into a definition and used as a way of classifying forms of governing: if it has the attributes specified in the model, it can be seen as 'policy', whereas modes of governing which do not should be called something else.
c Models may be used to subject practice to a normative test: to the extent that it conforms to the model, it gets a positive rating. The AIC model is a good illustration: if governing is the result of a choice, by the appropriate authority, on the basis of good evidence, to achieve a socially beneficial objective, then it can be considered 'policy' and normatively superior to alternatives like 'partisan allocation', 'what we're trained to do', or 'compromise'.
d We should also consider the extent to which the relationship of model to practice is the consequence of systematisation in our thinking. For instance, the AIC model assumes that practice in governing is a systematic attempt to achieve a specified outcome and can be labelled 'policy'. How much practice conforms to this expectation (and what other factors

shape practice) is a question for empirical research: it pushes us back to what people do and why it matters.

e   Validating practice by reference to a goal assumes one to have been chosen by appropriate decision-makers, and it is not difficult to find goals being articulated by authorised leaders. But we can see many other spurs to action: being in a position of authority ('people expected the government to do something'), having occupational routines (we've just had an epidemic: our health staff know what to do'), or relevant organisational capacity ('we had trucks that were not being used because of the floods'). Researchers should not assume that the public account of the participants is all that is needed to explain their practice.

This reminds us of the significance of context. Both the AIC and the CMP perspectives are in use and valid – *in context*. This is the dimension of organisation that Goffman was struggling with in posing a 'front stage' and a 'back stage' as an important dimension of organising. This seems to be well understood by policy practitioners, who learn that who participates, how the issue is discussed, and how the outcome is presented, will depend on where the action is taking place, and that the action 'back stage' is focused on constructing an outcome which the most significant participants can regard as acceptable on front stage.

The English-language distinction between 'policy' and 'politics' does not seem to have direct parallels in many other European languages, but it can be argued that order through authoritative choice, as a core element of the concept of policy, has been a significant part of the collective sense-making which validates governing. It tended to be assumed rather than demonstrated, and in liberal democracies, competing parties might make declarations of what they would do if in power, so observers could see the election as a contest between policies and declare that 'the electors' had 'chosen' the policies of the winning party. Social scientists looked for better analysis of what could be inferred from the electoral result, but also paid more attention to direction and intention in governing – that is, to 'policy' – and the ways in which it was shaped by knowledge and preferences.

So 'policy' as a focus of social science only dates from the middle of the 20th century, when attention focused on issues of authority, decision, and compliance: it was about the technology of rule in a modern liberal democracy. As the social science developed, there was more focus on choice: what data was used, what alternatives were considered, and to what extent the likely response of the subject population was considered. In time, more attention was given to how to assess the outcome, which led to the development of 'evaluation' as a sub-field in policy studies, and this raised questions about how outcome was to be assessed and who would participate in the assessment.

Underlying this social science attention was the fundamental ambiguity in the concept of policy: it implied a continuing order, but the order was established by an authoritative intervention – and could be changed by a new intervention. So, there was always a tension between authority and order, with those in authority usually accepting that they presided over a 'negotiated order'.

So, the study of policy has to be the study not of documents ('policies') but of what people do: the process through which roles and practices give significance to action, validate the outcome, and offer assurance that the situation is being managed – and how the concept of 'policy' is used in constituting this order, and labelling it, in a way that 'makes sense'. Policy has to be understood as a continuing pattern of practice by the people who care about the outcome, and can establish a claim to contribute to it, and in so doing, 'make policy'.

Where we go from here

This book, as stated from the beginning, wants to contribute to an understanding of how we are governed, and policy is one way to help reveal and make sense of governing practices. We have offered an alternative account of policy which understand the policy process as the continuing CMP, consisting of various processes – problematising, structuring, managing, and assessing – which function to organising and structure how we are governed. These processes are interrelated, socially constructed, and normative. In the preceding chapters, the contributors have brought their experiences and knowledge to bear on the many interrelated policy processes and practices. Collectively, these chapters mark the contours of *policy as practice* and provide a window into the diverse ways 'policy' helps us – practitioners, academics, the public – make sense of governing.

The concept of 'policy' has become so ubiquitous in our lives that we can mistake it for something discrete and fixed, forgetting that what constitutes 'policy' is contextually contingent and changing over time. While policy texts (policy documents, speeches, legislation) can be a means of entry in to sense making and to understand how we are governed, any inquiry must move beyond the confines of the texts and (re)examine social worlds in context.

Miller and Rose (2008, 28–29) posit that policy (and political) scholarship needs to move beyond comparative and evaluative methods, the kind that "make judgements as to whether and why this or that policy succeeded or failed, or with devising remedies for alleged deficiencies". They claim that to only go as far as identifying 'problems' and their various interpretations, and propose more 'solutions' is insufficient. This edited collection questions the organisational frames that constrain the study of policy and thus how we make sense of governing. As Colebatch (see introductory chapter) argues policy practices, including 'making' and analysing policy, involve attributing significance to some things rather than others, recognising some participants and some practices as being important and valid in preference to others. Over time, those things 'in focus' come to dominate and subsequently are taken-for-granted. The uncritical (re)production of the AIC approach and 'policy cycles' functions to replicate systems of rules, practices, and knowledges which reinforce and legitimise structural injustices, even when those 'creating' them are well intentioned and supportive of societal change.

Shifting one's frame of reference, attributing significance to other practices and processes, often creates space for new insights and understandings. Over the years, various scholars, including Carol Bacchi, Peter Miller, Barry Hindess, Iris Marion Young, and others, have highlighted the need to critically interrogate the mechanism that "shape, normalise, and instrumentalise the conduct, thought, decisions and aspirations of other" (Miller and Rose, 2008, 32) in order to open them up to critical scrutiny. A paradigm shift is an opportunity to break existing tacit assumptions that become embedded in taken-for-granted practices and processes, to recontextualise issues and open up the possibilities for sense-making. Throughout this collection, the contributors have shown that discursive practices, including policy, produce knowledge about the world that is bound to specific socio-historical contexts; that shape and delimit what it is possible to do, speak, and think about in relation to them. Several chapters in this collection draw attention to the importance of looking through a wider frame, or sometimes different frames altogether, in order to value different ways of *doing* policy.

It is important to recognise that how we discuss policy today can reinforce or challenge how we make sense of governing, as well as how governing takes place in the present, and into the future. The fact that so many policy textbooks uncritically adopt the AIC approach, policy cycles and their components, restricts the organisations, technologies, functions, participants, and what we understand as (and of) policy to the parameters of the status quo; implicitly (re)inforcing that it is 'the way we do things around here' (Brown, Chapter 5). Consequently, the one view becomes pervasive in our everyday lives. That is not to say it is wrong, but it is important to be cognisant of its limitations and critically question its taken-for-granted status. It is our hope that this collection expands what counts as the work of policy and contributes to a broader understanding of how we are governing, and we thank all those who have contributed to, and supported, this work.

References

Davies, Alan F. 1964. *Australian Democracy: An Introduction to the Political System*. Melbourne: Cheshire.

Miller, Peter, and Nikolas Rose. 2008. *Governing the Present: Administering Economic, Social and Personal Life*. Cambridge: Polity Press.

Index

Note: Page references in **bold** denote tables.

Aboriginal and Torres Strait Islander people 39–41, 44, 46, 108
Aboriginal community/communities 42, 45, 47
analytic concept (also construct) 6
analytical framework (also analytic models) 13, 18, 115
analytical techniques (also analytical approach) 55, 71, 93, 115
archetypes (Jungian) 92, 95–101
Asia-Pacific 4
Australia 1, 5, 8, 10, 16, 18, 19, 22, 27, 28, 32, 35, 61–65, 73, 76, 77, 85–87, 106, 107, 117
Australian: Agency for International Aid Development (AusAid) 61; Children's Education and Care Quality Authority (ACECQA) 11, 12; child support policy 81; Child Support System (also Child Support scheme) 81, 83; education policy 22 (*see also* Education Act); Indigenous policy 39, 46; local governments 28, 30; Policy Handbook 1, 5, 14, 92, 93, 95, 97–100; schooling system 19, 22
Australian government 11, 19–20, 24, 40, 60, 61, 62, 89, 116
authoritative instrumental choice (AIC) 1–5, 12–14, 70, 83, 115–120; authoritative choice model 70–72; authoritative choice 93, 119; authoritative decisions 93; *see also* collective management of problematic (CMP)

Bacchi, C. 10, 16–17, 19, 21–24, 71, 74, 82, 89, 120
back stage 5, 14, 117, 119; *see also* front stage
Beyond the Policy Cycle 13, 50, 115

child support 5, 81–89
childcare 9, 12; care of children 8–10, 12, 87
city councils 30–32
climate change 4, 27, 29, 32, 35, 53, 105
Closing the Gap 46

coal seam gas 31–32
collective management of problematic (CMP) 2–4, 6, 12, 116–120
community engagement 27, 29–30, 32–33, 34
council protocols and practices **34**

data 13, 20–22, 44, 50, 52–57; data analytics 54; datafication/datafied 21–22; *see also* evidence
deliberative principles 33
democratising local governments **34**
Department of: Agriculture, Water and the Environment 30, 61; Education, Employment and Workplace Relations (DEEWR) 61; Employment and Workplace Relations (DEWR) 61, 62, 63; Foreign Affairs and Trade (DFAT) 61; Health 73–74, 76; Home Affairs 64; Immigration and Citizenship (DIAC) 61; Jobs and Small Business 62; Social Services 82, 85–89
depoliticise 5, 82, 85, 86, 89

East-West Link 31
ECEC (Early Childhood Education and Care) 9; *see also* Australian, education policy; Australian, schooling system; childcare, care of children
education 2, 9–12, 16, 18–24, 98, 105; education tool 73
Education Act 22
employment 2, 9, 46, 60, 61, 63, 66, 81, 86; framework 67; laws 61; noncompliance 63; relationships 63; Department of Employment 60–64
environmental: conservation 77; policy 1, 27–28, 30, 32, 35; scanning 55
evaluation 4, 11, 13, 50, 70–78
ex-ante 13, 70; ex-post 13, 70, 72–74; *as* normative practice 74

Index 123

evidence 5, 10, 33, 4–45, 50–57, 63, 72, 73, 76, 81, 83, 84; evidence-based policy 44, 50, 52, 54–55

federal government 11–12; *see also* Australian government
Finland 10, 11
First Nations people 47, 107–110; *see also* Aboriginal and Torres Strait Islander people
front stage 5, 14, 95, 117, 119; *see also* back stage

Goffman, E. 95–96, 117
Gonski Review 19–20
governing practice 70–71, 74
government, as official form/authority 2–4, 9, 11–13, 17, 40, 42, 45, 53, 70, 71, 73, 81–83, 94, 103, 116–119
government outsourcing 51, 56
governmentality 17

health 9, 10, 12, 45, 74, 77, 117; community 28; public 53; *see also* mental health
Henderson Poverty Inquiry 81

Indigenous Australians *see* Aboriginal and Torres Strait Islander people; First Nations people
Indigenous policy 39, 41, 45–47
industrial countries 8
industrial relations 9; industrial awards/labour standards 63
instrument constituency 10

Jung, C. 92, 95–98, 101
Jungian Archetypes 96–97; *see also* archetypes

Kibbutz 8
kinship 8–9, 12
knowledge 1, 3, 4, 8, 9, 12, 17, 20, 29, 51–56, 72, 74, 76, 83, 84, **96**, 98, 99, 117, 119, 120; bodies of 2; expert 42, 44; knowledge assumptions 21; local 29, 42, 44–47; management/acquisition 52, 55; policy 50, 56; production 71, 72

learning metrics 19–23
local government 4, 10, 27–30, 32–35
Local Government Act 29
local government voice **34**

Machiavelli 93
mapping 3, 85
managing 3, 4, 12, 42, 51, 117, 118, 120
market-based model/approach 60, 62
mental health 74–76; care 73; policy 70, 73–75, 77; sector 4, 77; services 73, 76; Fifth National Mental Health and Suicide Prevention Plan 73–74

Meriba Omasker Kaziw Kazipa (For our Children's Children) Act 2020 5, 103, 106–107, **109**
models: AIC (*see* authoritative instrumental choice); CMP (*see* collective management of problematic)
Modern Slavery Act 65–67
Moore, M. 5, 14, 103–105, 108, 111

NAPLAN 19–21
Narrative Policy Framework (NPF) 95; policy narrative 35
narrative structures 94–95; policy cycle narrative 95, 97–99
New South Wales (NSW) 11, 31–32
New Zealand 61–62, 64
National Partnership Agreement on Remote Service Delivery (NPARSD) 40–47
normative 5, 11, 14, 22, 35, 50, 72, 118, 120; ideal 92, 93, 100, 115; practice 70, 72, 74, 78; power 70, 72, 74, 77; theory 71–72
norms 5, 8, 9, 39, 40, 43, 46, 47, 71–72, 74, 75, 95–96, **104**

organising concept 2, 9, 10, 120; model 2; process 3
organisational: actors 92; capacity 5, 14, 29, 119; complexity 6; culture 29, 32, **34**, 39; personas 97

Pacific Australia Labour Mobility (PALM), 61–62
policy: actors 5, 23, 24, 39–43, 45–47, 85, 92–95, 98, 100, 103, **104**, 105, 111 (*see also* organisational, personas); analysis 16–18, 39, 50, 56, 70, 92–93; analyst 74; community 117; convergence 21–22; cycle 1, 5, 13, 14, 27, 33, 50, 72, 92–95, 97–100, 115, 118; development 33, **34**, 53, 56, 73, 74, 83; environment 24, 109; evaluation 70–78, 118; implementation of (as a practice) 3, 74; implementation of (as a process) 1, 2, 5, 6, 8, 16; making 2, 52, 70, 84; policy analytical capacity 55; success 73, 100, 116; worlds 4, 39–41, 47
post-structuralism **104**; approach 24; post-structuralist 17, 24, 103
problem representation 16, **18**, 19–21, 23, 24, 74
problematisation/problematization 3, 6, 8, 9, 16–24, 76, 115; problematising 4, 17, 120
public performance standards 60; public value 5, 14, 103–106, **109**, 110–111

Queensland 65, 107–111
Queensland government 108; Queensland Parliament 106–108

rational comprehensive approach 92, 93; rational models 50; rational policy 54; rationalistic methods 76
reflexive modernity 93
roles 5, 32, 94–95, 100, 119

school 11–12, 20, 21, 23, 43, 107, 116; education 16, 18–24; systems 3, 9, 10, 20; underperformance/performance 19–24, 116
scripts 2, 92, 93, 95, 100; *see also* archetypes; roles
seasonal worker program (SWP) 4, 60
seasonal workers 62, 65
Sedex Members Ethical Trade Audit 66
state government 10, 11, 28, 30–31

Tasmania 65

underperformance 19–24, 116; *see also* school, underperformance/performance

values 27, 33, 53, 55, 71–72, 74, 83, 93, **104**, 106, 110–111; *see also* public value
Victoria 11, 29, 30, 51
Victorian Government 30–31, 50, 51

well-being/wellbeing 74–76; wellbeing indicator 77; *see also* mental health
wicked problems 5, 83, 84, 86
worlds *see* policy worlds
WPR approach (What's the Problem Represented to be?) 16–18, 19, 24